D1156191

The River Less Run

9/22/00

The River Less Run

A Memoir

Tim McLaurin

Down Home Press
Asheboro, N.C.

ISBN 1-878086-85-5

Library of Congress Control Number
00-133350

A portion of this book, *Below the Last Lock*, appeared in *The Rough
Road Home*, copyright 1992, University of North Carolina Press.

Printed in the United States of America

Book design by Beth Hennington
Cover design by Tim Rickard

Down Home Press
P.O. Box 4126
Asheboro, N.C. 27204

Distributed by John F. Blair Publisher
1406 Plaza Dr., Winston-Salem, N.C. 27103

There is a tide in the affairs of men
Which, taken upon the flood, leads
on to fortune;
Omitted, all the voyage of their life
Is bound in shallows and miseries.
On such a full sea are we now afloat,
And we must take the current while it
serves
Or lose our ventures.

Julius Caesar

—William Shakespeare

This book is dedicated to
Liza Ruth Terll,
who with a bottomless heart
and a ready smile,
goes quietly about her task
of healing the world

Acknowledgments

More than any book I have written, this was a collaboration of family, friendships, and hearts. While the list would be too long to thank everyone who touched the year chronicled within these pages, I do want to acknowledge the people who directly contributed to crafting this book:

Pat Conroy, Harry Crews, Clyde Edgerton, Kaye Gibbons, Gary Hawkins, Marvin Hunt, Doug Marlette, Alane Mason, Jake Mills, Carol Quaine, Lee Smith, and special thanks to Erik Bledsoe, my editor, Jerry Bledsoe, my publisher, and Rhoda Weyr, my agent.

The Winnebago Gang. Left to right, Meghan, Christopher, Mama , myself, Bruce, and Donnie.

One

Like the world turned upside down, the moon's laughing face is upon the water. Above, the heavens are spangled with threads of morning like a great pond rippled by the breeze. The sun is still below the tree line, and the world is cool and muted with fog. From this rock where I sit, the river flows only a few feet from my feet, silver and dappled with cumulus clouds that are really miles above. The effect is surreal, as though I were suspended between water and sky and sky and water, myself another particle of flotsam carried seaward from the mountains.

I'm camped by the Platte River on the second morning of a journey to the high tops of the Rockies in Montana. I've been to these mountains three times, but not in this exact body or same mind. Like this water flowing before me, my blood has circulated now for forty-five years, but the pulse I feel today is not the same as a year ago, or of ten years ago, or twenty. According to the principles of Zen, a person's forty-fifth year is particularly important, the multiplication of nines and fives, which in themselves are holy numbers. The body is replaced, each cell washed away and replaced with a new one, a sort of reincarnation within the same life. I do know this year has carried me to both ends of the spectrum.

The kids are still sleeping, nestled inside their down bags, their breathing slow. I watched them earlier when I was inside the Winnebago getting the fixings for breakfast. I watched them as I have since they were infants. When they were very young and deep within folds of sleep, I would touch a foot or a hand, needing to see that flicker of movement that

—11—

reassured me they were breathing. A father thing, but they are of my blood and bone, and will still be kids to me long after they are grown. They grew up so fast. Meghan is fifteen and Christopher almost thirteen, and these brief years seem to have flown by in a brilliant whirlwind of Christmas mornings and bouts of croup, birthdays and sick days, coloring books and algebra books and good-night hugs.

All the rest of the world seems to be still sleeping, my brother Bruce inside the tent I crawled from earlier, Ma inside the camper, Donnie, my brother-in-law, sleeping on a fold-out bed beside the kids. I strip away my clothes on impulse. For good or bad, I have allowed instinct to rule most of my life. Naked, I push myself forward crab-like on my hands and feet, sucking in a great breath as the cold water washes across my flesh until I am submerged to my neck. The water is so cold it burns; probably only a week ago it was snow. I dip my head backwards into the flow, slowly, until my face is beneath the surface. I have never let another man or woman dip my head; I don't think I ever will.

After a few seconds, I can't bear the cold, so I scuffle backwards out of the water again onto the rock, my body is puckered with goose flesh. Beads of water shine like diamonds on my skin. I stretch my legs and touch the long scars that run down both hips. Until I was thirty, I'd never had a stitch put in my body. Today, I have more scars than most people. But I do not begrudge the old wounds. Instead, I look at them as badges that show I have lived these forty-five years, diplomas of a sort that mark an accumulation of knowledge gained through confrontation.

In mythology, there exists a story about an ancient woman who sits at the gates of Heaven. Before a pilgrim can enter the Promised Land, she eats the scars from his or her body so that person may enter unscathed. If the person has accumulated no scars, she eats his eyes, denying him vision for eternity. Any person who has not suffered scars has not fully used the gift of life.

The scars on my hips are raised and purple. My right index finger is permanently stiffened from a bad copperhead bite. These, and other encounters left their story but gave me insight into what it is to be human. I am a wealthy man this morning. Jewels on my skin, my pulse strong in my ear, the people most important in my life within a rock's throw from where I sit. And ahead of me are two weeks of traveling into the inner fortress of this country, and I believe, a journey into my most protected center. We left home just two days ago, and already those long hours of driving have been swept into memory like the river current flowing before me.

• • •

We took off Saturday morning at eight, all of us packed inside this thirty-foot boat of a Winnebago. We're riding first-class. The bus sits high off the road and is equipped with nearly everything found in a house. The coffeemaker ran all night. We crossed the Blue Ridge on I-40 west of Asheville and rode that ribbon all the way to Nashville, where we began to slant northwest. Drove right by the feet of the Gate Way in St. Louis. My shift at driving rolled around again after midnight, and as I stared into the headlights, everyone slept except Bruce, who I knew would not let himself sleep because I could not. We have always resembled each other, but even more so since we shaved our heads the day before leaving on this trip. We figured we might get at least a sliver of respect with our tattoos and shiny scalps in the event we cross paths with wild, western biker types who hold in contempt those who travel in rolling mansions. I thought of this trip, and of the times I had followed this route in days of my history, of the people I had shared those miles with and the man who drove then, who he still is and who he is no longer.

I first crossed this land twenty-four years ago with Jenell. I was less than a year out of the Marines, and Jenell and I had been married only six months. She had just graduated from college, and I had quit my job as a CocaCola salesman so we could sandwich this trip between moving back to Fayetteville and the rest of our lives together. That first trip frightened me. I had never been away from home when the direction and duration of the trip was in my hands. During deployment in the Marines, I was always under orders, but on that first trip the map was spread across Jenell's lap and the steering wheel was in my hands. We had unplugged the clock.

I sped us through the journey, spending two weeks on the road instead of the month we had planned. I know now what scared me. At twenty-one years of age, I had been loosened from the umbilical cord and for the rest of my passage through life I was beyond the nourishment of my mother's blood, my father's protective hand, and Uncle Sam's restraining orders. Any horizon I crossed, the return navigation was up to only me.

Seven years later I transversed this same land on my honeymoon with Katie, my second wife, the woman who would be the mother of my children. The last time I followed this road, I was with Katie again, enroute to Seattle where a bone marrow transplant and my fate awaited me in a formidable gray hospital upon a hill. But I knew I would walk down from that hill, that I would breathe again the sweltering August heat of Dixie.

This trip is different. I've already opened so many doors, and now I am content to ride a circle through the rooms I already know. I am at a point in my life where I am no longer envisioning twenty years from now, but am content to take each day as it comes. There are doors I might open, but they will be opened by choice.

Turning away from the broad windshield as I drove, I glanced behind me at doors wide open. Ma was sleeping in the rear of the bus in a bed as large as the one she rests on at home. She had padded the mattress with a cushion of foam rubber to help ease the pain in her legs — muscles and sinews strained beyond healing from years of carrying child after child upon her hip and with the weight of a family she somehow had to feed. I knew she had not slept much during the night, had turned and tossed in an effort to distribute her pain, like flipping the hourglass, those minutes before suffering can collect in the low spots like rain puddles when we have more than we need.

Meghan slept beside Christopher on the fold-out couch. She had slept uninterrupted since midnight, and I wondered if she had dreamed of her sailing trip last summer through the Greek islands while this bus rocked her gently as a boat. She rested at one end of this vehicle and my mother at the other, and except for the color of their eyes and the blood in their veins, the two of them could hardly be more different in the position of their lives.

Ma has seen the most of her life. Her body is worn at sixty-nine from bearing and raising six children and the stress of living thirty-five years with their father. Her face is lined with the worry and knowledge that went hand in hand with her duties. Except for a few trips beyond the border of North Carolina, her world has been contained within a few square miles.

A Peace Corps baby, Meghan was born into romanticism and the exotic. She had to be cut from her mother, the umbilical cord wrapped twice around her neck. Raised in Chapel Hill, surrounded by the comforts and privileges of the upper end of middle-class life, at fifteen she has already traveled much of the United States and parts of Europe.

But she has not seen the Northern Rockies, and neither has Ma. They both possess the best qualities of their gender, that instinct to put loved ones before their own needs. And I am the father and the son, and on that morning, as I drove again toward the mountains they had never seen, we were immortal.

As the sun rose, the rain tapered off and shards of light broke through the cloud cover. The sleepers began to wake. Ma came down the hall and sat on the edge of the fold-out bed.

"You must be exhausted," she said to me, and put her hand on my shoulder.

"Naw. I'm OK. Actually, I feel pretty good. Did you sleep any?"

"I slept some. This thing sure rocks. I thought a few times I would roll out of bed."

She peered through the windshield at the flat lay of the land. Christopher sat up in bed.

"Where are we, Dad?"

"Almost to South Dakota. We're getting close to needing gas. We'll stop soon and fill up and get a biscuit to eat."

Donnie sat up. He's been married to my sister Karen for twenty-seven years; he repairs telephones for a living. Originally, Karen was to come on the trip, but a promotion at the insurance agency she works at cancelled her plans. Donnie did not withdraw from the roster. A part of me wished he had stayed home, but a larger part could not tell him no. He rides his horse and goes to redneck rodeos, and his dream has always been to see the real west.

Meghan slept on. I guess when she has already seen the blue-white waters of the Aegean Sea, a rain-soaked highway in Nebraska is nothing to wake up for.

• • •

I pull on a pair of shorts, then a t-shirt, the diamonds soaking through the material in dark spots. My heart still pumps hard, and my stomach rumbles with hunger, and I feel totally mortal and alive. Almost ten years ago to this day, a doctor said I could best expect to live maybe three more years before multiple myeloma killed me. I didn't believe him from the getgo. Submerged in the shallows is a Coors beer can. On my first trip west, I couldn't wait to get to the Rockies to buy Coors; back then in the South, where it wasn't sold, Coors was considered a magical beer. I've been six months now without even a sip of alcohol, and to the people who know me, that is magical.

The coffee is ready when I get back to our campsite. I pour two cups and add some milk and carry them outside the camper to the picnic table. I wash down a couple of Advils with a gulp of brew, to counteract any effects from sleeping on a too-soft air mattress. Both my hips were replaced nearly a year ago due to degenerative arthritis caused by the transplant

I survived. The hips feel almost as good as new. This cup of coffee I am drinking is hot and strong.

Leaning into the door to the tent, I say, "Bruce!" I repeat his name three more times before his head jerks up and he immediately slides from his sleeping bag into the chill air, naked except for a pair of boxer shorts. We look a lot alike and are only eighteen months apart in age. My bone marrow is his; my blood is his.

"I got you some coffee," I tell him.

Bruce blinks, rubs his face. "You didn't have to do that. How long you been up?"

"About a half hour. I took about a ten second-dip in the river.

Bruce pulls on his trousers, then sits at the table and lights a cigarette. I light a half-smoked cigar.

In an iron skillet, sausage is slowly frying. The smell is salty and fragrant and blends well with the fish odor of the water where bream are beginning to bed in the shallows. I have a box of instant pancake mix — add a little water and, presto, hot griddle cakes that are remarkably good lathered with butter and cane syrup. Christopher has gotten to where he likes a little coffee now in the mornings, but I dilute it about half with milk.

Fish are surface feeding, a sudden little "puck" sound, then circles of water ribbons spread outward where some hungry perch or trout has sucked down a dragonfly. The gathering sun is adding texture to the sky, high cirrus clouds catching the light and mirroring the rippled lake below. The foggy morning reminds me of how, when I daydream, the surrounding world loses focus and becomes a pastel print of colors that are softened and fuzzy around the edges. But as a man of forty-five, I know well that the world is made up of sharp contrasts and definitions, choices that have to be made, decisions and commitments adhered to or sometimes altered.

The sausage is browning around the edges; I've made a second cup of coffee, stirring the sugar with a twig from a willow tree. My head is clear, no hangover like those I woke up with so many, many mornings. I'm reluctant to wake the kids or Mama or Donnie.

I no longer rouse Meghan and Christopher each morning as I did for so much of their lives. Divorce is like the moon's shadow upon the sun. The blight comes and goes, and is not visible from every vantage point — another pledge once thought eternal now stored in the ashes of what has been. And I like sitting here with Bruce and talking with the world cool and quiet. Soon we will have to tear down camp and hit the road for the Badlands three hundred miles distant. Bruce smokes two cigarettes, then says he is going to the bathhouse to shower. Breakfast is getting close to ready and I need to start rousing the family.

Meghan's long blonde hair covers half of her face. She has changed so much in the past couple of years. The slender child to whom I once read bedtime stories now possessing the body of a young woman. She attends school dances, likes boys, and wears a trace of makeup. I rarely can talk her into wearing a dress. But she has not gotten so grown up that she won't sit in my lap occasionally, or hug me, or say she loves me when I am leaving. I am as quick to respond. My own father was dying from lung cancer, I a grown man, before we were able to speak those words.

Christopher is on his back, the soft wind of sleep whistling through his nose. He's tall for his age, a southpaw, slightly clumsy, with a trace of baby fat. Like his sister, he has my brown eyes and cheekbones, his mother's nose. He loves to fish, and now baits his own hook. The firemaster of the camp, he takes great delight in starting a blaze from scraps of paper and twigs, which by bedtime is a heap of embers. Like I did as a boy, he'll spend an hour poking the flames with a hickory stick, igniting the end and blowing it out and firing it again until all that is left is a nub. A wonderful change of focus from TV sitcoms or CD-ROMs. Last night when an owl screeched nearby, he jumped on my lap, then a minute later was piling more wood upon the fire.

"Rise and shine," I say inside the camper. "I want to hear toenails tapping on the floor."

That's what my father used to say. Ma chuckles from

her bedroom in the rear. I know she has probably slept little. Donnie rolls over. Christopher raises his head and stares at me for a moment, then flops it back down.

"Rise and shine. I got hot sausage on the griddle. I wanna hear toenails tapping on the floor." I leave the door open when I go back outside.

My canoe is pulled half on shore, the bow tied with a length of rope to a sapling. This is the first year I have allowed the kids to take the canoe out by themselves. They are both good swimmers, and the rules are to wear a life vest at all times and not to paddle out of sight.

Yesterday afternoon, Meghan and I took the canoe out, following the shoreline for about a mile. An adult bald eagle swooped skyward from a treetop, a flash of black and white against the cloud-dappled sky. Meghan's braces were removed last winter. When she was younger, I used to tease her that braces attracted lightning, but I do not joke like that so much now. She has been diagnosed with Obsessive/ Compulsive Disorder, a malady we caught early and seem to have under control. She is also the age when the flowing hormones stoke fears that are often irrational, but seem real. As a child, I feared that when I went to sleep, I ceased to exist, a beginning of the awareness of death. I would lie on my back, eyes wide to the dark ceiling, until I surrendered to fatigue and opened my eyes again, reborn to the clean light of morning.

Meghan steered the canoe sitting in back, me doing the power rowing from the bow. At first we zigzagged across the water, but by the return passage she had learned to sight on a tree or point of land and keep us true to course. So strange it seemed to me, a bit frightening and wonderful at the same time, to realize that the toddler in frilly dresses was no more, grown into this lithe woman-child, our destination this moment in her hands.

The sun is like fire in the trees. The mist still hugs the river and shoreline, but will burn away soon. The mirror will lift and the water will become slate gray beneath the overpowering flames of heaven. Upriver I can see a bridge, the muted arc nearly indistinguishable from the curtain of water and shore. I hear no cars crossing, but by mid-morning, the bridge will stand out like a steel thorn in Mother Nature's palm, a crossover from the primal world of waters to a time when hunters cut trees to build dwellings.

The sausage is nearly cooked. When it's done, I'll wipe the grease from the pan with a paper towel and cut the heat down on the propane stove. I'll make sure everyone is up before putting on the pancakes. They should be eaten hot from the griddle. I notice a bone lying in the sand at the water's edge.

Last night I cooked spareribs on a grate above a wood fire. The odor had begun to leak from the meat and fat, dusk was descending, when I noticed Christopher was still out in the canoe.

"Meghan, call your brother in," I said to her, as she sat at the picnic table reading. She walked down to the water and called his name, turning her head as she scanned the shore.

"I don't see him, Dad."

"He's right out there," I replied, leaning over the grate while flipping ribs. "Call him again."

Her call was clear upon the smooth waters, reverberating from the far shoreline. I turned from the fire and noticed that the river was deep in twilight, darkness only minutes away. The air was beginning to chill. I stood beside my daughter and lifted my voice to the sky, heard my sound return to silence. Meghan turned her face to me, her large, dark eyes wide with worry. Ma got up from the picnic table and walked over.

"Call him again, Dad."

I bellowed that time, surely a cry that could be heard a half mile away. Finding no sight of a canoe along the exposed shoreline where he was instructed to paddle, I felt a flicker of fear in my belly. Meghan continued to stare at me, her young forehead furrowed like someone much older. She was only six when I had the bone marrow transplant that cured me of multiple myeloma, but that memory in some ways has aged her beyond her years.

"He's fine," I told her. "Probably heading in right now."

"I'm worried, Dad."

"He'll be here any second."

I was praying at that time. I knew my fears were probably unfounded. A boy in a stable canoe wearing a life vest does not easily drown. But I lifted up my plea, as Ma had done countless times on summer afternoons when I or one of my brothers had wandered out of sight.

A full, long minute had passed when the bow of the canoe slipped past a distant point of land where he was forbidden to go, the boy paddling with long, sure strokes. He pulled on the port side and swung the craft along the shoreline toward us.

"That's him," I said, exhaling at the same time. "He was only out of sight."

"You should fuss at him," Meghan said leaning against me. "He knew he was not supposed to go there."

"You should skin him alive," Ma said.

I pulled Meghan to me and watched as Christopher came toward us, switching the paddle from side to side, then thrusting deep when he was nearly upon the shore to slide the bow several feet up on the sand.

"Boy, you're a little late, aren't you?" I said, trying to control the anger I felt. "We were getting worried."

"I was scared, Christopher," Meghan said, her voice thick. "You know you're not supposed to go out of sight."

He stood in the canoe and stepped into the shallow water. "Dad, you should have seen it. The moon is rising over the water, and it's as big as a basketball."

His face reminded me of the moon, luminous and golden and smiling. He had followed his eye to a point where I could not guard him, lured by the wonder of life and the draw of a vessel in his control.

"We were getting worried about you," I said softly.

"I wish you had been there, Dad. I never saw the moon

look like that."

He was before me then, and I clasped his shoulders and kissed his salty forehead. "Come on. Supper is about ready."

"You bubblehead," Meghan scolded. "I was worried about you."

I scoop the sausage patties onto a paper plate. I should awaken everyone, but still I tarry, looking once more toward the curve of the bridge. The structure is more evident now, the fog steadily lifting and forcing the earth into real time. No longer am I cast only in the mold of God, but am cobbled up now with man-made plastic and steel parts. Even the marrow at the core of my bones is not what I was born with. Part machine and part sibling, how much of my soul has leaked through the wounds? I won't dwell on that thought. Life passes quickly; I have made vows and broken some, and my children now hold the steering oars and seek the moon. Yet I hold faith of promise.

At the door to the camper I call their names.

Two

Following breakfast, Bruce, Donnie and I break camp, packing the tent and cables and hoses back inside the storage bins beneath the Winnebago. The sky is cloud-dappled, the temperature already in the sixties. Ma and the kids go to the park office to buy postcards, while I walk down to the riverbank. The water is silver and slides noiselessly seaward. I think of where I am on the continent, and what other bodies of water this river will mix with, what dams may hesitate her flow. I am in that gigantic valley between the eastern and western continental divides, so I assume that eventually this water will flow into the Gulf of Mexico.

If I could liken life to one thing in this world, I would choose a river. Rivers begin in the higher lands and flow drawn by the same universal force that pulls all matter eventually to the common plain, the sea, the level where nothing is higher or lower. And then the cycle begins anew, the molecules heat and lift once again into the air and are borne by wind currents to the altitudes where they collect into clouds and coalesce to fall in either raindrops or snowflakes. For the snowflake that settles against a glacier on a mountaintop in Montana or the drop of water that speckles a leaf on a bush in Central Africa, the journey starts anew. Moisture is drawn through the fissure or gully into the wordless streams and creeks that converge until a body is formed that is named and is drawn upon maps and twists and curves and turns back sometimes upon itself and eventually straightens before emptying and mixing once again into the ocean with the waters of a thousand other rivers.

Rivers are all illusions. All that really exists is the

time-sculpted path in which the water flows. The current that one stands and observes is not the same body that was there moments before, but a new vessel molded to the form of the journey. In the beginning, the path is quick and turbulent across rocks and faults, but toward the end it has widened and contains the bodies of so many tributaries, a multitude of currents that have mixed ions and shared the last miles. There is a gentleness where the fresh water merges with the primal salt of so many similar journeys, the wisdom of the raindrop that smoothed the stone.

During the past year, I have spent much time on or beside water, floating it, or fishing it. In many ways, this has been a cleansing year, flushing my mind and body of certain weights that had come close to drowning me. While watching the current, I think back to last July, to another river and a different passage.

• • •

Merrie was up and waiting, her coffee hot within the cup and steaming like the fog that still muted the land. Standing there smiling at me in her canvas shorts and tee shirt, hair pulled back in a pony tail, she looked like she might be seventeen instead of thirty-seven. She smiled, and I smiled back at her and pointed at the canoe strapped atop my car; it stuck beyond both fenders like the arrow on a wind vane pointing south to where the river flowed.

"You 'bout ready?" I asked, and she bobbed her head.

"Just need to load up."

We loaded up more than was needed for a one-night trip on the water, her pack stuffed with extra clothes and lotions and tools of hygiene, the red cooler heavy with prepared food in Tupperware dishes, energy snacks like M&Ms mixed with salty peanuts and chunks of coconut, and of course the fixing for coffee. She likes it sweet and strong with just a little milk like any Louisiana girl.

The backseat was full with my gear and hers. With all this weight, I worried about how low the gunwales would ride, and about the rocks we would have to slide between where the water was fast. At seven-thirty in the morning, the sun sat in the low branches, and the fog promised that tonight would be cool for July, very cool. The TV man said we might get down into the fifties.

"You ready to roll?" I asked.

"Yeah." She looked back toward the front door of the small house that I once told her looks like a Delta shack. Al was standing behind the screen, bare chested with his gut like the full moon, still warm from a bed that I knew before him.

"Let me say 'bye to Al," she said.

I followed her at a few paces and watched them hug, and then I shook his hand very hard.

I followed the bow of the canoe turned upside down above the car hood. Wind vane or compass needle, it led me, splitting air now instead of water, and I thought of how when ducks dive beneath the surface of ponds everything is turned in reverse, the elements and gravity, like suddenly being cast inside a mirror.

"You hungry?" I asked Merrie, and she nodded and smiled, and I had to lean and kiss her cheek. What a face, dark skin and cheek bones like walnuts from the part of her blood that is Choctaw, brown eyes and coral lips. She carries her Irish in her hair, red, but streaked heavily with gray, as if the fairy that painted her frozen-at-eighteen girlish face ran out of pigment.

Red. I flashed to a memory more than a year old.

Me coming through the door. Her sitting at the table with her legs crossed in a red, silk camisole with lace garters strapped to sheer, black hose. Red lips. Her eyes fasten into my sight like staring into a twelve-gauge, double-barrel. She is oiled, and I feel red behind my eyes. She has whiskey poured in two glasses, double shots served neat, and she is smoking one of her cigarettes rolled by hand....

The signs for several fast-food places were ahead. "What would you like to eat?"

"Doesn't matter. Whatever you would like." She wanted me to decide. She doesn't like men who won't decide, although she always knows exactly what she will eat and what she will not eat in the end.

Hardee's was just ahead on the left, so I swung into the turning lane and into the parking lot to the voice box where you order takeout.

"Get me some coffee." She went inside to pee while I ordered sausage biscuits with egg and cheese and two coffees and a carton of milk. We ate on the road, crumbs caught in the wrinkles across my belly. The sun was quickly burning off the fog, and we needed to get on the water. The clock was not the one that ticked above us on the wall of the Oak City Grill where we sometimes went after midnight when all the red had been rubbed from her lips. We would sit in a booth and eat slowly and not talk very much, intent on our current appetite and reflecting on the one we had just filled.

In Lillington, at a convenience store about a mile from the bridge, we bought more ice and candy bars and drained our bladders of what once was coffee. The rocks were in my thoughts. As soon as we pushed off from shore beneath the bridge we had to get quickly into midstream. There, I could line us up with the chute that spilled down the ledge to the slow, deep water. I wondered how low the canoe would ride with all this gear. If we were to swamp, she would not blame the white water and the rocks; she would blame me.

The bank was steep. We loaded the canoe first, most of the weight in the middle and toward the front so the craft would track better. The space-age plastic hull slid over the gravel and grass like a sleigh, no, more like a fat, green gator with its nose toward water. Where the bank was steepest, I hung on to the gator's lasso and leaned backwards, no desire to launch this vessel unmanned toward rocks that cut deeply as icebergs. Merrie was leaning against her rope, the muscles in her calves bunched when she slipped on the gravel and went down rump first. She was up again in an instant, half moons of dust pressed into those fine buttocks.

The bow was in the water at the end of the slide. I

breathed hard and felt the sting of a sweat breaking across my back. The underbelly of the bridge was above, and cars went *cha-chunk—cha-chunk* across the seams of concrete. They sounded like drums, as the river played string music, violins and cellos, the whisper of water through rocks. But I knew I must not listen too closely and become drunk like the sailors who listened to the Sirens. Two people had drowned here.

"See. Like I told you," I said to Merrie. "This river gives you a jump-start."

"We're not going to turn over are we?"

"No. We just need to get out to the middle and line up with that V and we'll slide right through. Nature's playground.

I distributed the weight a little better; that cooler must have weighed fifty pounds. I pulled tighter some bungee cords and re-tied a couple of knots. Even if we turned over — we will not turn over, I said to myself — the gear would not sink. An extra paddle. Extra life preservers to be used as seat cushions. I started to put on my life vest; it zips up the front and is supposed to keep a dead man floating face up, as if he really needs that. In pockets and hanging from straps I had a whistle, a compass, a first-aid kit and a serrated knife that would cut through bone. Boy toys. Could I really cut my own leg off at the knee if trapped underwater as one of the men who drowned had attempted?

"Put your vest on," I told Merrie.

"You said we wouldn't turn over."

"We won't, but you need to put your vest on."

She looked at me with her neutral stare, eyes that could range between those of a panda and a grizzly.

"Zip it up."

ZZZIIIIIIPP. With exclamation. She stared at me, one eyebrow arched, the other eye half squinted. Definite defiance, and for a millisecond I wanted to slap her backwards into the water, and even more, I wanted to strip her bare and do it in the shallows while the drums and violins kept cadence.

I soaked one tennis shoe pushing off from shore. Baptism in reverse. I seated myself and braced both feet against a strut and pulled the water at port side, swung the bow at an angle upriver, and dug deep. The water was like glass, and in that mirror I could see clouds and patches of blue sky and the skeleton of the bridge. At mid-river, I let the current swing the bow downriver like a second-hand turning backwards. I exhaled, my pulse in my ear, and paddled from one side to the other until we were at center with the rocks and the dark water went light.

"We're good," I shouted to Merrie, her back straight, paddle feeling the water.

We might as well be good. In the grip of physics, there was no turning around. Thirty yards distant the water was white and lifted and lowered like the backs of several white horses racing. No turning back, even if we weren't lined up with the chute, nature doesn't go in reverse, and if I were in the grip of Angel Falls, I would rather go over the lip eyes first and shouting than ass-backwards and crying in remorse.

The spray of water in the sunlight looked like shards from a rainbow, black, slick rocks and the roar of the current; the river's violin was now a fast-drawn fiddle. The bow pared left of a barely submerged boulder while Merrie pulled opposite and I backpaddled to swing us straight. We slid through, though a wave curled into her lap. Another wave and we dropped about two feet while I leaned backwards adding ballast to the rear, and as suddenly as we were in chaos, the water went flat again, and I swung us broadside to where we could look backwards to where we had been.

"You were great," I shouted to Merrie, her face spangled with rainbow drops, and she smiled, her shirt darkened with water. "Were you scared?"

"No. You said we weren't going to turn over."

I believed her. I know she has been horrified at some of the turns in her life, but I believe she has never, ever been scared of anything.

The sun was in the upper branches, but a paper-thin sheet of mist still drifted above the river. We were in drought, and the river was low. Sandbars were exposed, growing lush with aquatic grass that usually was shelter to minnows and the lesser creatures. Sitting erect, I scouted downriver and saw a quarter mile distant the next faultline, resembling a crack splitting a sheet of glass.

I was carrying a map of the river in my head from a solo trip I had taken earlier. I had counted the rapids, a dozen or so in the first half of the float, a couple I'd need to pay attention to, but most just gentle slides in knee-deep water. I had a campsite picked out about twelve miles downriver, a flat sandbar of white sand clean as the beach at low tide. It would be under water if the river were higher. I only needed to count the power lines that crossed the river. Just past the fifth set of strands, our landing waited like a flat, white pancake lying a couple of feet above the current.

I could hear the voice of the next set of rapids getting louder as we drew closer.

"The next few rapids are easy," I told Merrie. "There's a pretty good one a few miles down."

"This is wonderful." She laid her paddle across her lap and lifted both arms into the air. A breeze was to our backs. A heron lifted from a patch of grass, his wings going *fump, fump, fump,* then he glided downriver and settled again to earth. We slid between the next rocks with ease; the sun cut into the shallows like luminous, silver blades. June sun and water that smelled rich of life, white heron, and a woman in the bow of my craft — had it been that long? God, going on eighteen years.

Katie and I had launched below the big rapid beneath the bridge, pushing out in quieter water; we did not know each other very well. We had an inflatable kayak I had bought the day before with my Visa card, the smell of new vinyl overpowering the musk of slow water. Katie wore her hair long then. She was rail thin, her eyes very blue against her pale skin.

We had met a few months earlier in a dance class where we were learning to clog. With her long legs and her attraction to the spotlight, she stood out in crowds. We had gone out for pizza a few times. When I asked her to come with me on the river, she readily accepted; I knew little about her, except that she was from Memphis and she worked in a bookstore, and she could kick her legs very high.

We went through the first rapid sideways, two captains at opposite ends of the boat. Was that an omen? We managed to get our paddling in synch for most of the next runs of white water; the river was up a couple of feet and most of the rocks were covered. The kayak was better suited to floating on a pond than tracking miles on a river, and the float took us ten hours. But the sun stayed clear and we saw turtles resting on logs and a couple of deer along shore. We ate lunch on a spit of dry earth beneath willow branches. When we were about a mile upriver from the landing, I put my hands on her shoulders and kneaded the muscles at the top of her spine. She leaned backwards and I kissed her upside-down. On shore, we mashed the air from the boat and went for pizza and cold beer.

After several minor rapids, we were about four miles downriver. The vapor had burned from the surface. We passed several cows that stood knee-deep in the water drinking. I called to them as my father used to do when he and my brothers and I scattered bales of hay across the pasture in winter. *KOOOO-YAH, Ko-yah, ko-yah, KOOOOO-YAH.* A heifer trotted along shore, lowing. Merrie laughed. I was strong, my pheromones matching those of a bull's.

I heard the next big rapid when we were still a quarter mile away. I remembered from my earlier trip how the river narrowed there and dropped to both sides of a large boulder. I had backpaddled, trying to decide which way to go, then went left down a chute to the quiet pool of water below. I felt gnawing in my belly again; the water was even lower than on my previous passage and I wondered if we would hang up on the rocks, jam sideways, and swamp.

"This one is pretty good," I said to Merrie. "Last time I went through on the left."

I spied three men fishing just below the rapid, an audience to watch as we passed through or spilled. The knot in my belly tightened. The river was loud, the line of white water throwing up fingers of spray. No time to dally, we were in the throat now and left was good last time. I pulled us into the V current that narrowed to a chute between black rocks. Crack in a mirror, I could not see what was over the lip until we were upon it, but, Lord, she looked tough and rough. We would tumble down sideways if we weren't right with the flow. The men were looking at us. God, what a drop! About three feet, then a chute that zigged sharp right where the water piled against a rock, then zagged left. Merrie yelled and we slid over. She was digging with her paddle and the bow went under. We were tipping heavily to the side. Come to me, Karma. I have done much good in this life. My right foot braced against the strut, and I leaned far to the opposite side, and we straightened. I backpaddled just enough that the bow pared left of the big rock and stayed with the current, but the stern was going sideways so I thrust my weight to the opposite side and pushed against the stones with my paddle and the water piled against the bow and swung us straight. Sloop, down another slide of two feet, water spray and the grind of space-age plastic against ice-age boulders, diamonds in the air. As suddenly as the chaos began, we were upon the river of tranquility, although the water rolled in backward waves beneath us as it boiled up.

Merrie bent backwards laughing; she was soaking wet, and I, too, was laughing, and I lifted my hand with slight mockery to the men staring at us from dry land.

"Scare you that time?" I asked Merrie.

"I was terrified," she said. "I thought we were turning over. I want to do it again."

"Piece of cake, it was," I answered, but in my mind I was thanking God. Not that we had escaped death, for the water was not deep, the hydraulics not the keeper type that would drown a man or woman. We had escaped humility. We took the current that seemed best suited to our craft, and rode it with faith and drawn sinew, and for a moment — for a flicker of time — we understood the difference between being human and being the bovine that lows from shore.

Pileated woodpeckers hammered a dead pine limb, mallards swooped in, then flung themselves skyward at the sight of man; the heron kept his distance ahead of us like a vanguard; cooters sunned themselves on logs, and a banded watersnake slithered through the water. These were the minutes, and the sun showed us the hours, straight-up, where we beached the canoe leeward of an island cool under willow shade.

"You hungry?" I asked Merrie. The biscuits we had eaten earlier had been burned off in biceps and shoulder muscles.

"Yes!" she replied emphatically.

Merrie hopped from the canoe and pulled the bow onto shore. I debarked more slowly, my gimpy right hip slow to bend. She crunched granola and drank from an ice-cold Coca Cola, while I searched in the bottom compartment of my pack and fished out a can of Vienna sausages, a box of saltines, and a squirt-can of cheddar cheese. Soul food for rednecks. I took a cracker and placed a sausage on top, covered it with cheese and ate it down in two bites, washed down with cola, many calories and belly-filling.

"Want one?"

"No. I don't care for pork by-products."

"I do."

Vienna sausages have re-fueled me during breaks in the tobacco fields, atop mountain ridges on backpacking trips and during rest stops while canoeing through the Everglades. I remembered them in the VA hospital in Seattle along with longleaf pines and Carolina basketball. The difference between junk food and gourmet fare is all in the mind; once, while helping a friend prepare hors d'oevres at a party, I ate half a can of deluxe cat food on stone ground wheat crackers, thinking I was enjoying paté.

"You were great in those rapids," I said to Merrie. "I thought we were tipping over once."

"You had the easy seat. I got soaked."

I thought of the second hand on a clock, how she was on the short end where the circle turned within reach of her hands, while I rode the far end counting the numbers and hoping we made it full turn.

"We make a good team."

She smiled. 'Yeah, we always did good when a hurricane was on top of us. We just had trouble dealing with the calm times when the eye passed over."

And she was right, but I would still rather lean into the wind than stand erect when one has only to draw breath in order to live.

"Is that the same heron that keeps flying in front of us, or a different one?" she asked.

"There's only one heron in all the world. We just see it when we need to see herons."

"So I guess you're the only man in the world?"

"Yep. I don't see another one. You're the only woman in the world right now."

"Then shouldn't we be naked and dumb right now."

"No. We've already bitten the apple. We could get naked. But we can't get dumb again. That's the curse."

Smiling. "You're full of crap."

"No. I'm seventy-five percent water and the rest is Vienna sausage."

She stared downriver, and her gaze was intense, as though she saw way beyond the next bend, all the way to Slaughter, Louisiana, which she left years ago. I know and dread that she will return there one day.

I counted the power lines. We slipped through several gentle sets of rapids. The heron led us, and the sun reached her zenith and slid to the west. Three p.m. The sandbar shouldn't be much farther. We had passed by several good camping sites, but this sandbar was special, as though Nature had ordered the drought to expose this clean-washed sand, and along with the calling, exposed the river rocks to test our passage so that our landing would be gotten instead of given.

Twin power lines crossed the river ahead. The fifth set of wires, yeah, that was the count. I steered us to the east side of the river. I was glad the sandbar was on the east side. Beyond the east bank rolls farmland, and beyond the west bank is Fort Bragg. If visitors should come in the night, I would prefer that they be drunken farmers rather than drunken GIs. I have been both.

The sandbar was where I remembered it to be, high and dry and shaped like a pancake, about the size of a living room. Twigs and leaves littered the sand, fallen during thunderstorms; a rock shelf under knee-deep water ran out to mid-river, then dropped into a deep channel. Good footing for me and my fly rod or a bed to lie in and soak tired muscles.

"What you think, Merrie?"

"It's perfect. Looks like a KOA."

Except there was no camping fee higher than the price of the passage, and that toll had been low. I stabbed the river, pulled hard and ran the bow several feet upon the sand. Merrie was out of the canoe in a moment. I was slower. We had arrived at this garden spot midway in our journey, the big rocks behind us. The forecast was for an exceptionally cool night, and the moon, only a couple of days into the waning, would rise late and large. I knew an owl would haunt us from a tree branch downriver and a whippoorwill would call unceasingly, because I needed to hear that as did Merrie, and here on this spit of sand we possessed the only ears in the world.

Swept the sand clear of storm debris. Laid out the tarp that lies underneath the tent. Merrie helped me connect the aluminum poles, and the tent was erect in only a few minutes, the door toward the river so at night we could see and hear the water. Air mattresses down, sleeping bags unrolled. The last time I lay beside Merrie, we worked each other over four times, then split up two days later. I remembered the union much more than the division.

I dug a fire pit and lined it with flat rocks while Merrie set up the kitchen comprised of the ice chest, water jugs, mess kit and a Coleman gas-fueled stove. I laid out two flashlights, then filled the gas lantern and changed the mantles. But darkness would come late, and we would probably light candles and before midnight the moon would rise and shine white upon the river. I stood and surveyed the camp and everything was taut and placed and dry, and I was even more glad that Merrie knew not to stop paddling when the river was in her lap, and that I knew when to shift my weight to the right and then back to the left when the canoe wanted to roll over.

"Want to go swimming?" I asked.

"Yeah."

She changed into her swimsuit, while I took my keys and wallet and spare change from my pockets. The rock shelf was smooth and slick and pocked with stones. Sitting against a boulder, I submerged myself to my chin and smelled the sweet musk of fish and frogs and leaves in decay. A minnow tugged at the hair on my leg and I jerked, thinking of snapping turtles and cottonmouths.

Merrie went by me without hesitation, off the shallow rock shelf into the channel where the water beneath her was dark. She is intrepid, always has been; I will grip a rattlesnake by its neck, but I don't like to dangle my parts above sunken logs and beady, luminous eyes behind sharp beaks and fangs. I'm not scared of danger, but I like to see it coming and know its name, whether the letters spell canebrake or cancer. Merrie just seems to throw herself in, swallowed into the belly, and if the saints become sinners, she claws herself out and walks, never once looking back.

Fishing with a fly rod is not about fish. It is motion and meditation, the oblong circle of the planets around the sun, don't bend your wrist, feed out the line slowly, arm forward to ten o'clock, then in reverse before the leader flips over and whispers as it cuts the air, slung backwards and you feel that weight, two o'clock and the clock reverses, back and forth until you lay the line upon the surface in a motion like sending a wave down a length of rope. You might awaken to the pull of a snagged bass or bream, but fishing with a fly rod is not about just catching fish.

I got no strikes, casting over the lip of the rockshelf. I should have brought a Black Ant lure that would sink down to where the fish are. Instead I had only popping bugs that float too fast on the current. But that does not matter this afternoon, because I was here to enjoy the domain and not exert my dominance. I have done float trips where my food stock was only a can of lard and a bag of corn meal, dependent on snagging catfish on bush hooks, and I caught catfish and fried thick fillets in a skillet over oak embers and ate the flesh with my fingers while it was smoking. This night we would eat warmed-up spaghetti that Merrie had cooked the night before, and chunks of French bread warmed in a skillet and topped with slices of sharp cheddar and red onion and sprinkled with capers. This float was not about endurance and feeding from the land, but was rather a celebration of the senses, of hip bones replaced by nylon and steel, canoe bows that pare left with the white current, and a friendship no longer centered on a bed.

We washed plates and frying pan in the river and rinsed them with jug water. I heated water for coffee, then sat on a blanket with my back against a log. Merrie settled to the ground, then lay back using my legs as a pillow. As if I had dialed him up, an owl hooted once, then again from his perch downriver.

"I should have brought a pint of Jack Daniels for you," I told her.

"I don't want it. I wouldn't want to drink anyway if you're not going to."

"It's been two months now, and I don't miss it or want it."

She was silent for several moments. "Why is it that people always seem to straighten up and get real good when it's too late?"

"I don't know. I guess it takes a while to learn what's important. I'm proud of you for quitting smoking. That's harder than quitting drinking."

"I thought I was going crazy. I couldn't sleep for a solid month."

I recalled the time when she was with me and quit smoking for five days. She *was* crazy. We went to see *Dead Man Walking*, and as soon as we left the theater, she demanded I stop at the Quick Mart, where she bought two packs of Marlboro reds and smoked three on the way home.

The owl haunted us again, as if the spirits of the two who drowned upriver had followed. "This is nice," Merrie said. "You know, all the heavy stuff, we've already done. There's no tension now."

Yeah, all the heavy stuff we'd already done. About a thousand times. "I always did like you more for your mind."

She pinched my leg. I opened my mouth to tell Merrie how strange it seemed that I was here with her sharing this same river I paddled with Katie more than seventeen years ago, and that Katie was just a friend now, as she is. Two bodies of flesh cast into spirits and drawn back in memories as lonesome and rich as the owl's call. I did not see the maker, nor could I touch him, but still I heard the song. I decided not to speak.

The air had cooled, the moon in the trees, golden and shaped like a pumpkin flat on one side. In the tent, I lit the candle lantern and hung it from a cord. Merrie slipped into her feather bag, and I into my separate cocoon. We talked only a little. Her breath went slow and long. I blew out the flame, and rolled onto my belly and looked at the river. It was white in the moon's glow like a path of concrete, like a road before me, worn slick by the tread of those who passed. The road was one-way. No backing-up allowed to try the rocks again and get it right. A whippoorwill started up and called as steadily as the moon slips across the sky and the river slides. I was not the same man as earlier in the morning, nor the one seventeen years ago. I was a better man.

Morning was cool and draped with fog. The doves cooed. I tried to be quiet while building the fire to heat water for coffee. Merrie was up soon after me, just as the water was bubbling. I fixed her a cup of instant, sugared and cooled just a bit with milk.

"You sleep good?"

"Like a log," she said. "I wanted to talk to you, but I was so tired."

"I had a long conversation with the whippoorwill."

"What did it tell you?"

"I'm not sure. It was speaking in whippoorwill, but the words seemed so familiar, like I had heard them all before. I just couldn't quite understand."

Merrie blew steam from the lip of her cup. She did it again — raised one eyebrow and squinted the other eye. "The whippoorwill was a female."

We ate sausage and pancakes smeared with butter and dribbled with syrup, drank lots of coffee. We tarried; both of us visited the woods. Then it was time to break camp, and by mid-morning we were back on the water. I swung the canoe broadside and looked once more at the sandbar, flat and white and marked only by our footprints, and they would be washed clean when the rains began and the river swelled. What I carried away, framed within a separate wood and time would only brighten the colors, because that is the way I choose to view the pictures of my passage. If the whippoorwill spoke to me in a female tongue, I know I did try to listen, even if the words were not tuned exactly for my ear.

Noon passed and I refueled with Vienna sausages, Merrie more in health with nuts and fruit. We reached the landing, and there were men in boats powered with gasoline who cut their eyes at Merrie and probably assumed she was my good-looking daughter. I gazed back upriver where I once had been, and knew I had reached a spot where life starts new again.

Three

The exit off the interstate for The Badlands National Park appears at mid-afternoon. The earth has changed so much from the lush, damp green beside the Platte River, rolling, dry hills where pairs and trios of antelope are often seen grazing upon sparse patches of grass. At the park station, I hand the ranger eight dollars.

"I don't know why they call this a national park," Ma says. "It looks about like the rest of the land to me."

And it does at the passage through this gate. But the earth rises to a ridge in front of us, and I remember from my trip here with Jenell that beyond the lip the land will drastically change.

"Just hold your horses," I say to Ma. "Wait till we pass over that ridge."

The high ground swells above us like some great, brown wave and we begin to climb, the transmission automatically shifting down into low. A few minutes later, we crest the ridge, and there spreading for miles in a series of buttes and hills and cliffs and canyons, the earth looks clawed and gnarled, as though God had raked it with his fingers, and is colored within a range between lavender and deep purple. The road descends into the chaos and loops and curves in a thin ribbon that appears and reappears in the distance like the backbone of a snake in high grass. Within the vehicle, there is a scramble for cameras, and at a vista I pull over so the shutterbugs can get out.

Strangely, I am disappointed at the Badlands. I remember them as being so much wider and deeper and richer in color. But everyone else seems pleased, and at every pull-over the cameras start up again. Ma wants me to stop where she can get a rock. A Badlands rock. We already have Blue Ridge and Kentucky and South Dakota rocks on board. I explain to her that we are cutting through a corner of the park to a campground, that later in the afternoon we will drive deeper into the terrain to where there are a million rocks.

KOA. Dependable and clean and usually located within a few miles of the best sights. This one is about two miles outside the south entrance to the Badlands, situated on a narrow river and shaded by billowy cottonwoods. Meghan and Christopher are excited to see a pool. I haven't camped at a KOA since the trip with Jenell.

The camping fee has sure gone up. Thirty-three dollars for one night, but still much cheaper than a motel. I plan to save more money by cooking supper and breakfast. In the KOA office is a sign that advertises breakfast served from seven to nine in the morning, pancakes and sausage and eggs offered up in exchange for a few bucks. Certainly not like the old days. I wonder if they have a drive-through window.

Bruce and Donnie and I set to securing our rolling habitat. Have to get the vehicle parked level first, but within reach of the utility hookups. The Winnebago is equipped with leveling jacks, but we decide not to use them. None of us have ever lived lives that were exactly level and plumb. Connect a hose between the water spigot and our holding tank. Hook into the electricity circuit. Mate with the sewage dump. Bruce studies the release lever, then pulls it and a day and a half of waste vomits through the tube out of the vehicle. Everything takes about five minutes.

The tent goes up next. The Winnebago can sleep all six of us, but we would be cramped, and both Ma and Donnie snore. Besides, I prefer the open air where I am able to hear the night sounds. Doesn't seem like camping when you sleep two feet from a microwave. The tent goes up fast. Christopher and I slept in it once on the river and rain fell all night, but not a drop leaked inside. Next, we inflate two air mattresses. I've invested in an air pump. Much easier on the lungs. Inside half an hour, we have a movable home. My shoulders aren't sore from humping a backpack all day. In past time, I would have disdained such luxury, but today I am older — and wiser.

Late afternoon, and we leave the campground and take the road through the heart of the park toward Wall, a small town that is mostly one huge drug store. Wall Drug, the epitome of a tourist trap, sprawls over several acres and contains nearly every cowboy concoction so far conceived. I wonder if it has grown even more since Jenell and I were there.

The Winnebago groans through the turns and loops of the park, passing between layers of earth and rock gradually exposed through erosion over millions of years. The sun is lower now and the shadows and light across the buttes and cliffs more stark in contrast. During the twenty-mile drive, I pull into overlooks several times for photos. Ma points out two more large rocks she wants for her collection, and Bruce lugs them on-board.

"You can't get every rock you see, Ma," I complain.

"But, these are so pretty."

"You'll see about a million pretty rocks between here and home. We won' t have room to move."

I think about the dozens of rings she has at home, ordered over the phone from QVC, cheap jewelry that looks much prettier on television than when unwrapped from the package. Rocks, their nuclear half-life millenniums beyond the durability of bones.

Ma's eyes brighten at the gaudy expanse of Wall Drug. She'd choose a visit to a flea market in east Fayetteville any day over the Frick museum in Manhattan. Probably twenty more motor homes as long as ours sit in the parking lot. Ma complains when Bruce gets the collapsible wheel chair from one of the storage bins.

"I don't need this," she complains. "I can walk."

"Why hobble around and hurt when you can ride," I tell her.

"I don't want nobody having to push me." She stares at the chair, and in her eyes I see a reflection of pain, a humility that cuts me. She has carried more than her share of the load all her life. I remember when my hips were bad, and the doctor told me he could write me a permit for a permanent disability parking sticker. I refused it.

But she settles into the chair and tucks the hem of her dress between her knees. Immediately, Meghan steps forward and grips the handles.

"I'll push you, Granny."

Ma lifts one arm and lays her hand atop Meghan's. Ma, overweight and bent, Meghan in shorts with her long legs so shapely and tanned, both possessing brown eyes of the same genes; I am stunned by the beauty of the moment, and I silently pledge to complain no more about rocks.

The sun's light is nearly horizontal during the trip back to the campground, through the same hills and gullies and twists we have already transgressed. But the vision is different now, the colors refracted through a different angle and consumed through an eye still taut and viscous, but filled with water not the same as the eye through which I viewed life twenty-five years ago. I cannot see the same shade of vermilion I witnessed as I rode through this park with Jenell, because my brain now interprets shades in a different hue; I describe them in words uttered through a dissimilar tongue. But what I see are still rocks of time fissured and fractured and painted by through rubbing against the elements of age. I, and these stones, look different in twilight than in the shine of a vertical sun, but we are still basically the same, a few molecules washed away, but the wound tightening the pitch of the tuned nerve. I feel color more today than I see it.

If we cannot return to that same spot on the river because what flowed beneath us then is gone and part of the sea, we can still walk the bank to a spot beside where that current flowed. The bedrock beneath our feet is our bone and does not dissipate so fleetingly as our blood. I can look into the current and, though what I saw once has moved beyond me and is now a part of the mass and memories, the water is still flowing. The Badlands are still beautiful to the bone if I look at what is there instead of what I came back to see.

We all go to bed early, still weary from so many miles. During the next week, we will spend more time on foot instead of wheels. In the darkness inside the tent, I listen to a night bird, but it is not an owl or a whippoorwill, as I am used to hearing back home. Nevertheless, the sound is soothing, offering the assurance that when I slip into sleep and the realm of dreams, the bird's open eyes will tie me to the real world.

I often dream of an empty house. Rooms dusty and bare of furniture, linoleum curled at the edges and cracked, the air chilled and musty and dim with only the light that leaks through a drawn shade. I am always alone in that house, and the doorway into the next room is even darker. But, I know I need to go into that room, because inside is something I forgot to take with me, and I don't know if it is even still there. The dream is always of a place I have left, and it is stale and barren and ghostly, and what I have come to retrieve is not in the room where I stand, but in a deeper chamber I wish not to enter.

The light comes early in this high latitude, five a.m., and the inside of the tent is luminous and cool. I lie here and think about where I am and where we are to travel today. Bruce is sleeping. He always has trouble going to sleep, but has an equal difficulty waking up. I fall to sleep easily, but awaken seconds before the bell chimes. I feel pretty good, despite losing a full night of sleep driving out here. I think of coffee, and how good it would taste right now, a few puffs on a cigar.

I try to unzip the tent door as quietly as possible, then slide out without disturbing Bruce. He doesn't stir. Outside, the air is cool and very clear; through the cottonwoods I see the river and beyond to the first roll of the Badlands. No other campers are about, but I do spy a magpie hopping on a patch of grass. Black and white with long tail feathers. We have no magpies in North Carolina, and the sight of the bird furthers my realization that I am in another land. The dew is also missing, the grass under my toes dry. I think about how I stand on the boundary of a park sculpted by water, yet the morning lies as dry as old bones.

Inside the Winnebago, silence is thick except for the drone of Donnie snoring. He lies on his back upon the couch, did not unfold it into a bed. I try to be quiet, but the silence amplifies the sound of movements. I spoon some fresh coffee on top of the old grounds, then pour water into the reservoir and click the juice on.

"Son?" Ma calls from her bed.

I stand in the doorway. "Did you sleep OK?"

"'Bout like usual. How about you?"

"I was out like a light. I'm making some coffee. I'll try to be quiet."

"You won't bother me."

I doubt Ma has slept soundly since she was a girl. A wife at seventeen, mother at age twenty-one, she has always slumbered, one ear tuned for the wheeze of a child's breath laboring with croup, the sound of her husband's truck tires in the driveway on late nights when he came home drinking.

I watch the coffee make. Meghan's ears are muffled with innocence; she sleeps on her side with her hair covering her face. I study her shoulders until I see them rise with her breath. Christopher still sleeps like a baby, his butt thrust out and knees drawn; they are crowded on the narrow bed. A cup clangs against the counter top, and Donnie rolls to his side and mumbles, his face against the seatback. I rob the coffee pot of the first brew, not waiting for all the water to filter through. The liquid is black and rich and bitter. Add a little milk, the way Bruce and I drink it.

He's up when I walk from the motor home, bare-chested and sitting at the picnic table smoking another of the cigarettes that will probably eventually kill him. Woke up on his own as if on this morning away from the need of clocks, his own inner chime uncoiled.

"Got you some coffee here." I set a cup before him.

"You didn't have to do that. I thought maybe you had gone up to the bathhouse."

And there we sit for the next half an hour, talking and smoking and sipping coffee, while the world around us is waking, two brothers bound beyond the blood that flows in our veins to bone marrow; the same as twins.

When Bruce leaves to go to the bathhouse, I take a postcard and a pen from my shirt pocket. I look at a postcard I bought yesterday. The picture is of high, thin clouds above a mountain range, the vapors illuminated and colored by a low sun. I turn the card over and begin writing.

All of humanity, once part
of some primal, finite mass
for some unknown reason
has been scattered to infinity.
And everything from raindrops to people
who possess like ions
need at times to merge and share the same molecules.
To return home.

Scanning the words, I think about Lynn, a woman of whom I am especially fond, of the last time I was with her, and how this morning she lives among my memories. I write her address on the card and wonder what she is doing at this moment, and if she will receive the picture and the words before I am already back home. I need to start breakfast, get the rest of the family up and living.

Through Rapid City to Mount Rushmore to the faces blasted and chiselled and sanded into the likeness of men now dead. Makes me think of a man in L.A. who questioned my license to write about one year of my life; is my chief motivation the need to sculpt my own face and leave that profile out of fear that people will forget I lived? Through the Black Hills where the Indians say spirits live, but in this rocking, rolling tribute to the white man, I find it hard to feel the souls of a people who mostly walked and lived in wigwams. Ma needs a Black Hills rock, and at a pull-off, one is added to the collection. We cut through the corner of Wyoming, cross rolling grasslands, cattle country. Donnie is like a tour guide. Often, he talks non-stop, a monologue rolling off his tongue about where we are on the map, the history of the country we are cutting through, just about anything that happens to be on his mind. I look at Bruce and roll my eyes.

Donnie was born in Broadslab, North Carolina, a crossroads farming community in the eastern part of the state, tobacco-farming country, moonshine-making country; he talks in an accent that makes mine sound upscale. He is the son of parents who lived their lives as tenant farmers. He told me once that his father went to the store each morning and bought the food they would eat that day, and except for the garden and the yard chickens, no snacks ever rested in the refrigerator or pantry. Unlike most of his ancestors, Donnie graduated high school, then went on to get a degree in business from Fayetteville Tech.

"Somebody ought to make another pot of coffee," Donnie declares.

Yeah, somebody ought to, I think. I'm driving, and Bruce just got through driving; Ma is too unsteady on her feet, and the kids don't drink coffee. Who is that somebody who ought to make another pot of coffee?

Donnie stares at the coffee maker like he might will it to chug and spit and fill. "Yeah, somebody ought to make some coffee. Tim, you see some buffalos, I want you to stop. I'm gonna catch me a baby buffalo. Take it back home and put it in the pasture. I ain't seen no buffalos yet. Ain't seen any niggers, either. I ain't seen a nigger since we stopped for gas in St. Louis. Darlene, you want some coffee?"

Ma starts to grind to her feet, but Bruce slips up and beats her to the pot. "I'll make it, Mama," he says.

"You know, Tim," said Donnie, "that's why the Indians called niggers, 'buffalo soldiers,' 'cause their hair looked the same. I don't know how they come to call them that, though, 'cause I ain't seen any niggers out here. No buffaloes either. Plenty of Indians, though."

At the end of a long day of driving, we reach the KOA located about five miles from the Custer Memorial. Hook the

Winnebago up again, pitch the tent and blow up the air mattresses. As early as the dawn came, twilight drapes herself even later. Ma limps to the pay telephones to call Kelli, Donnie to call Karen; I remind the kids they need to phone their mother. I realize for probably the first time on a trip, I have no one I am obligated to report my whereabouts to — no wife back home, no steady girlfriend, my children and mother in tow with me. Standing beneath the dome of this big sky, I feel strangely small, as if the lifelines that have always buoyed my journeys have been cut, and I am adrift with only a compass that rests in my heart.

Our campsite is in view of the Little Big Horn River. Studying the light left in the sky, I pull my fly rod and tackle box from one of the storage bins and head for the river bank.

The water is mostly shallow and slow, but I notice darker holes toward the middle of the current where fish have wallowed out vantage points from which to feed. I oil the male joint of my fly rod by rubbing it against the side of my nose, then put the halves together, thread the line through the guides, then start tying a surface fly to the leader. Circles of expanding ripples spread out from where fish are already surface feeding and I hurry trying to knot the lure until I screw up and have to start over again. Slow down, get the knot right, then strip out several yards of line and flip it out. I strip more line and whip the rod back and forth until I can feel the weight, then cast toward the middle of the river. The line lies across the water like a wave cresting in reverse, then flips the leader over and the lure lands gently on the surface like an insect lighting. That's the way it's supposed to be done. When the lure slaps too hard, it scares the fish. Twice I cast, letting the lure float over the circles of darker water.

On the third cast, the lure implodes, and the line goes taut. I jerk backwards on the rod; the fish runs parallel to shore. The tip of my rod bends, and the line stretches until it stabs the water. I let extra line slip between my fingers. The fish leaps above the surface, writhing before smacking broadside, a big rainbow trout, his sides irradiating red and brown and ivory. He runs again and I allow him more line. I'm worried he might go deep and get tangled in submerged branches or rocks. But I can't fight him in; the leader is only a four-pound test, and the fish looks bigger than any I have caught. Feels like a whale on this light weight rod. Twice more he jumps, square tail fanning the air; six or seven minutes pass and the fish tires and I am able to land him. He is exhausted, gills heaving, wet sides fracture the sunlight and cast it back in rainbow colors. I grasp him by the lower jaw and lift, and when his mouth opens, I could put three fingers inside. This is a big one!

I think of him gutted and scaled, sprinkled with salt and pepper and dabbed with chunks of butter and rounds of sliced onion and lemon, wrapped in tin foil and baked till the pink flesh is barely flaky. His eye is black and flat, and I look into it and think of the last squirrel I ever shot.

I was living in the cabin then and hunted squirrels in the bottom land where the creek flowed. I had a twelve-gauge Remington pump, a big gun for squirrels, but I wasn't in it for the sport. I wanted the meat. One shot would knock the varmint down, and if he still kicked, I'd snap his neck between my thumb and fingers.

I already had four that afternoon, and the fifth I shot at through branches. He fell, but ran dragging one leg into a hole in the base of a tree. I poked the rodent out with my gun barrel, and he ran squealing between my feet. I whirled and shot again, but was short and only mangled his tail. The squirrel stopped and turned to me and stood on his hind legs, silent and motionless and scalded by shot and fire as if he knew that death had come and he wanted to see it in its form. When I pulled the last time, I was only a few yards from the animal, and the blast knocked him through the air several feet and ripped him inside-out. He was no longer good for living or for eating. And I hadn't needed that fifth squirrel; I already had enough for a meal.

I don't need this big fish in order to eat tonight either. Taking a tape measure from my tackle box, I hold the trout by his lower jaw and let him hang. The tape tips his tail fin at seventeen and a half inches, by far the largest trout I have ever caught. And then I put him back in the water, and he flips his tail and is gone among the rocks.

A pair of mallards are sitting onshore watching me. I wonder what the drake was thinking as I let that big fish go. Does he applaud me for my grace, or does he think, "You dumb sumbitch. Better fatten up now before the ice comes." I cannot know his mind or if he thinks at all, but I suspect sometimes that any intellect other than my own has more answers to the riddle of creation because my concrete knowledge is nil. Maybe the dragonfly skimming the water moved beyond clothes and cars eons ago, the duck not in need of the Internet any longer, that fish I just released a product of an evolution that has taken him beyond cablevision and bank accounts and the need of war to ensure such luxuries. Perhaps the animals and fish and bugs and plants view humans with disdain and pity at our nakedness and ignorance, their own minds in tune with one infinite, cosmic frequency.

And Saturn shines yellow because of her chemical make-up, and black holes gobble up matter and spit it out into another time dimension, and a big trout will lay thousands of eggs, but maybe one grows into another seventeen-and-a-half-inch trout, and if a Methodist or a Buddhist or an Agnostic catches it, the likelihood of the fish being eaten or released depends mostly upon how hungry the man is.

Everyone is tired, and we retire early. Bruce and I talk for awhile lying on our beds of air, moon and neon light mixing through the screen windows.

"This feels good, doesn't it," I say to Bruce.

"Yeah. I'm pretty tired."

"I hate you had to drive so much today. You must feel like you're at work."

"Naw. I'm enjoying this."

"I appreciate you coming. I couldn't do this trip without you to help drive and navigate. And keep me from choking Donnie."

Bruce laughs. "He can talk, can't he." He's quiet for

several moments. "Donnie is just Donnie. I've learned that. He means well."

"Yeah. You gonna be able to go to sleep?"

"I'll go to sleep sooner or later."

"You want a couple of Valiums? I've got some right here."

"I'll go to sleep all right."

I hesitate a moment, then roll over to where my trousers are and get the pill vial from one pocket. Bruce will never ask for anything. He will give you his last dollar, but he would not ask for a penny even if he was hungry. "Here, take these. Ain't no reason to lay awake."

"I hate to take your Valiums. You'll need them."

"I don't ever take any except when I'm speaking. I got plenty. Here." I put two in his palm. Funny how I always carry a vial of Valium around with me, my security blanket, as if I might be stopped at a highway license check and asked to suddenly stand up and perform.

"Thank you, Tim."

"It'll be good tomorrow. The Custer battlefield is pretty impressive. That hill. Grave markers. You can see how Custer stood there, all surrounded and no way out."

They didn't make Valium back then.

In the light of dawn, I can see against the horizon the hill where Custer and his men gathered. Steam lifts from my coffee, the pink, eastern sky stark against the dark rolling hills. I can't believe how many mornings I wasted sleeping off a fifth. And since I talked recently to Roy, my doctor, I guess my appreciation of the coming of the light is tempered by my renewed knowledge that my number of dawns is finite.

• • •

Roy Cromartie has been my doctor since I returned from Seattle after my bone marrow transplant nine years ago. He's about my age, his ears stick out and he is always pleasant and quick to smile, even though he works mostly with very sick people. A little more than a month ago, he sat behind his desk in his office at Kaiser Permanente, with me in a chair across from him. He had called me in to talk about my blood test drawn in my yearly check-up a few days before.

"You have a little bump in your protein level that hasn't been in the blood tests since you came back from Seattle."

I nodded and felt a little tightening in my stomach. I remembered that protein in the blood is a major symptom that shows up in people with myeloma.

"The protein is still well within the normal level, but anytime we see a spike that hasn't been there before, it's something to watch."

I nodded again. The hair holding the sword over my head had just thinned a bit.

"There are other things that can cause the spike. Statistically, there is a bit more than a fifty percent chance that if we test again, the results will be normal."

"OK. So when do I need to get tested again?"

"In three months. We need to give it some time. It's like when you see a person everyday, you don't notice changes, but if you go a while without seeing them, you notice things different."

Three months. That would be in mid-August, I thought. In mid-August I would already have made the trip out west in the Winnebago with Ma and the kids. I'll have already taught summer school and paid the extension on my taxes. Mid-August seemed like a long time, and I have never been one to worry too much about nothing until it is time to worry.

"Tim, I wouldn't be concerned right now. But, we haven't seen this spike before, so we need to stay on top of it."

I shook Roy's hand and left, and a whole new shade of light seemed to engulf the outside world, as if the crystal had turned and the light now shone through a different facet.

Ten years had passed since I was diagnosed with myeloma. After five years you're generally considered cured. The doctors told me when I was leaving the VA hospital that statistically there was a ten percent chance I would be disease-free in a year — a nicer way of saying there was a ninety percent chance the disease would return within 365 days. I didn't believe it would, just as I didn't believe I would die in Seattle, and after a year, I was disease-free and I have just kept running.

Several times after I returned from Seattle, I was asked to speak or write about being a "cancer survivor." That word pissed me off, "survivor," as if I was a man ravaged by a hurricane, left naked and dazed clinging to the denuded trunk of a palm tree with nothing left but my devastated life. Screw that. Maybe I was ugly for a while and weakened in some ways, but I pretty much picked life back up where I left off. Instead, I viewed myself as a "cancer scholar," a man who had gained an education and insight into himself and life that would have never come without the experience. Plus, it was one hell of an adventure.

But right now, I'd prefer the doldrums for a few years. The time to raise Meghan and Christopher and write a few more books and snag some more fish and finally catch up with my spirit-woman. That would be just too ironic and too mean to be where I am right now — finally have a nice little house and two new hips, sobriety, promotion at work and a little money in the bank — the potential of some good years ahead — and suddenly be thrown back in the fire. And this time, I'm honestly not sure I would make it out again like I was sure I would ten years ago.

And then the bubble floated up and I looked at it this way — better to be thrown back in the fire after gaining the satisfaction of owning a nice little house and good hips, sobriety, the title of assistant professor and a few extra bucks, than to get sick when you're homeless, hurting, drunk and broke. The glass is still half full.

Half an hour later, I was back at my house. I had bought two baby geese and a young turkey about a month earlier. They think I'm their mama, follow me around the yard, will squat at my feet if I stand still long enough. I like the way the goslings, Gomez and Lucy, cock their heads to one side and look upwards at me with one eye. The kids named the turkey Peaches, and when I told them it was a he instead of a she, the name was changed to Mr. Peaches. In my fenced back yard, George, my African spur-foot tortoise, was happily eating grass. He is about three years old and weighes probably twenty pounds, but with luck can live 150 years and grow to weigh 200 pounds. He rarely drinks water and can live on grass, but he loves bananas. I guess I'll have to include him in my will. Maybe sooner than later. Those thoughts kept popping up since I had spoken to Roy, and I tried to dispel them.

The backyard is fenced into two sections, and in the larger pen the dogs stand on the wire and speak to me. Lilly, the golden retriever pup, is growing so fast. I got her spayed, but I hated to do it. I would have loved to breed her to a nice, male Golden and have a litter of puppies for the kids to enjoy. I have fond memories of laying on the ground as a kid with seven or eight puppies squirming atop me licking my face. When the kids were small, I got them a female kitty from the animal shelter. She promptly got herself pregnant when she was of age, and when Valentine went into labor in Meghan's closet, I got Meghan out of school and let her watch five kittens come wet and fragile into the world. Valentine had another litter, and we kept one of the males; Katie talked me into having her spayed after that delivery. Tux still lives with the kids, but Valentine got run over eight months ago. Meghan and Christopher gave her a proper funeral, complete with flowers, song, and tears. And I think they were bettered by the cycle of joy and grief; too many kids grow up today with their only concept of the finality of death based upon what they see on television. When a fourteen-year-old girl kills herself because her boyfriend broke up with her, I can't believe she really comprehended the reality of death.

My bulldog, Roy Lee, warbled at me like some fat, wingless bird. I rubbed his head. His noggin is scarred from the fights he has picked with other male dogs. He's 7/8ths English and 1/8th Pit, but the American scrapper in him dominates his more genteel English heritage and makes "his mouth overload his ass," as they used to say down in Fayetteville. He's been with me more than three years, and I wondered who could love his ugly bone-head as I do if I was no longer around.... I stopped myself. I'd already beaten nine-to-one odds against my survival, so why was I letting a spike in my protein levels color my thoughts? But it felt as though a certain lens had been put over my eyes that made the world and my thoughts a slightly different hue, more acute and focused like ten years earlier when I first got the bad news.

And incredibly, I felt a distinct spark of excitement in my belly, a certain crystalline exuberance that is with me when I am poised above a poisonous snake ready to take it in my hands, or when I embark alone on a river trip, or when I'm lying on a gurney waiting to be wheeled into an operating room to have a chunk of bone sawed out. It's me and who I am and my grit and faith and a bit of luck that will go a long way toward seeing the situation either cured or killed. Draw on what I have learned, and the humility to trust in those I have chosen. And that instinct is primal. It may not dwell in everyone, but it does in me. Life without conflict is pretty mundane.

At three o'clock, I picked Christopher up at school.

"Hey, Bud. How was school today?"

"Good."

"What'd you learn?"

"Oh, different stuff. I got asked to be a marshal for the eighth grade graduation."

"Really! Man, that's great. I'm proud of you!"

Christopher smiled. He's growing so fast these days. Nearly as tall as Meghan. His voice is starting to change, cracks sometimes in mid-sentence. Meghan teases him. I don't recall my father ever asking me a single question about school. He had quit in the seventh grade to go to work. But, I remember when he was dying, and I was home fresh from Tunisia with a year left at UNC, and he told me he wanted me to finish my degree. When I finally got that piece of paper, I thought of him, of words he could never say, and of words I would make sure I said to my own children.

"Yeah, I'm proud of you, Buddy. You can be anything in the world you want to be. You just have to want it."

"I'm proud of you, too, Dad," and he placed his hand on mine, and my breath caught for a second.

"We're gonna have one heck of a trip out west," I told Christopher. "I talked to the guy again today about the Winnebago. We're getting the big one. Thirty-foot long. Big as a bus."

"That's going to be sooo cool, Dad."

The trip out west is the realization of a pledge I made to Ma years ago that I would take her to the northern Rockies before she died. It's time. The trip would be expensive, but if I had lived my life by what was affordable and rational and safe, I'd have a much tamer portfolio of memories. I've got good credit.

I picked Meghan up from her school at three thirty-five. God, I'm in love with that child all over again every time I see her. She seems to dance as she walks, rail-thin and shapely with brown eyes as large as continents. I had already gotten in the passenger seat so she could flaunt her newly-earned permit.

"Hey punkie-punkie."

"Hey, Dad."

How was school?"

"Good."

"What did you learn?"

"Dad, I want to get my ankle tattooed."

"You're not getting your ankle tattooed now. You wait till you're eighteen, and if you still want one, I'll take you personally to Bill Claydon's place in Fayetteville."

"Tema got her eyebrow pierced."

"That's Tema, and besides, it would hurt like hell. Too much metal in you and lightning might strike you."

"Daaad!"

"How did you do on your French test?"

"I got a ninety. What about getting my upper ear pierced?"

I thought on that for a moment. I realized her tactics. She has to lie down when she has blood drawn, and wouldn't really get her eyebrow pierced if I paid her. "I don't have a problem with getting another hole in your ear. What would your mom say?"

"She wouldn't care. I *am* fifteen."

Yeah, you're fifteen all right, I thought. Fifteen and clueless. At fifteen, I bagged groceries on weekends and cropped tobacco all summer. I hunted poisonous snakes. But, I wouldn't want her doing any of that. I never made a ninety on a French test. Didn't even take French.

"I can handle another hole in your ear," I said. "If you can stand the pain, I can stand the financial strain."

She smiled and started the truck. Ride, Meghan, ride. And I hoped I was riding shotgun with her for a few more years.

The sun crests the hill where Custer died, blood red and swollen.... I sip my coffee and puff on a stogie, listening to the birds chirp. I'm even more glad I let that fish go yesterday evening. He's probably enjoying this morning just like me.

A bluejay sits chirping from a nearby limb. I wonder what he is thinking or if he thinks at all, if possibly he has lost his mind in the sense of Eastern philosophy, no longer ruled by thoughts, but at peace with his mere existence.

I recall a man I did not know, who died of cancer a number of years ago. He was the brother-in-law of a man Katie worked with. I heard how in his last days his wife found him each morning sitting in front of the picture window of their house, gazing intently into the world. A hard winter was upon the land, and when I thought of the man, I found the image as chilling as the frost I walked out into each morning. Limited in the sunrises he had yet to observe, the dawn frozen and gray and without colors, weeks from the flocks of robins and daffodils that would crack the ice as the sap flowed northward. He knew he would probably not live those weeks, and I imagined he lamented all that he had not touched and smelled and tasted and heard and seen when the platter had been ripe within his sight and grasp. What a cold way to go out of this world.

But this morning I realize how wrong I may have been. I judged him by the measure of what I still lacked in my life, painted his vision with the textures and colors I wished still to see. This morning I speak for him with this tongue....

...This coffee is good, the bitter blended with the sweet, and I drink it slowly and look upon the land that sleeps chilled under a blanket of rest. I have not seen the sunrise as such, the ascending light not hazed by veils of vapor, but rather crisp and crystalline and silver. What I see is not barren. History is only as real as memories, and I have stored volumes behind my eyes. The dawn is like a naked canvas that can be dressed in any cut or shade of clothing, and what I see through this portal, I can clothe with the recall of 10,000 mornings that dawned between the polar ends of chaos and calm. If I am faced with a stark canvas, let me dress it with remembrance of what I did not turn from when that moment beckoned. I am the helmsman who steered the vessel between the tides that ebbed and surged twice within each cycle of the sun. The narrow blue passage through rocks with my hand upon the wheel and tempered with the knowledge of what is right and not right, I slipped between the shards of stone left cracked and rendered by the anger of Moses, learning that no law is etched in stone, but is scribed in a unique cursive in each man and woman's heart. And by passing within reach of the rocks, did I not hear better the surf and see the sprays of splintered spectrum, and sail within the grasp of that person marooned and drowning? Calmer water would have given more ease of passage, but also would have remained solitary and flat.

This frigid canvas is mine for the coloring, and what I bear to the grave will be the portraits of what I did not turn from when the vision of seeing hurt my eyes but held such aching beauty more treasured by the simple truth it would have been so much easier, but emptier, to have simply closed my eyes....

This is what I now choose to believe the man saw on those white-cold mornings because I can know only my heart, and *these* are the pigments I would draw upon in my own last visage of dawn.

And that hill is impressive in an ignoble way, where Custer and his men fled to the high ground when they realized how seriously in trouble they were. The knob of ground isn't much higher than the surrounding hills, but the earth from it slopes down gently to the Little Big Horn River where the shallow water is shaded with willows and cottonwoods. Bruce and I broke camp and had us on the road before the rest of the troupe was out of bed, and at nine a.m. I'm standing here on the crest, trying to blot out of my mind the other tourists and imagine what it must have felt like on that Sunday afternoon when the Indians were circling and yelling and soldiers were shooting and falling and the air was acrid and blue with smoke.

I never was a Custer fan. He brought death to many Rebel soldiers during the Civil War. He seems also to have caused the demise of about 230 pony soldiers on that Sabbath afternoon when he failed to heed his scouts' reports and military logic and rode into an ambush with two of his brothers and a number of civilians along. He was arrogant and brash and despite the Hollywood version of the battle, an Indian eyewitness said, "It took about as long to kill the soldiers as it takes a hungry man to eat." I do have sympathy for him, though, because he had his brothers with him, and I bet if he was any kind of man, he hated worse than losing his life what he had done to his blood.

A breeze blows up here and the river shines in the distance. A number of white grave markers dot the hillside where soldiers dropped trying to make the water. I think about the squirrel I last killed, how I was as big as an army to the creature, and when it knew there was no escape, it stood at the top of a rise of land and faced me. I like to think that's what Custer did when he realized he was not going to make the river nor the next morning, that he dropped his pistols and stood looking into Crazy Horse's eyes with the sun warm on his hair and his chest bowed out because he knew death had come for him, and he wanted to look it in the eye and not over his shoulder.

That's what I want to do if the myeloma has come back. I'll fight it again — fight it hard — but if I see that I am on a hilltop and surrounded, and the ammo has run out, I don't want to go out scrambling and clawing and lying on my back, all dignity shed and dependent on a machine for my breath.

I think about John Parker, one of my doctors before I went for the bone marrow transplant. About five years after I returned from Seattle, John was diagnosed with lung cancer at age fifty-seven. His brother had already died from the disease. John studied his case and his options for treatment and cure, and he decided that instead of enduring radiation and chemotherapy that might add a few months to his life, he wanted to play his piano and read Shakespeare and drink good wine and die. He did, and the squirrel died facing me, and Custer dropped his guns and lifted his chin, and I ain't dying in no hospital bed. Next year, or thirty years from now. Not if I see death coming.

I'd like to cook breakfast, but the road is calling, about five hundred miles of blacktop between where Custer last stood and our next stop at Saint Mary's on the eastern edge of Glacier National Park. So we load up again, Bruce lugging on board a five-pound Little Big Horn rock for Ma's collection. I pull into the next McDonald's down the interstate.

"Let's do this quick," I announce. Meghan scribbles on a piece of paper what each person wants. Donnie is silent.

"What you want, Donnie?" I ask.

"Nothing. I brought my food."

Before leaving home, Donnie lugged on board a cardboard box filled with canned goods. Mostly Vienna sausages and crackers, lunch meat and a loaf of white bread, instant coffee and honey buns.

"You don't want a biscuit?" I ask him.

"Naw. I brought my food."

"Y'all hurry," I tell Meghan and Christopher. Bruce stares at me for a moment. After the kids scamper from the vehicle, he rises from the driver's seat and walks outside. A few minutes later, he returns with the kids. They start passing out the food.

"Here, Donnie," Meghan says, handing Donnie a bacon and egg biscuit.

"I didn't pay for this."

Meghan pauses, her arm extended with the food. She glances at Bruce. "The woman must have messed up the order," Bruce explains. "Got a free biscuit, Donnie."

Donnie stares at the food, then reaches and takes it. Bruce turns toward the windshield and cranks the engine. Donnie consumes his breakfast in about the time it takes a hungry man to eat.

We roll northwest, crossing broad plains and rivers and small mountain ranges, counting antelopes beside the highway, prairie dogs often sprinting across the asphalt in front. Many have been mashed. Donnie keeps his eye tuned for a buffalo herd. We stop for gas and a chance for everyone to get out and stretch their legs. When I go to the door to pay for the fuel, a man is sitting beside it, his back against the wall. Tattered clothes, several days of stubble on his chin, between his knees is clasped a paper sack with the neck of a bottle sticking out. Wine probably, fortified, cheap wine that will do the trick in less time and for fewer coins than a good bottle of Chardonnay. I've known my share of drunks. Some drank Mad Dog wine and some drank Johnny Walker Black Label scotch, but they were all trying to get to the same place. I think of the taste of Gibson's vodka, a triple shot mixed with Mountain Dew soda pop, and I shudder at the memory, and just six months ago, I could easily have been mistaken for the man against the wall.

Four

Where in the hell was I? A bed. A small bed. A large picture window in front of me. Through it I could see the tops of several buildings. I must be up in the air. Sun just below the horizon. Red sky. Beyond the buildings, the earth rolled to the crest of several ridgelines; the earth was blue, the way it looks when the air is cold. That red, red sky. Red in the morning, sailor take warning. But was the sun rising or was it setting? I looked at my watch and it read seven, and the sun at this time of the year is already set at seven, so it must be the dawn. Where the hell am I? I turned my head, and to my right was another bed, and in it beneath the covers I could see the form of a person.

Then I knew where I was, the realization curling over me like a tidal wave. I closed my eyes and tried to blank out all thoughts, tried to fall backwards into a deep, black hole without thoughts or dreams.

The sun was probably an hour above the ridgeline when I opened my eyes again. A black woman was standing above me beside a cart.

"I need to take your vitals," she said.

She stuck a thermometer in my mouth. "How you feeling?" she asked.

"I'm all right," I mumbled around the glass rod.

She fastened a blood pressure cuff around my bicep. The machine hummed as it pumped air, then made a chugging sound to the tempo of my pulse. The machine hissed as the air was expelled, and I watched the numbers appear, one-fifty over ninety-six. Pulse is one/thirty. That's fast.

"I'll get your meds," she told me. "They'll be bringing up breakfast in about half an hour."

I closed my eyes again and tried to fall back into the hole, but the person in the other bed was stirring now, and I watched him through cracked eyelids. About my age, clean-cut, he acted like I was not even in the room. Slipping on a pair of jeans, then a shirt and loafers, he walked into what must be the bathroom because I immediately heard water running.

God, I didn't want to think, but memories kept coming back to me. I remembered being in the waiting room in the emergency unit with Dave; I remembered lying down on the floor. I recalled lying on a gurney with an IV in my arm, a bag of fluids running into my arm. The nurse was pretty. Dave was sitting in a chair.

"He's been drunk about three weeks," he told her.

"How much were you consuming a day, Tim?" she asked me.

"About a fifth."

I remember a nurse rolling me in a wheel chair, and she stopped at a window and spoke to another woman, and then the door in front of me hummed and clicked, and the nurse opened it and rolled me inside.

South Wing at North Carolina Memorial Hospital. The same hospital where I saw Christopher born, where I went through four-day sessions of chemotherapy before I went west for the transplant, the same hospital where I spent three nights after the copperhead bit me, same place where both my hips were replaced. I'd survived about every ward in this joint, and now South Wing, where the drunks and crazy people go.

The guy looked at me when he came out of the bathroom.

"You all right?" he asked.

"I'm breathing."

"I didn't hear you come in. Must have been late."

"They don't bring you breakfast?" I asked.

"Not unless you can't walk. They're into the group thing here."

"How long you been here?"

"Nine days. I get out tomorrow. That is if the doctors say I can."

I thought about that for a minute. If they say you can. What the hell have I gotten myself into, I wondered.

"You don't have to do none of this stuff if you don't feel like it," he told me. "I didn't hardly get out of bed the first three days I was here. Course, if you do, you might get out a little quicker."

He turned and left the room. Don't have to do what stuff? A woman knocked on the door. I waved her in.

"I have your meds," she told me. I assumed she was a nurse, but she was dressed in street clothes. She held a paper cup in one hand, and a glass of water in the other. "How are you feeling?"

"I'm OK. What are these pills for."

The names of the pills didn't ring any bells, but I understood that one was a tranquilizer, one to slow down my pulse, another just a common vitamin.

"Why don't you try getting up and coming out to the dayroom. Breakfast is being served."

After she left, I sat up and swung my legs off the bed. The room was pretty sparse. Two beds, two desks with chairs, no television. A table separated the beds. On it was a pile of folded towels, hospital greens, and a bath robe. A man stuck his head through the door.

"Our first morning group session is beginning in twenty minutes. We'd love to have you join us." He moved on. I heard him talking at the next room.

I looked down my chest to my belly. Wearing a t-shirt, a pair of jeans. When I stood, the jeans hung real low on my hips. No belt. I felt for my wallet, and it was missing. I bet I'd lost ten pounds. Three weeks on a vodka diet will shed the pounds. Might as well start facing the music. I wasn't hungry, but I knew I needed to eat.

My room was at the end of the hallway. I wasn't walking so good; I'd still probably have blown a twenty on a breathalizer.

All right, McLaurin, pull out the Moe-rine in you. I can hack.

I been through worse than this. Feet forward and back erect.

You got yourself in this shit. Now get your dumb ass out.

As I passed the nurses' station another woman looked up at me. "You look like you're feeling better."

I flashed a smile. "I'm fine," but we both knew better. The day room was large, a dozen tables in the middle, couches lining the walls. A television in one corner, a bookshelf filled with books. Maybe twenty people were sitting at the tables, eating from plastic trays. A couple of them paused and looked up at me, but most just concentrated on their food. A metal cart with shelves still held several trays.

"Mr. McLaurin," the woman behind the nurses' station said. "Let me help you."

How did she know my name? Searching through the trays, she pulled the one out with my name typed on a slip of paper. She placed it on a table across from a young black woman. I thanked her, then sat down and glanced at the woman, but she ignored me. Carton of milk on my tray, container of orange juice. A plastic wrapped set of plastic eating utensils, napkin, salt and pepper. Beneath the plate cover, I had a wad of scrambled eggs, two slices of bacon, grits, I guessed, in a small bowl. I drank the milk and juice and ate the bacon. I couldn't deal with the eggs and grits.

I surveyed the people around me, and most of them looked pretty normal. To get admitted to this unit, you needed insurance, and people who have insurance look pretty normal. Mostly white people in their middle years, most of them slender, some gaunt in the face. One older man with a gray beard had his arms folded and was rocking back and forth, his face down and weeping. I didn't look at him very long. I was starting to feel worse by the minute, hands beginning to tremble. Spent trays were placed back in the cart. I gripped mine very carefully and slid it back on a shelf.

"Mr. McLaurin, we need to get your weight while

you're up," the nurse said to me.

I stepped on the scale, watched the numbers stop at 178. Damn, I had lost some weight. Ten pounds like I guessed. I wished I had a belt on.

"What day is this?" I asked the nurse, embarrassed.

"Saturday. Do you remember coming in last night?"

"Sort of."

I'd been lying back in bed for about ten minutes when a man poked his head through the door.

"You have a phone call from your ex-wife. Do you want to take it?"

"Yeah." I swung my legs off the bed.

"The phone is on the wall by the day room."

Lord, I didn't want to take that call. But I had to. Start facing up. Got myself in this shit. "Hello."

"Hi. Are you all right?" Katie's voice sounded tight.

Exhaling. "Yeah. I'm OK."

"Dave called me this morning and told me he had brought you there."

"Yeah. I needed to come. I just couldn't get over the hump this time. So I had him bring me here."

"Everyone needs a little help sometimes," Katie told me. "You did the right thing."

"I'm sorry. Are the kids OK?"

"They're fine. They're worried about you. When do you want me to bring them up."

"Not today. I need to straighten out a bit. Maybe tomorrow."

She put the kids on the line. I told them I was all right and that I loved them and would see them soon. And I do love them. Love them more than I do my own breath. Suck it up, homeboy. This elevator had gone as low as I'm willing to ride.

Saturday? Where had the last three weeks gone? Withdrawal was beginning to kick in; my hands were getting shakier, had chills even with the covers pulled up to my neck. Then the dry heaves set in, the urge to throw up, although there was precious little in my stomach. After a couple of trips to the toilet, I set a cup by my bed and every few minutes rolled to my side and retched until yellow bile came up. My stomach muscles knotted, the sweating started, a cold sweat that made me shiver even more. A nurse came in to check my vitals again.

"How are you feeling?"

"Not too good. When is the doctor coming around?"

"They're making rounds. Weekends are a little slower."

Pulse was still fast, my blood pressure was a little better. I resisted the urge to puke until the nurse left. I touched a strawberry above my left eye and wondered how I got it, rubbed my jaw that was furry with whiskers. Saturday? What's the date? Finally decided it had to be December 12th. Two days till my birthday. Less than two weeks till Christmas, and I hadn't bought the first thing. Tried to remember what was the last day I could post grades at school. Hated to even think about school, missed the last three classes. Several of my students called to ask if I was all right. Told them I had the flu. Mama called several times; she knew I didn't have the flu. Several friends stopped by to talk to me, me either in bed or lying on the couch, a half gallon of vodka within reach.

"What the hell is going on?" George had said. "Man, you got to get a grip on yourself. Your mama's called me. Your sister. What I need to do is just beat the shit out of you."

"Why don't you just shoot me, George."

"You ain't getting out that easy."

How the hell had I gotten into this mess? But I knew, just like the times before, except they never got this bad. The Friday before Thanksgiving, me feeling good, the kids with their mother for the weekend, a good ballgame on television.

"You been mighty good for several months," the voice told me. "You've been good pretty much the past year. Gone through all that pain with your hips, but now they're fixed. Finally have a house. Have a little extra cash in the bank. Ought to get a bottle and enjoy yourself. One night won't hurt anything."

Then the good voice broke in. "You don't want to get

drunk. You'll feel bad the next morning. Be disappointed in yourself. Drinking has brought you enough problems already."

"Yeah, but it sure feels good. Drink good just tonight and stop again tomorrow and go dry for another few months. Ain't nothing wrong with that."

Sixty/forty, the odds in favor of drinking, me standing in the middle of a tottering see-saw. I am very strong at standing up to pain and confrontation, incredibly weak at resisting pleasure. Fuck it! I drove to the liquor store and got a jug, stopped by the Quick Mart for a bottle of Mountain Dew, some beef jerky and a newspaper. At the house, I poured a triple shot in a glass and added some soda, threw the glass back and drank it straight down. I shuddered at the aftertaste. Clicked on the tube to watch the evening news, unfolded the paper and started scanning the headlines. The alcohol kicked in, fingers tickling my forehead, a calmness descending over my mind like a warm blanket. By midnight, the ballgame was over, the paper well-read, I watched an old movie on television and the liquor was gone. In bed, my breath was long and slow, and then I slept without dreams.

Morning, and that familiar cloudiness was in my head. You dumb ass. Drank the whole damn fifth. I lay in bed for about another hour, then got up and drank some juice and puttered around the house. Outside, the day was bright. I had planned to start putting up gutters, but my motivation was low. Noon passed, the voice flickered in my head several times, but I ignored it. The words got stronger.

Another ballgame on in the afternoon. The day's paper was unread. Hell, it's just Saturday, and you're not supposed to see the kids today. Sure would be nice to kick back and relax and get drunk again. You've got tomorrow to sober up. You deserve it; you've been so good.

Midnight, and another fifth was empty. On Sunday I drank beer because the liquor store was closed, tall Ice Houses, about fifteen. Monday, the liquor store reopened. I called Christopher's school and said I was sick and could not pick him up. Cancelled class on Tuesday because I had the flu. Wednesday, Katie and the kids left for the mountains to spend

Thanksgiving with her family. I would miss being with Meghan and Christopher on Turkey Day, but also would be apart from Meghan on her birthday. But I did have five straight days in front of me without an obligation except the bottle. Thanksgiving Day I was supposed to go down to Fayetteville to share the holiday with the family, but I spent it lying drunk on the couch, watching television and feasting on leftover pizza. Never before missed Thanksgiving dinner in my life, although on many I was half drunk.

Monday rolled around, and it was time to sober up. It is finished, I told myself. I am not drinking today. Will hurt bad for awhile, but I've been through that. Mid-afternoon, I had the dry heaves and was starting to shake. Physical addiction had me in the grip. Not going to drink. Tough it out. Class is tomorrow. The kids need me. Suck it up. Draw on those reserves of will power I learned in boot camp, that resolve that brought me home from Seattle. Pace the house. Retch. Sweat cold water.

Fuck it! Why am I doing this to myself? A triple slug will set things straight. Need to taper off slowly. A triple shot now to stop the shakes and the dry heaves, another before I go to bed and I will sleep through withdrawal. Next morning I'll be OK and can teach, go by and see the kids. That's the plan.

The week rolled by on automatic pilot. I got tired of people calling, so I unplugged the phone. Thursday night I was asleep on the couch and was awakened by my children. Meghan and Christopher were standing above me, sweet, loving faces etched with worry and fear.

"Dad, you haven't seen me since I turned fifteen," Meghan said.

She was so beautiful. So tall and lean. Christopher so handsome, his foot nearly as big as mine. My babies growing up so fast. Just yesterday I was changing their diapers.

"Let us be your addiction, Dad," Meghan said. "Let us take the place of liquor."

Christopher nodded. Katie listened from the next room, and I hugged them to my chest and wept. The roles were reversed — the father is the weak one, the children guardians. I promised them I would quit from that second forward, but as soon as they were gone I downed a triple shot to get back into the free zone where nothing matters.

The next afternoon when Dave came by, I knew I couldn't quit this time on my own, and I asked him to drive me to the hospital, to this ward where the door is locked.

A knock on the door, and I saw a group of people standing at the threshold. "Come in."

A couple of doctors and several medical students. This is a teaching hospital, and I was a piece of the day's puzzle. "How are you feeling, Mr. McLaurin?" a tall man in a white trench coat asked. He must be a psychologist, I thought. Has a graying beard, wears glasses, must be a shrink.

"I'm OK. Feeling a little rocky."

The other doctor was younger. The students stood to the rear in a semicircle. Everyone stared at me. "How about telling us why you're here," the older doctor asked.

"Well, I just got on a big drunk. I knew I couldn't quit on my own this time, so I came here."

"How long were you drinking?"

"About three weeks."

"How much were you consuming a day?"

"About a fifth. And some beer mixed in."

Heavy silence for several seconds. "Do you have any thoughts of harming yourself?"

"Noooo. Nothing like that."

"Do you have any thoughts of harming anyone else?"

I grimaced. Shook my head. "Absolutely not. I don't want to hurt me, and especially not anyone else."

"Any problems in your life you want to discuss?"

"I have no big problems. Look, I was just feeling good and I decided to drink, but I let it go too far. I just need to get sober and get back to school and post grades. That's why I came here."

"Have you heard any voices? Seen things that weren't really there? Suffered delusions?"

"No. I've never had any problems with that."

Everyone continued to stare. "This place sort of reminds me of One Flew Over The Cuckoo's Nest," I said. "Except I haven't run into nurse Rachet yet."

The younger doctor laughed. The older one did not. I wanted to ask how long I had to stay here, but was afraid of what I might hear. "Could I get some tranquilizers in me. I'm feeling pretty shaky. I've been throwing up, too."

"I'll prescribe something for you. Have you attended AA in the past?"

"A few times. It doesn't work for me."

"When you leave here, you need to get into a recovery program. You're on the way to killing yourself."

The group shuffled out, on to the next room, the next drunk or crazy person. I wished I had told the doctor I was not trying to kill myself these past weeks, but was actually curing myself, but the way I looked, he might have ordered a straight jacket.

Through the window, beyond the flat-roofed shorter buildings, the view was handsome, gray hills rolling east to where the sky meets. Beyond the hills, I knew the earth flattens into the coastal plains that gradually lower to where the land borders the sea. And beyond the ocean a few thousand miles on almost this exact latitude lies North Africa and Tunisia where Meghan was born just fifteen years ago. I recalled the afternoon of her birth, where from a different window in a strange hospital I gazed west across the Atlas Mountains and beyond the sea toward home.

Katie had been in hard labor for several hours, the sun was setting, when the doctor made the decision to do a cesarean. Studying the fetal monitor, he announced in heavily accented English, "The baby is a girl, the cord is wrapped around her neck, and she is going into fetal distress. We need to take her now before we lose her."

I kissed Katie's forehead and tried to gulp back down my heart as she was wheeled out of the room into surgery. Cynthia, the Peace Corps nurse, told me I would not be able to go into the operating room, and suddenly I was as alone as

I had ever been in my years, staring through a plate glass window at the sky streaked with flames. The hospital sat on a hill above Tunis, and lower on the hill, I could see the grid of the national zoo where wild animals were caged. I paced the floor as I had seen a lion do earlier, my pulse racing, wanting to roar my fear and frustration. My mind whirled with memories.

Evening had settled when I returned to our small, cinderblock house in a village on the outskirts of Siliana, coming home from working out in the field where olive groves spread green to the base of purple mountains. Katie stood smiling at the doorway and took both my hands and spoke to me in Arabic, "Hibla." Stunned and speechless, I listened to her tale of going to the clinic where the Russian woman doctor told her she was three months pregnant and asked whether she was happy, and when Katie nodded, the doctor hugged her. And I hugged Katie and knew the world had been transformed with her one word, and in that moment had not loved a woman more....

I watched the last crescent of sun slip beyond the horizon while I prayed, my pleas trying to drown out the doctor's last words. *"Before we lose her."* The baby we had conceived while on a four-day vacation on the Isle of Malta, the child I had watched swell within Katie, had felt kick and roll within her mother — God could not be so cruel. *I know you are not cruel, God,* I prayed. *Forgive me for my many sins and let this child live and I will change my life and be good and pure. I will dedicate my life to you, and I will not drink any more or cuss and I will tithe and bear witness.* I left no promise unmade while darkness descended until I could no longer see the zoo below me.

Cynthia was smiling when she came through the door and told me the baby had been taken and was fine and that Katie was fine. I exhaled in a long, warm breath that seemed to last for minutes. Within the hour, Meghan was brought to me, bathed and wrapped and sleeping, and looking at her pink face, I realized why I had been born and why my father had been and his father and all the fathers back to Adam.

Fifteen years later, I lay in a detox ward with the dry heaves, so many vows and promises broken, locked in like that caged lion pacing at the zoo in Tunis. In wean of alcohol and thirsting like the big cat's dreams of when he lapped warm blood. I am not an animal, although I have acted like one. Am I a man now? Have I drunk enough vodka to stain my white collar blue and quicken the blood in my jugular vein till all my neck is red, the colors matching those of the men in my lineage who have worked with their hands?

What constitutes the life of a man? Open the east Fayetteville directory and flip through the pages until you find a Billy. Of the Billys I know, his history reads more often than not as such: Born in the county hospital, as a baby he had colic, got a bad case of the measles and came close to dying, nursed his mother's breast until age two. He liked to play with toy trucks as a toddler; his daddy drove a truck for Roadway. In grade school he got A's in PE, usually got a B- or a C in Citizenship. Received three paddlings from the school principal for fighting at recess. In the ninth grade, the school counselor told him he needed to channel his aggression, so he started playing football. Started dating as a sophomore, worked weekends bagging groceries at the local SafeWay. He went steady twice during his junior year in high school, flunked algebra, but made a B+ in biology because he liked cutting open frogs. Decided not to take the SAT. Why bother? He wasn't going to college. No one in the family had ever been to college. Why study like a fool to make an A when a C would keep you on the football team? The football team went six-five his senior year, and he played end and snagged eleven passes, two for touchdowns. He went straight in the Army following graduation for a two-year hitch, and Kathy waited for him. Following his discharge, he went to work for South River Electric. He and Kathy got married, and they went to Myrtle Beach for a three-day honeymoon. Twenty years rolled by, and he was still climbing power poles, hating when ice storms come and his crew is called out to work all night. After the divorce, Kathy remarried, but they have stayed friends, mostly because of the kids. On weekends he likes to work in his yard and drink Bud Lite, but he is prone to get into the Seagram 7 if he doesn't watch himself. He smokes Marlboro 100 now instead of reds. Watching his old man die from lung cancer got him off the reds. Sometimes when he's deep inside a fifth, he likes to remember that pass he caught against South View that won the game. Later that night was the first time Kathy gave him some. And now she gives it to another man. In fifteen years he can retire from the power company and maybe open up a small engine repair shop behind the house. He always was good with motors.

In east Fayetteville where I grew up there are many Billys, their combined stories creating a narration of manhood that is at once very familiar to me and as distant as Tunis is from Billy's engine repair shop. What defines the life of a man?

The definition does not include: sits atop a desk in front of college students two days a week. The first class starts at 1:05 in the afternoon. On the other three days of the work week, he tries to put in three or four hours in front of a word processor sculpting words. Prefers listening to Keith Jarrett playing jazz piano rather than Merle Haggard. Spent two years in the Peace Corps and has drunk wine in the morning beside the Grand Canal in Venice. Has made the police blotter a couple of times for DWI violations, but has also had a full page review in the New York Times Book Review. Can't back up a tractor and trailer or fix an air-conditioner, but can point out Saturn in the winter sky. It shines yellow.

The t-shirt I was wearing didn't have a collar, but I would bet those medical students who stared at me lying there with a two-week beard, shaky hands and a flushed face, would dress me in a blue shirt with my name above the breast pocket. Would believe me if I told them I had an associate degree from a technical school in automotives and worked repairing cars at the Ford dealership. I might not be able to whip the biggest man on the block, but I can drink him in the ground.

Maybe only my fingertips are calloused, but my liver has a few scars, my claim to a respected slot in my lineage.

A nurse brought me a pill in a papercup, told me it simulates the effects of alcohol. Told me the lunch cart was in the day room, and I ought to get up and eat. I didn't feel like eating, but I got up and started down the hallway. Tried to keep my bearings on a fixed point so I would walk straight. Shaking pretty bad now. Buck-up, dude. Grip your tray tight, don't want to drop it here in front of all these drunks. If you couldn't hold your liquor, you must at least hold your tray. Baked chicken, some sort of potato concoction, garden peas and a roll. I drank my milk, ate the skin off the chicken, three bites of potatoes and two of peas. This time I left my tray on the table. I had just lain down again when the man told me I had another telephone call. Mama this time. I told her I was fine. Told her she ought to wait till Monday to come and visit. Monday was my birthday. Wasn't that a dandy place to spend your forty-fifth birthday? Well, it's better than the grave.

Finally a doctor showed up at mid-afternoon. "How are you feeling, Mr. McLaurin?"

"Not too good. I've been throwing up a lot. Shaking pretty bad."

"Have you thrown up any blood?"

"No.

"Any delusions? Seeing things that aren't really there?"

"No. Nothing like that."

"Do you have any thought of hurting yourself or hurting other people?"

"Nope. I just need a little help coming down from this drunk. Can't you up my medicine some? If I could sleep, I'd feel much better."

"We can do that. There's no reason for you to be uncomfortable. I'll write orders for the nurse to give you medicine every half-hour. Get your blood level up to where you're comfortable."

He was good for his word. I got a shot in the hip to

stop nausea. The nurse started dosing me twice an hour, and I slipped into a fog that whited out most of the pain and the memories until the sun was lifting once more above the horizon.

Sunday was a bitch. Full grip of withdrawal, wasn't throwing up anymore, but sweating cold and shaking to beat the band. The medicine didn't seem to help much, but I hadn't had any DTs or seizures. I knew a guy who tried to stop cold turkey. Two days out, he decided to go squirrel hunting, to get his mind off the whiskey. Said he looked up into a tree, and the next thing he remembered, he was on the ground, and it was dark and his tongue was bleeding. He died a couple years ago from liver failure.

I began eating a little better. Tried to read a magazine, but my eyes were blurry. I talked to my roommate a little bit. He was supposed to get out tomorrow. I still didn't know his name.

"When I checked in here," he told me, "I was seeing snakes and spiders and tigers."

I thought about that. I could handle the snakes. I dream of snakes pretty often. The snakes are always neon colors, and there are more around my feet than I can stuff in a bag. I could handle the spiders, too. I used to dig up tarantulas down in Puerto Rico when I was in the Marines. I don't know about tigers. I owned a lioness cub once for about six months, back when I was doing snake shows. She ripped up the inside of my van and nearly ran me broke feeding her raw chickens everyday. I could do without visions of tigers. I guessed I was getting out of this drunk pretty light, having only the shakes and blurred vision.

"What's the deal for getting out of here?" I asked the guy. I'd been avoiding that question. Today was the 13th, and I had to have my grades turned in by the 16th.

"I've been here two weeks. When you admit yourself, you're in for seventy-two hours automatically. The doctors have to evaluate whether you're a threat to society or yourself before they'll discharge you."

I was no threat to either. Seventy-two hours would get me out of here Tuesday morning.

"How come you've been here for two weeks?"

"I guess it was the snakes and tigers. They've got stricter since that Williamson guy shot those people."

I knew who he was talking about. About two years ago, a guy named Williamson was in South Wing, got out and ended up shooting up Franklin Street about one mile from here. He killed two people, pleaded insanity and won, then sued the doctor who let him out, and won that case, too.

The entourage of shrinks came around. The bearded doctor asked me some of the same questions. I asked him when I could get out.

"Probably after the minimal stay. We'll need to get you established with an outcare program. That's one of the requirements."

Probably? I considered that word. I hadn't seen any water coolers around here big enough to lift and throw through the window like the chief did in *Cuckoo's Nest*. I needed to appear very sane; I am very sane.

I noticed a couple of new faces at lunch. Weekends must be the busy time around here, I guessed. One woman stood out particularly. She was blonde and blue-eyed, petite and pretty, looked to be in her late thirties. Had on a white bathrobe and pink, fuzzy slippers. Her hair needed a brush. After finding her tray, she sat beside me at the table. I wondered why she was in here. Too many whiskey sours? She didn't strike me as a druggie. Her nails were manicured and painted red. She looked fragile, almost brittle. Probably a mental case. Depression. Could be suicidal. I tried to think of something to say to her, but how do you start a conversation in a psychiatric ward. "Nice day, isn't it?" Nope. "How are you?" I didn't want to know. "Do you come here often?" That, I really didn't want to know.

I finished what I was going to eat, then stacked my tray. The woman glanced my way a couple of times.

"Are you going to eat your bread?" she asked.

"No. Would you like it?"

"Yes." She thanked me.

"You want these crackers?" I asked her.

She nodded. "I'll save them for later."

"You seem to have a good appetite," I told her. "I can hardly eat."

"I didn't eat for four days before coming here."

"I guess you are hungry."

"What are you here for?" She asked.

"Drinking." She didn't give her own reason, and I didn't ask her. I wondered what she looked like under her robe, if she was wearing anything else. One of the rules was that patients of opposite sex could not be alone in a room with the door closed. I thought about Billy in *Cuckoo's Nest*, when he finally got some and quit stuttering. Maybe I would quit shaking if I got some. Might shake more.

Monday morning, I was feeling better. Actually slept for a few hours. I watched the sun coming up over the ridge, giving birth to a new day, a special day, at least in my mind, almost forty-five years to the hour that I arrived naked and crying.

Forty-five years of drawing breath and not one of those years I would erase. If I had the power to reverse the sun and follow it backwards over time to any previous sunrise and live that day again, would I live it differently? Probably not. Despite lying there on that cot in a detox ward, I liked myself, liked what I have done with my life. Apparently there are people who like me and like also what I have done in these years, warts and all. My glass is definitely half full.

An early-summer dawn when I was a child, my brothers and I playing in the yard, barefoot and bare chested, not a coin in my pocket and no need for a coin. Mama was cooking breakfast. When she came to call us in, I was holding a wisteria blossom, a Japanese beetle clinging to the moist, purple petals, staring at the flower and the bug after my siblings had run inside.

"What are you doing?" Mama asked me.

"I'm frinking," I told her, in the accent of the slight speech impediment that colored my words until I was ten.

And here I was all these years later, watching the sun rise, bare footed and bare chested. Breakfast was being cooked; not a single coin in my pockets. I was thinking about when I used to frink, and what was then is the same now — I have all the rest of my life left.

I needed to shave. My whiskers were mixed with gray and made me look like a drunk. I was as sober on this day as I was on the morning of my birth. The nurse gave me a razor and a can of shaving cream. She told me I had to bring the razor back when I was finished shaving. I lathered my face good, then started scraping off the beard. The job was slow, and halfway through, I returned to the nurses' station and asked for another razor. I assured her I would bring both of them back. Thirty minutes later, my face was pink again, a couple of nicks on my chin, but I looked much better. I showered for the first time in a couple of weeks. Washed away the old skin, sort of like a snake shedding. I had the whole rest of my life out front and even if it was only a matter of hours — knock on wood, I rapped my knuckles against my head, closest thing to wood in this shower stall — the future was virgin and pure.

I ate most of my breakfast. A birthday greeting was printed on my name slip. They knew a lot about you around here. I looked for the lady in the white housecoat, but she was absent. Maybe she was an angel. Maybe beneath her robe, she was not only naked, but also had a pair of folded wings. Maybe my bread she asked for had been poisoned, and like Tinkerbell, she intervened. I should not say that to the bearded shrink when he made his rounds, I thought. He might decide I needed another week here. But at least I was still frinking. Still frinking after all these years.

"You're looking better," the doctor told me, when he came into my room an hour later, followed by his flock. On my lap I had positioned a copy of *National Geographic* and a copy of *The New Yorker*. The covers were up. Crazy people don't read such.

"I feel better, doc. I need to get out of here. I need to get back to school and post my grades."

I had no intentions of hurting myself, I assured him,

and especially not someone else. Told him I'd start attending
AA. I'd join Triple A if that would help.

"We'll discuss your case in session," he told me. "You
can probably leave tomorrow morning."

I ate all of my supper — pork chops, rice and gravy,
corn, a fruit cup, another roll. Drank my milk. Another birthday
greeting on my name slip. I had a little boxed cheesecake on
my tray. I hoped the staff wouldn't sing me Happy Birthday.
Back in my room, I brushed my teeth and hair and tidied my
bed. I was reading when Meghan and Christopher appeared
in the doorway, backed by Mama and Katie and my little sister
Kelli. The kids had tight smiles as they came to me, but they
did not hesitate, wrapped their arms around me and hugged
me. Their warmth is the best medicine in the world. Mama
hugged me, Kelli. Katie didn't, but I couldn't blame her.

They brought me wrapped presents, a birthday cake.
Sang me Happy Birthday. Meghan and Christopher sat on the
sides of the bed, kept touching my arms. My voice was a little
shaky.

"I told you I was going to get straight," I told the kids.
"I'll be out of here tomorrow."

I thought of how just a month ago Meghan and I were
in Manhattan tramping the streets and gazing upon Van Gogh's
Starry Night. I remembered thinking just a week before
Thanksgiving how I was looking forward to this year's holiday,
and then I recalled a conversation I had with my brother Keith
on Thanksgiving the previous year.

I was drinking again, had been for a couple of months.
I was in Mama's living room alone when Keith sat down close
to me.

"You know," he began wearily, "this might be your
last Thanksgiving."

"No, man," I told him. "I'm getting straight. You just
wait and see."

How did I go from the Guggenheim to the detox ward
so quickly? Well, at least I didn't cut off my ear. I have a way
of making the world relative.

The kids hugged me long and hard as they were leaving, assured me they loved me. I told them I loved them too, that I would see them at home the next afternoon. I escorted them to the door. Meghan and Christopher peeked at the patients in the day room. The door clicked as it locked behind them; through the thick glass I watched them leave, raised my right arm, and said I love you in sign language.

I got a new roommate. He had already been there ten days, but was sleeping in a room close to the day room that he said was too loud. He was a talker, a good-ole-boy sort, had a couple of homemade tattoos on his forearms. Like me, he was hoping to get out the next day. He came in for alcohol.

"Hell, I don't drink nothing but beer," he told me. "I ride my bicycle most afternoons down to this little bar where I have a few. I got into a little argument with the law. That's why I'm here."

He snored. I lay awake much of the night. My mind had cleared pretty well, but with the clarity came the full realization of what I'd done. Probably in a little trouble at school. But the semester was nearly over anyway. If I got out tomorrow, I'd be able to post grades. Fortunately, my stock was pretty high at school, so I ought to be able to ride this out. God, Christmas is ten days away, and I hadn't bought the first present. Hadn't paid all my bills that were due the first of the month. What was I going to owe for this hospital stay? Insurance probably wouldn't cover it. Katie was going to put the clamps on me; I couldn't blame her.

Was my neck red enough now? Had I earned respect with the spirits of my elders, men like my Uncle Dewey who drank his vodka mixed with grape soda; Carson Autry, who was called Kingfish and drank cheap bourbon and chased the taste by gnawing on a length of liver pudding; my grandfather Huey who would stand splay-legged in his wagon and lash his mules as he rode home, where my father would hide in the barn until Huey sobered up; my own father who never hugged us unless he was drinking. Is my neck red and my collar blue, despite the fact that only my fingertips are calloused?

I was told in the morning I could leave as soon as some paperwork was completed. I was scheduled to see an alcohol counselor immediately at my HMO, Jerry Williams, a fellow I'd already been in to talk to about three times. I started packing my stuff. My roommate came in. He'd had a conference with the doctors; they'd told him they wanted him to stay in the hospital a few more days. Some concern still about his aggression. He lay on the bed with his face turned from me, and in his voice I could tell he was close to weeping. I was about to leave the unit when a nurse told me my blood labs showed my B12 level was low, and they wanted to give me an injection of the vitamin. An hour passed before the nurse brought the needle and stuck it in the top of my butt. I remembered a story I read about circus clowns and how so many of them were drunks; often before performances, they took B12 shots so they could go in the ring.

At the front desk, a nurse wished me good luck, then pushed a button that released the door lock. I pushed the door open, then heard it click behind me. Dave, who brought me here, was picking me up at the front of the hospital. I sat on a bench outside and waited. The air was cold, and when the automatic doors opened and closed as folks entered and left, I heard Christmas music playing in the lobby, sweet songs about birth and innocence.

Jerry Williams sat at his desk facing me in a room that was dark except for the glow from a lamp. I'd already told him I was serious this time, that I'd go to AA or whatever was necessary.

"Why don't you just quit? You ever thought about that?"

"Can it be that easy?" I asked.

"It won't be easy. I'm not saying that. But you started drinking on your own. Quit on your own. For some people, that's the surest route."

I had never thought of it quite that way. Most everything I've accomplished, I did pretty much on my own. Made sense. I looked Jerry in the eyes.

"All right. I quit."

Five

In the mid-afternoon, we pass through a small Montana town, main street lining both sides of the blacktop, a couple of restaurants, a bank, two bars, a filling station, maybe a couple hundred buildings and homes constituting the whole settlement. A small school sits off the road, fronted with a raised American flag. I doubt it would hold more than a hundred students.

"Hey Meghan," I say. "How would you like to live in a town like this?"

She gazes out the window, then turns her head and looks behind us. "What town?"

I bought my house back in Carolina last autumn, the first mortgage I have ever signed on my own. Prior to buying the house, I lived for a year in a cabin on ten acres of remote wooded land that Katie and I had bought. The land rose gently to a ridge where we planned to build our dream house with a view over the orchard I would plant and the pond I planned to flood where a stream ran through the bottom land. I remember the afternoon when Katie and I signed the loan papers together in a lawyer's office, then took a bottle of champagne to a boulder that lay on the crest of our land and toasted the future. Five years later, separately, but in front of the same lawyer, we signed our divorce papers.

I bought my house the same way I buy a pair of shoes. I go into one store and look over a few pairs, buy one, and walk out. This house was the second one I looked at with the realtor on the first day of house hunting. I walked inside and studied the rooms for a few minutes, went into the yard and walked the boundaries, then told the realtor to put in a bid. A

month later in a lawyer's office, I signed away my ownership
of the land, the cabin, and my time spent living like Walden
minus a pond, and in the next minute, put my name to a deed
that married me to this small dwelling.

What hath Tim wrought! A small brick house on a
corner lot, a half acre of earth for a yard, several large oaks
for shade; I could throw a rock and hit my nearest neighbor's
home. A far cry from the cabin where the closest living
creatures were deer. Did I not swear I would never own such
as this? A rectangular house on a rectangular lot, one grid in a
rectangular neighborhood one mile and a half from downtown
Hillsborough. Is this the final step, this house like a Norman
Rockwell depiction of the American dream, possibly minutes
but I hope years from being laid in a rectangular grave in a
garden of gray marble contained within boundaries both
physical and eternal?

But the house is right for now, and now is all of
existence. The next minute when it arrives, or next week or
next year will be now. The future is only speculation, the past
only memories, and what I hold in my hand this second is
what is real. This house is real. Brick exterior, the box
measuring 1,060 square feet, a carport tacked on the end with
a utility shed. The lot is on the corner of a gravel road that
frames two of the boundaries. The house was built about thirty
years ago, the neighborhood a mixture of houses similar to
my own and contrasting with a newly completed structure
across the road from me that sits beside a mobile home with a
stick-built room nailed on the front.

Assets? Central gas heat and air-conditioning. A toilet
and hot running water — no more bucket baths and squatting
in the woods. Only twelve miles from Meghan and
Christopher; they have their own bedrooms. The drive to
school takes just thirty-five minutes, and best of all, with the
money I put down, my payments are only four hundred and
eighteen dollars a month. Hillsborough is expanding like much
of the New South and the price of houses is shooting up. My
new claim is in a good school district, so the investment is
like a savings account. Six years from now when the kids are

in college, I can sell and reap a pretty good return and retire maybe to some acreage in Montana beside a stream at the foot of a mountain, or to a whitewashed block home with a walled garden in Eleuthera, Bahamas, with a view through the front door of the water to the west where the sun sets blazing.

This house holds no ghosts for me, and although the rooms are bare, I have no history here to search for in the dream world. In the three decades of this house's existence, the vapors of recall that float within these rooms are not mine. I wonder of the children who have lived there, of the parents who bore them, people who live within different walls now. In their dreams do they return here in search of something they lost or forgot to bring with them, not even fully sure what that possession or knowledge is?

The walls are all painted beige, blank, like sheets of paper waiting for the words. In the paint I can see the marks where whole sentences have been erased — nail holes where pictures were hung, family portraits, Jesus at the last supper, kittens in a basket above the bed where a little girl slept. Could have been a Monet print of water lilies upon a pond, "God Bless This Home" stitched and framed. A couple of the ceiling tiles are dark where the roof has leaked, a corner of baseboard chewed by a puppy that grew into a dog who whined to be let in at night. The possibilities and combinations are almost endless, and I wonder if the boy or the divorced woman who drove the nails to hang the pictures, who swatted the puppy with a rolled up newspaper or placed the pot where the water dripped, I wonder whether that person still returns here in dreams to fetch what was left. Their words are not my own, but then every syllable in language has been cast and recast a billion times, no sentence spoken that is not the echo of another's tongue. What I write upon these beige pages will be personal, but not unique.

• • •

The Saturday after I signed the deed, Al and Merrie came over to see my bare, new house. We went out to the cabin where I had piled the furniture I would not keep to burn.

A ratty mattress, an old couch, bags of trash. Atop the heap was a worn blue recliner. One of the padded arms was chewed through to the wood from Roy Lee when he was a puppy.

"You're going to burn the recliner?" Merrie asked me.

"Yeah. It's pretty worn out. There's roaches in it, and I don't want to get them in my new house." Ed went into the cabin to call in his predictions for a football pool.

She was silent. I soaked the bottom of the pile with kerosene, and when I applied flame, it spread in a whoosh with a speed that surprised me. Within a few minutes the recliner was on fire, and it burned fiercer than anything else. The foam padding sizzled and dripped like streams of lava, the flame was blue and out of it boiled moist, black smoke. The wooden frame popped and sizzled and sighed like voices. Merrie stood erect with her hands clasped and stared, her shadow huge upon the ground. In not much time the pile collapsed into itself, the flames had eaten all they could digest, and all that was left of the recliner was the red-hot springs that looked like bones.

"It burned so fast," Merrie said, her words drawn long and thoughtful. "It's all gone. All burned away, just so fast."

Her face looked hard in the flickering light, shadows that masked her youthful features, and I knew why she was so serious and what she was thinking. I thought of the same thing.

"It was better to burn it," I told her. Sort of like you do a flag. I'd rather burn it, than throw it in some dump.

She nodded. "I just can't believe how fast it burned up."

And I remembered back more than a year when we lived in the house on Kilcullen and that blue recliner was in the living room. I would sit in it and she would often curl in my lap with her head against my shoulder. We sat that way often, listening to thunderstorms or to music from the stereo. We shared that chair when Hurricane Fran roared over and the wind rattled the window panes, and I said to her, "I never have made love during a hurricane." She was quiet for a moment, then spoke the truth as she did always, that she had done so once because there were lots of hurricanes in

Louisiana, but never in a North Carolina hurricane. I smiled and pulled the lever so the footrest came up and the back of the chair went almost level with the floor. We still had electricity in our house the next morning when everyone else I knew was in a blackout for days.

"It was better to burn it," I said again, "than throw it in the dump."

She turned her head and looked at me, one side of her face illuminated, the other half in shadows like a half moon. The steel springs reminded me of the ribs of an animal that once breathed and was warm with blood, now plucked clean by the friction of time.

"I just can't believe how quick it was gone. Just ashes now."

I reached and touched my fingertips to the dark half of the moon. "No, Merrie. It will always be a blue chair."

• • •

We roll past the sign marking the town's boundary, heading into more rolling, brush country. As much as I sometimes would like Meghan to live in a small town removed from shopping malls and kids with studs through their tongues, I suppose I am being idealistic to think she would be protected in a place like this. I remember speaking once at Woodberry Forest School in Virginia, a boys' prep school that costs $19,000 a year to attend. The young men were extremely polite and manicured with short hair and neat clothing. A couple of years afterwards, a young man stopped me in the hall at N.C. State. He wore his hair in dreadlocks and had metal piercing his eyebrows, nostril, lip, and ears.

"Mr. McLaurin," he said extending his hand. "I heard you speak at Woodberry Forest two years ago."

"You were a student there?" I smiled. "You've sort of changed your image since then, haven't you?"

He hunched one shoulder. "Yes sir. I guess I have. But I'm carrying a three-point-nine here at State. I guess that discipline did me some good."

Yeah, and he was also still polite. And I guess Meghan

is better off submerged in the varying currents of real life, gradually exposed to influences both good and bad, instead of diving headlong into the pool, naked and ignorant. I stare at her, and the tiny stone in her upper ear sparkles and looks pretty in tandem with the earring in her lower lobe.

I took her to get the higher ear pierced about two weeks ago. To the mall in a small shop where I had to sign a paper consenting to the damage. Meghan hopped right in the chair, excited and nervous at the same time, fearing the procedure would hurt, but willing to stand any pain that stood in the way of the passage. I couldn't watch the woman apply the punch to her ear; instead I stared directly into Meghan's bright eyes. I have been stuck with needles hundreds of times, but I will not watch a needle go into my skin, or into anyone else's. If in an emergency I had to give an injection, I would do so to myself or anyone else, but so far I have not been called upon. I asked God that if there were any pain to come to Meghan, that I be allowed to bear it for her.

The woman mashed the handle of the machine, and it was done, without Meghan even flinching. She touched the stone with her fingertip, her mouth formed in an oval, then curled upwards into a broad smile.

"It looks good, baby," I told her. She studied the new earring in a mirror while the woman told her how to care for the wound. "You ready to get yours?" I said to Christopher. "Jump in the chair, and she'll do you right." He smiled and shook his head.

"I wonder what Mom will say?" Meghan said for about the tenth time on the way home.

"You're going to be grounded for a year," Christopher informed her.

I knew Katie wouldn't really care. I would not have taken Meghan if I knew Katie truly did not want her to have another earring. I knew that Meghan, by choosing to get the piercing without full consent of her mother, had taken a small step into adulthood. She was willing to pay the price for the possession, whether the bill came in the form of pain or condemnation by her mother. And I realized that I should not always wish to bear her pain, or Christopher's; both of them must learn there is a personal toll for their passage.

Meghan watches the small townscape expire to another expanse of bush-studded grasslands. Katie took a week in noticing Meghan's new earring. At first Meghan was shy with exposing her ear, expecting Katie to seize on the new stone the first time they stood face to face. But as the hours passed, then days, Meghan took to displaying her defiance, wearing her hair above her ear, actually touching her ear lobe while talking to her mother. Finally, it was Andy, Katie's boyfriend, who noticed the change when he looked at Meghan at the dinner table. At his words, Katie jumped to her feet and bent to examine her daughter's ear, disbelieving at first that the defiance had taken place days before. Katie was not mad; I'm sure if a spider or scorpion had been clinging to Meghan's ear, she would have noticed it in the first second. Step by step, we should wade into the pool of indulgence, lose our innocence in increments where we have time to heal and learn from the pain and the scars. Meghan — do not leap in front of me or your mother or brother with a wound that gushes blood, for it is our instinct to thrust our fist into the fracture and try to stem the flow.

And even here in this small town, I realize it is not Mayberry RFD. I sight on a house set back off the road, and in the front yard beside a junked car is a television satellite plumbed to the urgent, hormone-drenched frequency of MTV. Once America was bound together loosely through units of miles and weeks. Now she is wired tightly within a jumble of steps and seconds. When I was Meghan's age, the family's yearly voyage to the ocean for a day was a big event. And here Meghan, at fifteen, is riding in a deluxe Winnebago on her way to the Rockies, having already traveled thousands of miles since her birth in Tunisia. As a child, I hoped mightily to travel one day to the moon. I know now I will not. I hope Meghan or Christopher will one day visit the moon for me. I hope even more that they will want to. Moon glow and the pale flash of a firefly. I did not make it to the moon, but I have held a firefly within the dark dome of my clasped palms and imagined.

• • •

Last November as an early birthday present to Meghan, I took her and her best friend, Tema, on their first real visit to New York City. Both had passed through the city before, but only in making connections enroute to elsewhere. This would be the girls' first chance to experience the Big Apple, and all the city's glitter and crud. I felt Meghan needed to share the experience with someone her own age. So for the next three days, she, Tema and I would be tourists, with all that implies.

"There it is!" Meghan squealed, her face pressed against the jet's window. Tema, leaned and looked over her shoulder. I sat in the seat in the next aisle, and pushed against my seat belt and peered over the back toward where Meghan was pointing. The jet was rolling gently to our side, and through the window I could see blue water and then the Statue of Liberty shining very white against the bay.

The jetliner hummed and bumped as it descended toward LaGuardia, the New York skyline stark against the horizon. Please God, bring us in safely, I prayed. The girls were smiling. If ever I must be in a plane crash, may it be on the return flight when I can die with memories instead of anticipation.

Miss Liberty slid out of view, I could see the World Trade Center, further up the island the spiny point of the Empire State Building, the green expanse of Central Park further north. Like the downside of a Ferris wheel, the jet lowered, cars were visible, roof tops, more water, then we were above the runway and the engines went quiet and the wheels yipped and bounced, yip, yip, then a roar as the pilot braked hard.

"Yep, mama, gonna make it, gonna make it now. Yep, mama, gonna make it, gonna make it now." I whispered the words. I recite the same words every time I'm on a jet when it lands. I don't know why. I just do it.

. . .

The first place where we could see the ocean was from the apex of the bridge that crossed the inlet into Carolina Beach. We always swore we could smell sea air many miles inland, my brothers, myself, sister, mama and daddy, all of us packed into an old Ford sedan that was heavily rusted around the wheel wells. Making our yearly summer trip to Carolina Beach for the day.

"I see the ocean," I shouted, expelling the air I had held in my lungs when the car began to climb the steel and concrete hump. "I see it first!"

"I see it," Keith shouted. "I saw it before you did."

We argued over who had seen the water first. The glimpse of the sea disappeared as the bridge curved downward. The tires thumped crossing the joint where the concrete joined the asphalt as if breasting the threshold of another land. An alien place where spiny palmettos grew, live oaks gnarled and weathered, gulls wheeled and shrieked on a cool breeze that always blew, where I could stand on the shoreline and stare east, and the only things between me and infinity were the limits of my imagination.

"We're gonna make it, mama," I said to my mother who sat in the front seat by the window, my sister Karen between her and my father who drove. "We're gonna make it!"

. . .

We'd carried on all our bags, so getting out of the airport was quick. We almost trotted as we headed for the baggage exit where the taxis waited in a long yellow line. I had Meghan and Tema on a short leash; I had pledged to Katie and Tema's parents the girls' safety, had sworn to keep them in sight at all times and within arm's length, to not have a sip of alcohol. I patted my pocket again to ensure I had my wallet, it fat with a thousand dollars in cash. I wore it against my thigh, safer from thieves, our return plane tickets under my coat against my breast.

We climbed into a cab. Yes, the driver was dark-skinned, looked foreign. "Forty-ninth and Lexington," I said with authority, like that was my home address. I hadn't been in New York for six years.

"Where?"

"Forty-ninth and Lexington." I spoke slower. "The Roger Smith Hotel."

"OK."

He punched the meter, and I looked to see that it wasn't set at one hundred dollars. "Fasten your seat belts," I told the girls. The driver zipped away and wove through traffic until he was on the expressway heading toward the river, where the gray skyline of Manhattan rose steep as a wall. The sun had gone below the horizon, and lights were coming on in the buildings, a beacon for the millions of individual lives contained within walls, diverse races, ages, and personalities, but each with his or her own stories, their own histories and visions. So different from my own, but I suspect so similar. I have always been amazed at how a rat terrier will recognize a Saint Bernard instantly as being of the same species, and will wag its tail or growl depending upon temperament.

If I liken America to a body, I consider the South the blood, heated and tuned to a certain pulse and typed B+, not the usual run-of-the-mill. But New York City is the belly, where all tastes and nutriments are blended and churned; the Museum of Modern Art sits within a stone's throw of three differing ethnic restaurants, a rifle shot from stages where people act out the lives of souls they are not.

And I felt swallowed up when the taxi rolled off the bridge and entered the city, like diving underwater where the sky is reduced to a patch of blue above. Distinct as I am in the capsule of my body, immediately I was part of a great mass, assimilated within the juices of an island that seemed as tall as it was wide. My cell walls dissolved and my body was one with the plasma of that great multitude.

In my voice I will remain intact. My accent is who I am and have always been and will remain. The taxi driver did not look very different from me in body, but his voice whispered of curry on his eggs and the morning call to prayer from a mosque in a small town in Pakistan, of mountains I had not seen and waters I had not dipped my hands into. On an earlier trip to Manhattan, I had driven a truck and delivered furniture to be ferried to showrooms. The terminal was down on the eastside, where I stood on the dock without a union card. I asked how I might get unloaded, and the foreman cocked his head and looked at me as if I might be from Mars to not know the order there. His voice reminded me of a guy I served with in the Marines who was from Jersey, who I considered had a heavy accent.

"You from Mississippi?" he asked me.

"No. North Carolina."

"You sound like a guy I was in the army with from Mississippi. We called him Hambone."

"I just need to know how to get unloaded," I said. "Then I'll get out of your way."

He shook his head, looked at another guy, walked to him and he pointed at me as they spoke. You can call me Hambone. You can call me Hambone and Collards if you want to, as long as I can back this truck in here and get unloaded. Y'all.

Both guys stared at me, and finally Pastrami on Rye walked back over, his chest a little bowed, sort of like the Saint Bernard walking to the rat terrier, having recognized him as a fellow dog, but knowing the terrier will have to stretch his neck when they sniff butts.

"Back it on in. Union would raise hell, but I'm the boss right now."

"I 'preciate it." I nodded at the boss, then at the other man. "Y'all have a good day."

Most of the world became vertical when we entered the city. Meghan was looking up, and I pointed to a rooftop where trees were growing. The driver headed down Roosevelt Drive toward midtown, and I counted streets and watched the meter click through the dollars until it had passed twenty bucks, and then he turned onto Lexington and stopped in front of the marquee in front of the Roger Smith. The Roger Smith is an old hotel that was refurbished a few years back, a place Katie recommended, medium price for Manhattan and within walking distance of Rockefeller Center.

Our room was as large as any southern motel room, two double beds, television, wet bar, large bath, but cost about five times as much. Once I stayed with Katie at the Algonquin Hotel, the famed waterhole of writers, and remembered how tiny the room was, the elevator operated by a black man who pulled a lever to take you up or down. The martinis they mixed in the bar were good, if, in reality any martini actually tastes good. I sat on the bed and studied a map of the city and decided we could easily walk to Rockefeller Center, but would probably need a taxi to the Empire State Building. As a kid, I thought the famous skyscraper was called the Entire State Building, and I guess, in a sense, it is.

I was the herdmaster, the shepherd, the sergeant-at-arms and head bouncer, caretaker of two nubile young ladies; my head turned three hundred and sixty degrees like a radar, my brain tuned to danger like a radio to the police channel. I walked between the girls, held their arms at crosswalks, scouted every potential pervert as we approached him, zigged and zagged across town until a street opened into a square brightened by Christmas lights where people slid and wove their way around a skating rink.

"Look, Meghan! There's the Christmas tree." And above us was a giant blue spruce, surrounded by levels of scaffolding, the same tree I read about in the newspaper that came from a midwest farm. The tree was yet to be decorated, and looked dark against the many surrounding lights. Below the tree, people glided upon the ice, moving mostly counterclockwise, against the wheel of time, seeking seasons when the spruce was only head high and rooted and what was the future is now the past.

In a deli a block from Rockefeller Center, we ate pizza, Meghan and Tema their usual pepperoni, my slice heavy with garlic and feta cheese. The air was slick with grease and the odor of Italian herbs; the men behind the food counter had thick black hair and wore it combed back like Elvis Stromboli.

I checked my wallet again, then pulled the map from another pocket and studied the distance to the Empire building.

"We'll take a taxi," I told the girls, and they smiled.

"Yes! Let's take a taxi."

"Finish your pizza. This is real pizza. Domino's would go broke in this town."

The girls went to the restroom, so I tagged along with them up a stairway to where the bathrooms were and waited outside the door in case a secret panel should open beside the toilet stall where pretty young women were snatched into the underworld to be sold as white slaves. I must cover every angle.

Beside Fifth Avenue, I lifted my arm and instantly a cab veered from traffic and stopped beside us. I got in first in case the driver was really a kidnapper. Told the girls to put on their seatbelts. The ride took only a few minutes, the fare a bit more than three dollars. I gave the man a five and told him to keep it. He probably had nine children at home, and Christmas was approaching. We had to look nearly straight up to see the top of the skyscraper, the spine illuminated with blue lights. The line was long to get on an elevator, but it moved fast, and we were soon packed inside a lift where everyone was quiet. The floors zipped by, my ears popped, and we were spit out into another line to wait for another elevator, but finally were at the top standing on the observation deck where the earth below us blazed like the heavens reversed.

• • •

Our trip to the beach usually took place in July, on a Saturday or a Tuesday, the days my father did not work. We would leave home when the sun was still in the trees, the car trunk packed with towels, a couple of old quilts to sit on, and a cardboard box packed with food. We kids would wear our swim trunks. The trip took nearly three hours to cover the hundred miles to the coast with time allowed for a bathroom stop. At the town of Riegalwood, still thirty miles from the ocean, we always swore we could smell sea air, would hang our heads out the window and breath deeply of the sweet smell.

What we actually smelled were the emissions from the paper mill, but that did not matter. The odor was foreign to our noses and conjured up images of white sand and sea oats and salt water.

I was always glad to see the arch of the bridge that led from the mainland to the string of long islands that form most of the Carolina coast. When we crossed the bridge, we were there. Our old car had more than 100,000 miles on her. Once, the driveshaft had gone out when we were halfway to the coast, and we had spent most of the day at a garage before the car was fixed, and it was time to turn back toward home even before we had smelled the sea air. I didn't care if the car broke down on the way home. By then, I would be sunburned and have sand in my pockets and memories in my head. I knew my father would get us home. If we just made the top of the bridge and then the whole motor fell out, I knew we could coast down the long incline to the first garage, and still be within a hike of the water.

• • •

At the east side of the tower, we stood and gazed at the man-made Milky Way beneath us, millions of lights illuminating millions of lives, the expanse stretching to a thin line of black where the sea begins. Just above the ocean, the heavens curled backwards in reverse, black and star-studded; the galaxy below our feet was finite and ruled by clocks, the universe above infinite and timeless.

"If I threw a penny off of here," Meghan asked, "would it really kill someone on the ground?"

"That depends on how much Penny weighed," I answered. "If you threw a Sally off, it would be the same thing."

"Daaad!" Meghan said. She leaned against the bars and looked down, and I gripped her arm, even though I knew she couldn't slip between the steel rods.

"Where is the Statue of Liberty?" she asked.

I scanned, and finally located the statue where the river flows, where the lights are thinner. "There." I stretched out my arm and Meghan and Tema sighted down it and finally saw what I was pointing at.

"That's where I want to go most," Meghan said. "Mom said we should take the last ferry out there in the afternoon, so when we are coming back in, we can see the lights of the city."

We slowly circled the observation deck. Cars below us on Fifth Avenue looked like ants.

"Would a penny really kill someone?" Meghan asked again.

"Probably not. The penny would only fall so fast. Not like a bullet."

"Then why do people say that?"

"It's just a rumor. Don't ever believe something just because people say it. You could drop a rattlesnake off this building, and the only way it would kill someone is if the snake dove fang-first into the top of their head."

"Or if they had a heart attack," Meghan said and laughed. "Imagine a rattlesnake hitting your head at ninety miles an hour."

In the souvenir shop, Meghan and Tema handed pennies to a man, who for two dollars each, would mash them flat in a machine with an imprint of Miss Liberty or the Empire building. The pennies come out oval and paper thin. I wanted to throw one off the building, because I imagined it would whirl as it fell like the winged seeds from a maple tree, that it might catch a breeze from this altitude and fly into Connecticut and land lightly on the bridge of a man's nose as he stood at a bus stop waiting to go home. Startled, the man would lift the wafer from his nose and look into the sky and recall when he was a boy and used to lay pennies on the train track and wait for the express to rumble by.

Times Square had changed since the last time I was there. Clean. No street people curled atop grates on beds of cardboard. The atmosphere reminded me of the state fair, people moving through each other, blinking neon lights, noise and food vendors. I couldn't resist any longer and stopped at a vendor and bought each of us a hotdog New York style. The weiner popped in my mouth when I bit into it. Chestnuts. I wanted to buy some roasted chestnuts before we left. We walked down to 42nd Street, and it was clean too, no prostitutes, no apparent drug dealers. I remembered how it used to be, recalled another trip I made to unload furniture and stayed overnight, the kid who rode with me, in his first year of college, a preacher's son who wanted a taste of the wild side.

I took him to 42nd Street. The strip off Times Square had the feel of a tee shirt that had been worn too long, warm and stained, the smell of rubbing against a body where the pulse throbbed just beneath the skin. Neon signs advertised "Live Sex On Stage." As a teenager, I had frequented the 500 block of Fayetteville, the playground for the 82nd Airborne, had pulled shore leave on floats with the Marine Corps. I thought I had seen about all the perversion that was offered. Live Sex On Stage? I wondered what the gimmick was, just how far it went.

Paul and I had drunk several beers each. I asked him if he wanted to check out one of the sex joints, and he said he did. I flipped out a ten, and we entered through a narrow doorway into a dark hall that led into a small theatre. All the seats were taken, so we had to stand against the back wall. The theatre was lit by red floor lights, the air heavy with cigarette smoke. The audience seemed to be all men, some slumped in their seats, others leaning with shoulders and heads close. The room was hot and stank. On stage, a black man with a large penis and a white woman were copulating animal style, only a few yards from the people in the front row. Not a film, no mirrors or trickery involved, just too people screwing. The only sounds were men who sometimes coughed and oily strip music from a cheap sounding set of speakers. I glanced at Paul, his eyes fastened on the stage.

After several minutes of doing it doggie style, the man withdrew. While the woman climbed on top of a bare table, the man jiggled his penis up and down to keep it erect. The woman lay on her back, legs dangling off the table. She was chewing gum. The man lifted her legs across his shoulders and entered her again, moved slowly back and forth. She didn't move at all. No passion was involved, no emotion displayed, the two seemed little different from people who had punched a time card and were performing routine tasks on an assembly line.

Paul began to slide down the wall. I looked at him, and his head was slumped forward. I caught his forearm just before he collapsed, got his weight against my shoulder and guided him outside. In the cold air of the street, he revived quickly.

• • •

I was afraid of the ocean. The ocean was so huge, and it moved. In the twelve years of my life, my world was one of concrete boundaries that lay before my eyes. From our yard, the first boundary was the green wall of the forest that lay across the field. That wall did not move or change except for the colors that varied with the seasons. Beyond the forest lay another field, then more woods and finally the river that separated the world I knew from town, the wide streets and subdivisions and shopping centers.

But the ocean had no boundaries. It was flat to the horizon and could be blue or gray depending upon whether clouds covered the sun. The water rushed inward in tall waves before collapsing into foam; the out current pulled at my ankles. Early in the day the tide would threaten to wash over the sand dunes into where the sea oats grew, then later would back off to where the beach was wide and sprinkled with shells and starfish. I would look at that water and know that if I could walk on the surface I could journey straight forward until all that was to my back was ocean and all that was before my eyes was ocean with nothing to stop my progress until I walked into the African coastline. I was afraid of the ocean in the sense I feared if I ever started walking, I might never turn back.

• • •

I awoke to the sound of horns and wheels, lay still for a few moments and got my mind in tune. Sunday morning, but Manhattan was alive, and from our fifth-floor room the sounds of traffic below on Lexington ebbed and surged not unlike the ocean surf. Meghan and Tema were still sleeping; I looked at my watch and saw the time was a few minutes past seven. A siren began many blocks away and wailed as the police car passed the hotel like some fleet banshee. Meghan stirred.

The sound of morning for me as a child was that of mourning doves cooing from pine tops. Their call was sad and haunting, but it spoke to me of another dawn and the possibilities of that day. Meghan and Christopher grew up within a hundred yards of a large boulevard where rush hour traffic was the predominant sound when the sun was low, not the call of doves. At times I have lamented that my children's morning song is piped from steel and vulcanized rubber instead of through the throat of nature. But if that mechanical song represents for them a time of renewal, of the new day and what it might bring, are the lyrics less worthy? When I was Meghan's age the dove's coo might herald a trip across the river to Sears; the banshee that just woke Meghan crows of Central Park and the Statue of Liberty.

In the hotel café, we ate bagels with cream cheese and raisin muffins. The girls drank milk and juice while I swilled coffee. I pulled out the map and scouted the streets. The morning was sunny, so we decided to hike the distance to the Museum of Modern Art. I was even more thankful for my new hips. The mourning dove of yester-dawn could not have provided me with artificial sockets, but the mechanical bird did.

The bells tolled from the tower atop St. Patrick's Cathedral, the gray, sculpted stone in sharp contrast against surrounding buildings of steel and glass. People were entering through the huge wooden doors.

"Can we go in?" Meghan asked.

For a moment I hesitated. The church is Catholic. Meghan was sprinkled Presbyterian as an infant; Tema is

Jewish. I claim fellowship in the Congregation of the Universe, where my baptism is renewed in the water droplets of each breath I exhale. Am I an infidel?

The domed ceiling of the church arched above us, the tall windows ornate and painted. We stood with other tourists in the rear of the church and listened to the choir sing. I suddenly remembered I was still wearing my cap and snatched it from my head. A marble bowl atop a pedestal contained water; I watched several people dip fingers into the liquid and cross themselves. Beside the pedestal was a brass donation box with a slit on the top. Taking a few dollar bills from my pocket, I handed one to Meghan and Tema, and they looked questioningly at me. I'd never done that before, painted my forehead with holy water, would it sear a cross into my pagan forehead? I paid up first, slipped a bill into the brass box, then dipped my finger and traced a cross above my eyes. The sensation was cool; I did not turn to ashes. Meghan and Tema did likewise; they did not sprout wings and fly off to heaven. I was out three bucks, but when I walked back outside to the bright street, traffic was stopped by a red light, and a dove — I swear it — a dove cooed from one of the trees on the church grounds.

Van Gogh's *Starry Night* was not a disappointment. Once I saw the *Mona Lisa*, and it was disappointing, so small, when I had expected something so famous to be yards high. But *Starry Night* was large enough and raw enough and beautiful enough to imagine Vincent sitting before a bare canvas with a mad vision of the night sky in his eyes and a knife in one hand.

"He cut off his ear for a woman," Tema said.

"Would that impress you?" I asked her. "Somebody cut off their ear and sent it to you in a box."

Tema whispered into Meghan's ear, and they laughed.

"He wasn't THAT crazy," I told them.

Rembrandt, Dali, Cezanne, many names I knew, just as many I did not recognize. Meghan especially likes Mary Cassatt and we studied some of her paintings. I prefer Monet.

In his gigantic canvases I see myself on a pond at sunrise fly casting for bream surface feeding in the shallows.

"That's the way art is supposed to work," I told the girls. "It moves you in a personal way."

"How does this move you?" Meghan asked me later as we stood in front of a coiled rope.

"This one I would have to think on," I told her. "Could be a statement on capital punishment. Could be someone lost a rope."

Outside again on the streets, we hiked north to Central Park, feasted again on hotdogs while sitting on a stone bridge. Beyond us through the trees, people slid upon a frozen lake. Must be a man-made frost for God's hand today was warm and the sun was bright, this island of nature stark, surrounded by a forest of glass and steel grown by man. Can't see the forest for the trees, and I was glad that Meghan and Tema were here in Central Park on this day, and I was even more glad that they did not always live here. I remembered the movie, *Hair*, and the hippies dancing and singing here in the park, thought of Simon and Garfunkel, of the concert they performed here, voices lifted up under the sun. And at night, these same meadows and woods are often crossed by rapists, muggers, and murderers. I thought of Van Gogh and his chiseled vision of night and Monet in soft colors of water and morning, each with hands capable of holding either a paint brush or a knife. Meghan and Tema smiled and clowned as they sat upon a bridge over water that flowed to a pond where the molecules chilled and slowed until they changed to ice. Do not ever sit for long, Meghan. Dance and twirl, but not for the man sitting in the front row; he is the same fellow who hands two twenties to the woman leaning against the street lamp. Dance because you want to and your critic lives within, and the steps you follow are from the music of your mind.

"Let's rock and roll," I said to the girls.

"Can we go to the Statue of Liberty now?" Meghan asked.

"We can go anywhere in this city," I answered. "All

we have to do is stand up and take the first step."

• • •

We took a taxi down the island to Battery Park. Cruising down Broadway, we passed through different hemispheres. Soho, trendy and eclectic, Washington Square where I thought of Joan Baez singing "Diamonds and Rust," through the edges of Little Italy and Chinatown, cultures so different, yet sharing boundaries. Wall Street where so much money is made and lost. I checked my wallet again for about the hundredth time. At the park, I tipped the driver too much, but what the heck. The wind was chilly off the water as we hurried to catch a ferry. We got seats by a window, and within a few minutes the engines started and we left land.

Miss Liberty, newly cleaned for the coming of Y2K, looked white as alabaster against the clear sky. As the ferry slid by the island, she loomed higher and taller; I tried to imagine myself as some poor immigrant cruising in from Europe, my head full of visions of the promised land. I have researched a bit of the lineage of the McLaurins. We came from the highlands of Scotland. History shows we were always poor and subject to fist fights. No kings or queens in the family tree. I do have an ancestor who was hanged for stealing horses. But the legacy of a thief is easier to transcend than that of a king.

• • •

Around noontime, we packed back into the car and drove down the North Carolina coast about five miles to Fort Fisher at the end of the island. On the way, we passed the Fort Fisher Ferry that carried cars across the wide mouth of the Cape Fear River to the town of Southport on the far shore. I always hoped that one day we might take the ferry across that wide water; a school friend had told me that hovering sea gulls would pluck bread from your hand at the rear of the boat. I had never been on a boat, unless I counted the cypress logs my brothers and I had lashed together and floated upon in our irrigation pond.

Fort Fisher had been a Confederate stronghold during the Civil War. From the earthen berms, Rebel soldiers had fired cannons at Union ships trying to come up the Cape Fear. The end of the island was windswept, the converging waters of the river and ocean subject to rip tides. Picnic tables sat in the shade of gnarled live oaks above the ocean, the beach unusual for Carolina, steep and rocky. Incoming waves at high tide exploded against the rocks and boomed like distant thunder. I liked to imagine the noise was cannon fire directed against the invading Yankees. Under the grove of oaks sat a small museum; inside, through paintings and models, the battle was depicted. Displayed were artifacts — old cannon barrels, musket balls and tattered uniforms. The paintings showed desperate soldiers surrounded by fire and blood. At that age, I had never heard of Vincent van Gogh.

My mother would spread an old blanket upon one of the picnic tables in view of the water. From a cardboard box, she placed bowls and platters on the blanket, fried chicken, potato salad, deviled eggs, a loaf of white bread, a jug of sweet tea, plastic plates and forks. I'd scramble to claim the gizzard; we'd wolf down our food, hungry in that cool salt breeze, gulls wheeling above the table, begging for scraps.

After eating, if the tide was low, we children would venture out onto the slick, black rocks that covered the beach. An alien world waited there in knee-deep pools caught between the boulders, starfish and sea urchins, blue crabs that skiddled and swam backwards. I was the bravest, and would wade furthermost out to where the waves still sloshed over the rocks. With a ship made from a paper milk carton, I became the captain of a schooner and battled whirlpools and tidal waves and giant sea beasts. Deep within the fantasies of my mind, I shouted orders to my crew and fought inside the throat of disaster until my mother called me back from where I had gone too far from shore, back to the white sand where my younger brothers played.

• • •

Meghan had hoped to climb all the way to Miss Liberty's torch, but we found that we could only go to the crown because of work going on higher up. A line waited at the base, but it moved pretty fast. Meghan and Tema hammed it up while we shuffled forward, working on a dance step set to a tune by Jewel. They laughed and hung on my arms, smiling and totally uninhibited by the strangers who watched them. Two gorgeous young women, gushing with life and prancing to a tune only they heard. I thought of young women the same age who steamed past this island many decades ago, some of them already holding a baby in their arms.

We began climbing the steps, selecting them over an easy ride in the elevator. My hips felt good; six months earlier, I had to step sideways while climbing stairs. Slowly up and up, like the switchbacks on a mountain trail, we climbed, like blood cells in a vein beneath the lady's gown, higher upon her thighs and loins, her belly, across her breasts to the heart, where we were recharged and propelled to the brain.

The view from the top was not spectacular; it did not show every horizon like we saw from the Empire State Building. But the view was historic and was visible long before any of the tall buildings on the island existed. The view five feet above a milk carton schooner seemed epic to me as a child when that was the most lofty vision. I took pictures of Meghan and Tema leaning against the platform railing, the jagged skyline of Manhattan framing their heads. On the return ferry, dusk was falling, and just as Meghan had hoped, the tall buildings were lighting up like a forest of Christmas trees.

For the first time in New York, I felt uneasy. Where we exited the park, no taxis were cruising; using the map I had navigated us to an almost empty Wall Street. In front of the New York Stock Exchange, I studied the map again. A few cars passed. Only a handful of people were about, but they did not look like the type to be carrying switchblades. Meghan stared at me, her big, brown eyes like a fawn's.

"Which way do we go, Dad?"

"Just a second here. Let me get my bearing." I looked at the street signs. "Tomorrow morning this place will be packed with people."

But it wasn't right then. I imagined a gang of young men in hooded sweatshirts walking out of an alley and sighting in on the girls, me with not even a pocket knife for defense. But I had my fangs and claws. I would spit the fire of a Scottish dragon if someone raised his hand.

"This way," I raised my eyes from the map and pointed. Up one block, left down another, and suddenly we were again beside Broadway. I lifted my hand, and like magic a taxi appeared before us. "Chinatown," I told the driver.

"Monkey," I told Meghan. "Probably either monkey or cat."

"No, it's not!" She stared at the piece of meat on her fork as we began eating in a Vietnamese restaurant. "What is it really?"

"Most likely chicken," I said. "Just plain ol' chicken. Wouldn't you rather it be monkey, or something unusual?"

"No. Monkeys are too cute to eat."

Chinatown was a different country. Like jumping the ocean in the span of a few blocks. Marquees and store fronts painted in Chinese scroll, vegetable stands that spilled out of shops and bordered the street. People jammed together. Spicy odors in the air. A far cry from the empty, sterile street of Wall we had just hiked.

I chose the run-down looking restaurant over the fancier places that advertised in English. I ordered for Meghan and Tema by pointing at a spot on the menu, for me, by pointing at a guy at the next table shoveling a bowl of noodles into his mouth. I wasn't too worried about getting hepatitis. The girls had been vaccinated; between the Marines, Peace Corps, and the bone marrow transplant, I'd already had all three types.

"You think an animal that's considered 'cute' has more right to life?" I asked Meghan.

"Don't start, Dad!"

"I guess that's why thirty years ago, the Americans and Vietnamese were killing so many of each other. Didn't think each other were cute enough."

"I'm not listening, Dad."

"Eat your monkey."

I spiced my noodles up with dollops of fish sauce and a liquid that was red and hot, ate pretty successfully with a pair of chopsticks. The girls picked at their rice and broccoli with forks. Both of them piled the little pieces of meat on a saucer. Most any food I'll eat, as long as I see someone else eating it first. In Tunisia, one of my favorite dishes was sheep's head. Once, when dining with a couple of Tunisian friends, after I ate the sheep's eyeball, my friends offered me theirs. Afterwards, whenever I ate sheep's head with Tunisians, they usually offered me the eyeball. I only found out later, they were not just being generous, but were amused. The eyeballs were edible, but no one ate them — sort of like the Pope's nose on a chicken back. But the American would eat them — a dozen if you offered him that many.

"You're not eating," I said to the girls.

"This tastes funny," Tema said.

"I'll get you some pizza or another hotdog when we get back uptown. You know what they put in hotdogs? Pig lips and buttholes."

"You're so stupid, Dad," Meghan squealed, but she was smiling.

"Do you know what perfume is made of?"

"Daaad!"

The theaters were letting out on Broadway, people getting into limousines, clad in tailored suits and evening gowns. Going to pop a bottle of champagne and maybe do it in the big back seat while the driver made a swing through Central Park before delivering them back to their apartment in the Dakota. Or, more likely, back to their flat in Brooklyn to face another work week on the docks to pay for this birthday luxury. Regardless, the girls were impressed.

"Wouldn't that be so cool!" Meghan said.

We ate again at a bistro a block from our hotel. I ordered a pastrami on rye, and with a bit of melancholy, a near-beer, recalled drinking martinis at the Algonquin with Katie, but I did not remember much else of that trip. The girls ordered a large order of fries and Cokes.

"Where are you from?" the waiter asked when he brought the food.

"North Carolina."

He chatted for a minute about UNC basketball and Dean Smith, looking more at the girls than at me. I don't know why New Yorkers have a bad reputation for being rude. I've always found them to be friendly and talkative. Especially if you talk to them first. Even more especially if you have in tow pretty girls.

Back in the room, I propped up in bed against the long pillows. The hour was approaching midnight, my legs were tired, but the ache felt good, one of satisfaction of miles walked and steps climbed and memories stored. Meghan and Tema had shifted out of their intellectual mode and were typical teenagers again; they flipped through the television channels.

"Turn it," I commanded when they paused at Jerry Springer. "How can you watch that junk after seeing *Starry Night*?"

"We're resting our minds," Tema said.

Two fat women were fighting. Most of their language was bleeped. "Those people are all insane," I told the girls.

"You said Van Gogh was crazy," Meghan answered.

"Maybe. But he painted canvas instead of his toenails. Turn it!"

Bay Watch, MTV. "Leave it there!" I shouted when a rerun of *The Andy Griffith Show* appeared, but the image of Goober flashed by. Meghan turned and smiled at me. They finally settled on a re-run of *Pretty Woman*. A hooker wasn't Aunt Bea, but she was better than Bevis and Butthead. From the street, I heard the wail of another siren, a foreign cry from the coo of mourning doves or the cry of a whippoorwill, but I must think in relative terms. Even I, with my nearly forty-five-year-old brain, had to admit that Julia Roberts was much more pleasant to gaze upon than Goober. Soon the girls' heads lowered to their pillows, and they were sleeping sweetly like the babies I still considered them, and I flipped the channel to MTV and rested my brain.

• • •

The spiral lobby of the Guggenheim was like some cosmic worm hole, the paintings and sculptures spinning on the edge of the vortex. The girls and I were swept along through a cram of culture, then finally spit back out upon Fifth Avenue, where we re-entered the real world by eating street-vendor hotdogs, heavy on the mustard. I took a couple of shots of the girls standing in front of the museum, then we grabbed another taxi down to the bottom of the park. We debated going to the zoo, but it was already noon, and there was still much to see before we needed to take another cab in the early evening back to the airport. I reasoned that a lion in a cage in Central Park was not so different from a lion in a cage in North Carolina. But Saks *was* much more expensive than Sears, and F.A.O. Schwartz much more fun than Toys R Us, and the Plaza Hotel much grander than Holiday Inn.

Meghan snapped a picture of the chandelier in the lobby of the Plaza, and one of the front desk where the kid checked in the hotel in *Home Alone Two*. Across the street, both girls stood on the giant piano keys in F.A.O. Schwartz, just as Tom Hanks had done in *Big*. Meghan and I bought a concoction of jelly beans and giant gummy worms for Christopher. In the span of half an hour, the girls had gone from art connoisseurs to kids again.

But an hour later, again beside the skating rink at Rockefeller Center, in a crowd of people, I lost sight of Meghan. In an instant, she was swallowed up in the belly of the city, my eyes not upon her, nor her arm within my reach. I walked for a few yards, then planted my feet and scanned the crowd, a trickle of fear cold inside my stomach. Only seconds ticked by, but time seemed stretched like single beats on a tom-tom. How could I, in this swift flood of people, lose my grasp on my baby's shoulder; she could be sucked down into a gutter in just an instant. And then I saw her, where I had already looked several times — right in front of me standing against the railing above the ice, her eyes upon the people skating; she was smiling, a strand of her hair blown across her mouth. She was not searching for me, did not look alarmed or lost; I could not believe I had looked right past her.

And I realized in that instant, the child I had raised was now just a memory; a young woman stood there looking into life. If I had created art, my masterpiece was in her, but she would rest no longer in the frames I had constructed. My arm had reached its length, and I could not continue to stay her. But my eyes would always search for her, singular in my vision, and if she stood alone, I would come, sighting her against any multitude.

I walked to Meghan and placed my hand on her shoulder. "What are you looking at, baby?"

"The ice. I was thinking about how ice is really just water."

And I was thinking of young women and how, to any father worth his breath, they are still babies in a different form.

• • •

The sun was in the western sky when everyone jammed back into the car. Sunburned and salt-crusted, we had stuffed a paper bag full of sea shells, sand dollars, and starfish. My father's legs were pink; in the bushes, he changed back into his usual trousers. I knew he wished he were home, tending to his cows and hogs on soil that was his own. Although he grew up only a hundred miles from the coast, he had first seen the ocean at seventeen when he joined the Navy. Taking time off from work to play was not in his nature; he never went into the water, but he watched us with hawk eyes.

A few miles from the beach, we stopped at the Tote-Em-In Zoo, a family-run place filled with a collection of animals and oddities. George Tregembo had moved south from Vermont following World War II and opened the zoo, expanding his interest in the exotic discovered during his service in Burma. An elephant was chained out front; inside the walls were monkeys and snakes and lions and parrots, a shed filled with artifacts from a cannibal tribe from the Far East.

I think for my father, the whole trip was made bearable

by our zoo visit. His natural love for animals crossed all boundaries and borders; a lion was at least distantly related to a bobcat; a coata-mundi was cousin to a raccoon; if my father did not know the animal, he could find a common kinship through the ark. The animals were drawn to him, would often press against the bars or fence when he was near, he would cluck in his throat as though speaking in some strange animal verse. I understood my father best when he was with animals. Unless he was drinking, he seldom laughed; as a child I do not recall him ever hugging me first or saying he loved me. But on chilly March nights when he brought a kid goat from the barn into our house to dry its birth water by our wood stove, I knew he did not need to speak. If I were wet, he would dry me.

Last stop was Faircloth's Seafood House on the outskirts of Wilmington, a ramshackle dwelling with many rooms, the whole structure slightly twisted on the foundation and leaning. They served only fried seafood, breaded and smoking hot from the grease. I always asked for an oyster platter. I was the only one in my family who would eat them, the furthermost thing I could imagine from pork chops and fried chicken. My father always ordered flounder and shrimp; my mother chose shrimp and deviled crab.

Back in the car, I would feel full, my skin tingling from too much sun. I would get sleepy as the car rolled west into the black night, but would try to stay awake and remember what I had seen and done. I did not care then if the car broke down.

We had been to the shore; I had consumed my yearly quota of oysters. Maybe next year we would get to ride the ferry, and maybe in a year soon to come, I would start walking where the rocks ended, and never once look back. But that was of time to come, and with my father driving and my mother beside him, I knew I would eventually get home safe, and nestled against my brothers, I would sleep.

● ● ●

Time was running out while we wandered through

the maze of Sak's department store. We needed to pack soon and leave for the airport. Hell for me would be to have to follow a female for eternity on a shopping trip.

"What about one of these little shirts?" I said to Meghan, pointing at a rack of black tank tops. At least they were less than a hundred dollars. She squinted one eye, then turned and headed back toward a rack of skirts she had already looked through twice. I followed, mumbling.

"What about lipstick? No one else at school will have lipstick from Saks."

Meghan glanced at me with a look of dismissal that said, "Shut up, Dad. You know nothing about lipstick. You know even less about what is cool to wear at school, and you are totally ignorant about shopping."

I was heartened when finally Meghan and Tema decided to buy replicas of the Empire State Building encased in a water-filled globe. Snow swirled when the globe was shaken. I had not totally lost my daughter to estrogen.

I was standing outside the hotel with my bag when finally the girls emerged from the lobby. Meghan stopped in her tracks and stared at me for a couple of seconds as if I were unfamiliar. I opened the rear door to a white, stretch limousine I booked earlier that day. Meghan's eyebrows shot up, and she squealed. A black man in a slightly ruffled uniform took the girl's bags and loaded them into the trunk. Both girls jumped up and down and hugged me.

On the way to the airport, they mugged and posed for pictures on the big, pleated, wrap-around seat. Meghan begged for me to open the sunroof and let her put her head through, but I resisted. I wasn't tempting some lunatic with a rock or a gun. We made faces at people riding beside us, knowing they could not see us, and recalled how we had stared at the tinted windows of other limousines, wondering who rode within and what went on there. In front of the terminal, the girls were wired; they posed like vamps against the hood of the limo and asked the driver to be in a picture with them. I finally had to herd them away from the car. About double the price of a cab, but worth it.

• • •

And now, all that separated me from bringing the girls safely back home were these last miles of descent when the pilot reduced power and lowered the flaps. The view was straight toward home, whether that sighting was taken from a jet's window enroute from New York, or from the arc of the bridge that separated Carolina Beach from the mainland. I lifted silent prayers again. As a child, I only wanted to arrive. But as a father, I now think like my own dad must have felt as he stared through the windshield of our old car headed through the night loaded with sunburned, sleeping children. We must return home to rest, to our roots and who we are, to dream and realign our sights so that we may venture forward again.

Six

The northern Rockies jut from the earth like a wall and hang cloud-like against the horizon. Blue-gray and spangled with facets of white, the immense tonnage of granite reminds me of the vanguard of a summer storm that mounts slowly and steadily higher and steeper in the western sky. I think of long-passed August afternoons as a child when I stood gazing across the pasture at home where a thunderhead boiled black above the oaks and sweetgum, the hot air heavy and still but the leaves on the trees trembly as if the roots remembered and feared the coming of wind and white fire. Ma would always call me into the house, her voice shrill in that deep silence between the growls of thunder when birds and crickets had ceased to twitter and chirp, to shelter behind the panes of glass and sheets of roof tin.

"Looks like it might storm," Ma says to me from her seat behind me as I drive.

"That's the Rockies, Ma. Those aren't clouds."

Ma leans and peers through the windshield and studies the wall of rock. "Those are mountains. They sure don't look like the ones back home."

The Blue Ridge Mountains back in Carolina are feminine, rolling gently into folds and mounds and gradually higher into peaks, but the Rockies are masculine, angular and erect and more violent in nature. I think of men like Jim Bridger and Jeremiah Johnson drawn here on the scent of something bigger and harder than themselves.

The campground at St. Mary's is situated beside a racing creek that flows out of a lake at the eastern entrance to

Glacier National Park. Peaks tower on three sides above the campground, blades of granite softened by fields of white snow. We get the Winnebago hooked up, and although ten p.m. has just passed, the sun still reflects off the snow fields. I change into my swim trunks and go with Meghan and Christopher to a hot tub that is built into a deck under the stark dome of mountains and clear heavens. On one of the peak flanks that faces west, a rooster tail of blown snow wafts upon a high wind. But here in the valley, the air is calm and chilly.

"I can't believe how late it gets dark," Meghan says.

"It's the high latitude," I explain to her. "Won't get dark until about eleven, and then the sun will be back up about five a.m."

I push the button that starts the water roiling in the hot tub, stick my foot in and take it out. The kids go right into the water, submerging up to their chins.

"God, that's hot!" I say.

"Get in Dad," Christopher says. "It's not hot once you get all the way in."

I take it slow, one foot, then the other, submerging up to my testicles. "Yiiiii!" Christopher laughs. Splash water on my flanks and chest. Go under up to my neck, and for a few seconds I feel like I'm cooking, but then it feels real good. Sitting here in steamy water not far from midnight with the sun shining on frozen snow fields. This ain't North Carolina.

I remember the last time I was at St. Mary's seventeen years ago. About a week earlier in June, Katie and I were here on our honeymoon.

"Me and your mom hiked over Red Gap Pass just north of here," I tell the kids. "I think we were the first people to cross coming from the north. Didn't see a single other person the whole four days except one guy at the pass coming the opposite way, sitting on a rock and smoking a joint." I tell the kids about the trout in a high, crystal lake, how we had been warned about the grizzlies in the area, and at night I'd listen to Katie sleep and wonder what I'd do if a bear clawed through the wall of the tent, me holding only a bowie knife.

"That was a long time ago. You guys weren't even thought about yet."

"Do you think you and mom wouldn't have gotten divorced if you hadn't drunk so much?" Christopher asks.

I feel a pang in my stomach. "I don't know, buddy. Probably. I admit the drinking didn't help, but me and your mother were a lot different."

"You could climb mountains together," Christopher says.

"Yeah," I answer after a few moments. "We were always strong when things were tough. It was just trying to live normal life together that was hard. I think we ran out of mountains."

We soak here in this man-made hot spring for half an hour, sometimes emerging to sit on the lip of the tub where the chill air causes the water on our skin to waft in fingers of vapor. Submerge again to our chins. I wonder if Jeremiah ever stripped down and soaked his tired, cold bones in some magma-heated pool with his eyes on his flintlock and these same peaks. I wonder if he ever thought of some woman he had left back east and of the children he might have sired had not his wanderings led him so far from her bed. I think about when Katie and I stood atop Red Gap Pass and looked toward this same valley with no idea I would return here years later with the children of our shared blood, but without her. I did not thirst away our marriage, but I did drink too deeply of the intoxicant that made me want to keep walking over the next ridge, not content and trustful that the valley I stood in was lush and green. Fastening my sight on the plume of blown snow, I think of Lynn, of how I wish I could rise from this water and walk through the snow field barefoot to a farther valley where she sleeps beside a fire she kindled from long deadwood, and there I would toss my trail staff into the flames and settle beside her on a blanket she wove where I would kiss her forehead and wake her, and the walls of rock surrounding us would no longer be what I must ascend, but the peak from where I finally recognized I had hiked exactly the numbered steps.

• • •

A lone dog is barking from somewhere within St. Mary, his voice singular and sharp in the chill air past midnight. I lie a couple of feet from where Bruce sleeps, his wind slow and regular.

From deep folds of sleep I would awaken when a child, fearful at first of what had torn me from my dreams, would lie there still and warm under the quilt and stare into the dark ceiling and listen to my brother's breath whisper. And then I would hear again the noise that had surely jostled me from my slumber, the voice rising again, like a night bird. My father, in the woods walking leaves crusted with frost, his hands cupped and shouting to his hounds. His voice would rise to a pitch that reverberated in the clean, cold air past midnight, and the dogs would answer, baying short from the top of their throats, blood hot in their noses with the fresh scent of the raccoon's flight. And I would sit erect, the covers clinched up to my neck, and look through the window beyond the gardenia bush bare in the moonlight and white with ice toward the forest where my father ran wild with the chase. And he would stop and cup his hands to his mouth and his voice became a trumpet that urged the hounds on; the bitch bluetick in lead, yelping in frenzy. She ran vanguard, and I — I would have to make myself breathe. And finally deep within the trees there came the bellows of hounds surrounding a sweetgum, their front paws upon the bark and noses toward the sky, where above in the branches the treed raccoon looked down with eyes matching the stars. My father's trumpet then changed and became long and sorrowful and matched that of the dogs and spoke that he was coming through the bramble of blackberry bushes to them with the rifle to knock the animal down. Sorrowful was his call, almost mournful, and I wondered if my father's sad cry and the hounds' bay in mourning lamented that the hunt would end in death or if only that the hunt ended. Maybe an hour would pass, possibly only a few minutes, but finally the sharp crack of a rifle would sound, and I knew a new pelt would be nailed to the barn wall and my mother would serve us raccoon baked with onions and yams. Lying back in bed, I would burrow against my brother's naked flank, and deep within my throat, silently, I would mimic the hounds' tree bellow and wish my father would run to me, shouting as he came and ask me what was it I chased and why.

My father has been dead for fifteen years, but he speaks to me now in the voice of that dog. I hope that in the years after I have departed, Meghan and Christopher will recognize my image and voice in some form within nature that ties me still to the earthly living.

I feel very alive right now, breathing chill air but warm within my sleeping bag. I am aware of my pulse in my ear that seems in sync with the mechanics of the earth that turns silently beneath me. What a ride I am on, this particular journey to Montana, these forty-five years of hitching a lift on Earth's spin around the sun. These past six months I've been walking an upgrade, lifting myself from the muck and mire of alcohol, through the cleansing rivers of life as they come to me.

• • •

My house was still there. Roy Lee was still in his pen, fed and watered by Dave. The dog licked my hand. I told him I was sorry about the past few weeks, that tonight he would sleep in the house. Inside, the place was a wreck, newspapers scattered on the floor, empty pizza boxes. The trash can was full of liquor and wine bottles. Their sight made me want to throw up. One of my stereo speakers was leaning against the wall, the corner embedded in the sheet rock. I touched the strawberry above my eye. My message machine had so many phone calls on it that the tape had shut off. I sat on the edge of the bed.

I felt as though a mountain were on top of me. But, I had to start digging out. Tomorrow I was supposed to turn in my grades. Nine days till Christmas. I had a stack of unpaid bills scattered about the house. I felt as if I'd been deep fried, not shaking any longer, but fragile. If I were to jump up and down, I felt pieces of me would fall off. But, the electricity was still on. The heat was working, so I had gas. I located my wallet between two cushions on the couch. About fifty bucks inside. One shovelful at a time, I just had to start digging my way up.

I called school, told the very concerned-sounding secretary that I would be in the next day to post grades. Called the kids and talked to them awhile, assured Meghan I was all right, and that I would be over to see them the next afternoon. Gathering my bills, I started paying my dues.

While I was drunk, I had bought a puppy. A female golden retriever. I had been meaning to buy a puppy for the kids, a companion for Roy Lee, and I did so, mailed off a check for $250 instead of making the house payment. One of the phone messages told me the puppy was ready to pick up. At least that was a golden spot in an otherwise gray world. I did have one Christmas present. Once when he was drunk, my dad brought home a young pony in the back seat of our old Mercury. That's hard to top.

I was up early the next morning. Couldn't sleep, anyway. Started cleaning up. Before noon, I drove into school. I sat down with the chair of the English department and told him what had happened. He was pretty good about it, very concerned, but I knew I'd lost the high ground I had gained over the past years. My vision was still pretty blurry, and I spent more than an hour penciling in the little circles beside each student's name on the grade forms. When in debate over a grade, I went with a B+ instead of a flat B, considering I had missed the last few classes.

Mid-afternoon, I arrived at the house where the puppies were. A lady and her son told me my puppy was their favorite, the runt of the litter, one they feared might die soon after birth. But she was eight weeks old now, much smaller than the males, but frisky and quick to lick. Puppy breath, I love it. I drove away with the dog in a box on the front seat, trying to keep her inside while I wove through traffic towards Chapel Hill. I still felt brittle as glass.

Meghan and Christopher were home from school. Katie was still at work. The puppy was a total surprise; the kids shrieked and cradled the pup, and hugged me at the same time.

"You guys get to name her," I told them.

I know. A psychiatrist would probably say the puppy was a ploy to distract from my negligence of the children the past weeks. Bullshit. A puppy is a puppy, and I could not be more aware of my failures, and I do not need to grovel or whip myself over the past.

"You name her, Dad," Meghan told me.

"Nope. You guys. Any name you like."

Linking arms, Meghan and Christopher cuddled the pup like a bassinet. Half an hour later, Katie pulled into the driveway. The kids stared at me. Katie is not a dog person. Especially not a puppy person.

"She won't mind," I assured the kids. They moved the puppy off the rug.

"Hi. How are you?" she asked upon entering.

"Much better."

The kids were beaming as they held up the pup. "Isn't she cute?" Meghan asked.

Katie's smile was tight. She rubbed the pup's head. "When did this happen?"

"Got her today. Full-blooded golden retriever. Why don't you let her run around?" I said to the kids.

The puppy romped on the floor for less than a minute before she suddenly squatted. Before I could act, she spread a small puddle of urine upon the carpet. Katie went ballistic.

"Get that dog out of here!" she shouted. "Take it to your house, and do not bring it here again!" Her eyes glittered like chunks of ice. I opened my mouth to argue, but stopped. The children looked scared. Taking the pup, I hugged the kids, told them I'd call later that night and left. In the car, I cussed a blue streak. But, I couldn't blame Katie's anger. Her wrath was not about puppies.

Later that night on the phone with the kids, we decided to name the pup Lilly. Lilly slept beside my bed that night. She did not whimper. Occasionally, in my broken sleep, I reached and rubbed her soft fur.

Katie called the next morning. Her voice sounded very weary. "I'm sorry for losing it last night," she told me. "It's just that I have been under incredible stress for the past couple of weeks."

"It was my fault," I told her. We talked for a while. I told her about talking to Jerry, that I was seeing him again early next week. I told her that I was through drinking. I knew she believed that like the man in the moon. Both of us being very restrained, we discussed me bringing the kids over that afternoon so they could play with Lilly.

"I just can't trust you anymore," Katie said. "I want to. The children love you and need you so much." Her voice was trembling. "It's so tragic, Tim. I used to love you so much, and now I don't. That just kills me."

A long, painful pause. What could I answer to such words? "I've quit drinking, Katie. I *just quit*. I don't expect you to believe that now, but you will see in time. A year from now, you'll take me more seriously."

"It can't be that easy, Tim. Years ago you could have 'just quit'."

"No. Always before, someone else was saying quit. This time, I'm saying it."

I kept mining my way toward daylight. Fortunately, I knew already pretty much what I was getting the kids for Christmas. A trip to the mall took care of most of the shopping. Christopher likes things that deal with science or the outdoors. That's easy for me. Meghan's list is tougher. Thinking like a fifteen-year-old female is alien to my brain. She requested a VCR for the television in her room, but I balked at that. Instead, I bought her beautiful quarter-carat diamond stud earrings from a jeweler I like and trust in town. The tiny stones will last long after I am dust. One expensive present for each, several lesser gifts. For me as a kid, a large part of Christmas was opening the presents.

The children helped me string some Christmas lights outside my house. Lilly was growing so fast; Roy Lee tolerated her chewing on his neck. He looked at me sometimes when she was annoying him as if he were thinking, "Pop, why in the world did you get this thing?"

One of Christopher's Christmas requests touched me. A hardback copy of each of my books, signed personally to him. At Barnes and Noble, I found a copy of one of my books I didn't have at home. I was on my way to the clerk when I stopped in front of a display. A big book on how to make your face up like different celebrities, photographs and step-by-step drawings. The book cost close to forty dollars. In my hands, I already had an equally expensive book that contained copies of famous paintings through history. Meghan's final present. I glanced from Mona Lisa's face to Madonna's. Finally, I put back the rational choice and picked up a copy of the logical choice.

Meghan had recently seen the real *Starry Night* with her own eyes. Let her be fifteen while she has the chance.

Christmas Eve was unusually cold with freezing rain. I couldn't remember freezing rain on Christmas but once in my life. The kids were over early in the evening, but I took them home before the roads got bad.

"Why don't you stay here tonight?" Meghan asked. She was worried about me driving back so early the next morning.

"I need to stay home. When I come, there won't be any cars on the road." Since the separation, I have come to Windsor Circle each Christmas morning before the kids get up. The situation always seems strained, but Katie and I have visited enough pain upon the children by divorcing; as long as they are young, they should awaken to the joy of Christmas morning with both parents in the same room.

And finally, it was Christmas, and I was driving over before the sun had risen, the back seat of my car piled with hastily wrapped gifts. The roads were not icy, but the trees along the way were, their branches glistened in the car lights. The sky had cleared, and Venus shone bright against the eastern heavens, and could not be in the sky at a better time. I came to the children bearing diamonds and books, the stones cast from the long roll of time, the words the meter of one man's passage.

And I, not bound in tissue and lace ribbon, but in flesh, worn but still warm, was what my children wished for most.

• • •

New Year's Eve rolled by. I spent it alone at my house, watching the apple drop on television. The kids called me a few minutes past midnight. I was sober, and could not remember being so on that date in the previous twenty-five years. I slept well and woke up to a whole new year — 1999.

I needed to set some long-term objectives. Way back as a young man, I pledged that I would live to see the turn of the century. At the time, forty-five seemed impossibly old, and now I am that age, and do not feel so ancient. My body shows some wear and tear, but my brain seems caught somewhere between adolescence and adulthood. I have pledged to take Meghan to Tunisia to see her birthplace, so if willpower has anything to do with longevity — and I think it does — I have more years ahead of me than the one that has just arrived. I have pledged to raise my children to adulthood, and what I do know at forty-five is that being grown has nothing to do with size.

1999. An ominous year. I have worried a bit about the turn of the century since childhood. All those predictions about the end of time. At a second past midnight will trumpets sound and the sky turn to fire, Mama and Meghan and Christopher and Roy Lee disappear into the rapture? Leave me behind facing Armageddon with snakes tattooed on my arms?

I was reading the Sunday paper, when a story in the Metro section caught my eye. Another kid had committed suicide, a twelve-year-old boy. He shot himself. I read on and suddenly felt as if I have been punched in the stomach. I knew the mother. Diana had roomed at college with Jenell, my first wife. She is a junior high teacher; a few years back I spoke to her class about motivation and overcoming the obstacles in life. Last October, her sixteen-year-old son was killed in a car wreck. I wrote Diana a note of condolence; she wrote back. Before pulling the trigger, the younger boy left a letter explaining that he no longer wanted to live without his brother.

Diana was in the hospital under sedation.

And I think my life is tough sometimes! I imagine for Diana, the end of time may have already arrived.

The new semester at State began. A few of the professors asked me with sincere concern, "How are you doing?" Word had circulated about my drunk. I'm doing fine. I used to drink. Don't now. Simple as that.

The buzz of conversation ceased when I walked into the first meeting of my first class at 1:05 in the afternoon. I didn't speak. I was wearing sunshades, jeans, and a polo shirt that rode high on my biceps so part of my tattoos showed. At the front of the room, I dragged a table into position, then sat on top of it. I rested my feet upon a chair. The room was very quiet, all eyes upon me. After studying the class roster for half a minute, I slowly leaned forward and pulled my shades down low on my nose and looked upon the faces trained at me.

"Boy, did you guys screw up!" I growled.

A few people chuckled. Some glanced nervously at classmates. Most just stared back at me. I knew what they were thinking. Who in the hell is this half-bald sucker with tattoos hanging out of his shirt perched on top of that desk? He sure doesn't look like an English professor.

Then I smiled, and most of the students returned my smile; I recognized a couple of faces from previous classes. "Do any of you honestly think you will carry an A out of this classroom?" I arched one eyebrow. More smiles. "Well, right now all of you have an A. You have to earn a B or C. We're here to learn about writing fiction, and study life and have some fun in the process. I can't teach you to write good fiction. You learn to write good fiction in the outside world. I can only guide you in the mechanics of writing, criticize your work and encourage you. There is no syllabus in this class. Learning to write fiction cannot be done according to a set schedule."

I took the roll then, asking for any nicknames. "Take a sheet of paper and write down your name, where you come from, any writing experience you might have, favorite author, and any interesting fact about yourself you might want to share with the class.

After I collected the papers, I told them about myself, and how I came to be sitting there on the desk — snakes and snails and puppy dog tails. Then in turn, I talked to each student and asked questions about their lives. I discussed the class requirements and told the students I give extra credit for doing something challenging for the first time — as long as the deed is legal and moral — basically. Class ended a little early. At two-thirty, my second class began, and I went through the same routine. Again at six o'clock. Maybe I act a little bit, but writing fiction is like being on stage, too.

Amy and Michelle sat right in front of me in my first class. Both were seniors, both very pretty, wore make-up and skirts to class, legs tanned and shapely. They sat so close, I could smell their perfume. Both girls paid attention in class, asked questions and always did their reading. I would be lying to say they did not give a boost to the day. If it is sexist to admit I prefer to look at pretty young women more than knot-headed, half-asleep, hung-over guys, then I am guilty as hell. Beyond looking, even if the possibility existed that I might touch one of the young ladies, I would not. They are children, only a few years older than Meghan.

Snake day. Once each semester I bring a few reptiles to class. On this particular day I had a cornsnake, a kingsnake, a canebrake rattler, and George, my African spur-foot tortoise. George was an instant hit with the students. His head resembles ET's. He ate a banana from my hand.

I held up the cornsnake, glossy with colors of brick-red, black and cream painting his scales. "OK, the cornsnake is not like a short story. A short story must have a conflict and resolution. There must be a theme or moral to the story. Cornsnakes do not bite. They are not poisonous. They are pretty to look at, but there is no conflict. Sort of like a scene you might write about Bill and Mary on a summer picnic. You describe the weather, what Bill and Mary look like, what food they have in the basket. The scene — like the cornsnake —

can be very pretty, but there is no conflict. That is not a story. A conflict must occur. Maybe Bill and Mary get into an argument. Maybe a bull runs up or a thunderstorm starts to brew on the horizon. Conflict."

I put the cornsnake in a pillowcase. Then, from an ice chest, on the end of a snake hook, I took out the rattler. He was four-foot long and buzzing, the tip of his tail a blur. A murmur rolled through the class. I held the rattler in the air. "Now, there is a definite conflict in the rattlesnake. The rattler will bite you. He is poisonous. Now, the resolution may be that I will pin the snake's head and milk his venom into that glass and then put him up and everything will be cool, or the resolution might be that I screw up and the snake bites me, and y'all get out of class early while I ride down to the hospital." I arched my eyebrows; the class laughed. "Either way, there is a conflict and a resolution. Thus, with the rattler, we have a short story."

I prefer the former resolution to the story. A few years ago during summer school, I brought a copperhead to class. While driving back to Chapel Hill in my pickup, the copperhead escaped through a hole in the corner of the pillowcase. Upon arriving at Windsor Circle, I discovered the escape and cautiously looked under the seat. No copperhead. That night, I left both doors open on the truck, knowing the snake would more than likely let himself out. The next day in class, I told the students about the copperhead escaping. We joked about the snake crawling out from under the seat while I was driving and biting my ankle. For the rest of the week, someone asked each day if I had found the copperhead.

The weekend rolled around, and Sunday night I was coming home late, when right in the middle of the road was another copperhead. I pulled over and pinned the snake's head with my shoe, then gripped the serpent behind his head. I didn't have a pillowcase to put him in, debated the issue for a minute, then decided to drive the couple of miles home while holding the snake. Using my wrist, I got the truck in gear and popped the clutch. I had gotten up to third gear when the snake started struggling. Because I was driving, I was unable to stop his thrashing with my left hand. The copperhead twisted just enough to sink one fang into my index finger. I felt the bite, but still had to steer. I didn't want to sling the snake down, because at least I knew where his fangs were. By the time I got off the road and stopped, the snake had administered a pretty good dose of venom. I got him off my finger, tightened my grip and drove on home where I put the copperhead in a cage. Within thirty minutes, the swelling and pain told me I had gotten a bad bite. Three nights in the hospital.

Monday morning following the bite, a secretary walked into my class.

"Mr. McLaurin will not be in school today," the concerned woman told my students. "He got bit by a copperhead and is in the hospital."

The whole class burst out laughing, thinking the copperhead under the seat had finally crawled out and bitten me. The shocked secretary scolded the students for being so insensitive.

I couldn't blame the copperhead for biting me. But, I had to get back on that horse. When the swelling had left my hand after a couple of weeks, I pinned the snake and grasped him again around the neck. I cussed him a blue streak, then released him to the woods. The knuckle where he bit me is permanently stiff. Another scar for the old lady to gnaw away.

In front of my class, I pinned the rattler without much of a struggle, then milked twin squirts of amber-colored venom into a glass. When I put him back in the cooler, the class applauded. "OK, we have a nice ending to this short story. I didn't get hurt. The snake didn't get hurt. What is the moral of this story? That's up to you. The interpretation of literature is subjective. You might say that some Southern writers are lunatics who will pick up rattlesnakes. But, you might also say that some Southern writers have the guts to pick up serpents, and that is one reason Southern literature is held in esteem. Either interpretation, you have a story."

At the end of class, I allowed the students to hold the cornsnake. Amy was brave and draped the kingsnake around her neck. Black, glistening reptile scales against the alabaster flesh of her throat. I thought of the Garden of Eden and the benefits of sin. But immediately, I purged that thought.

Several students thanked me for bringing the snakes. Maybe I was running the risk of another bad bite, but these students would remember what they had seen that day.

Friday afternoon, and my weekend with the kids. I picked Christopher up at five-till-three. Meghan at three-thirty-five. They packed their bags, called their mother at work. At five o'clock, we pulled into my driveway.

I'd cleaned the house up pretty good. The air smelled of incense I burned to mask the odor of dog urine. Lilly wasn't housebroken yet, although she was nearly paper-trained. She missed sometimes.

"What you guys want for supper?" I asked.

Pizza. Meghan wanted cheese and pepperoni. Christopher wanted the full deal like I did. I ordered a medium pie of each. The delivery man arrived with three minutes to spare before I would have gotten a discount. We had three movies to watch, a vampire flick, a love story, and an adventure movie.

"You guys decide which one is first," I told the kids, and they debated — not each for his or her choice, but for the other to decide. Finally, I shuffled the plastic cases like poker cards and drew one. The love story, *City of Angels*. That's what I would have chosen. I hadn't seen the movie, but the kids had, swore they wanted to watch again. Nicholas Cage is good in anything. He scared me in *Leaving Las Vegas*, shaking and retching when he needed a drink. Too real — I have known the feeling, but if I were in Diana's shoes right now, mourning the loss of my two children, I think I'd do the same thing. Knock on wood. I'd cash a check for about a thousand dollars, drive by the liquor store and buy a stock of good vodka, and a month or so later I'd be out of here.

I had to insist that Meghan eat a third slice of pizza. Lilly got the crusts. Roy Lee slobbers so much that I usually wait until bedtime to let him in. Very good movie. I enjoyed the score, liked how Cage quoted from Hemingway's *A*

Movable Feast. Phone calls interrupted me a couple of times, but Christopher hit the pause button. The ending was a gut wrencher. Meghan kept glancing at me,

"Do you think that is the way it is?" she asked.

"The way what is?"

"How people die?" She leaned against me. I rubbed her shoulder.

"I like to think so. I don't think death is anything to be afraid of."

"I hope I die before you," Meghan said.

"I hope I die before both of you," Christopher said.

"Nooo. I get to die first," I told them. "Years and years from now, and then I can be there for you two when it's your time."

"I wouldn't want to live if you weren't here," Meghan said.

"I'll always be here. Just like the wind. You just won't be able to see me." I thought a quick prayer. I said one for Diana.

We started the vampire movie. The flick was a classic, with a real plot instead of just special effects and gore. Christopher burrowed between me and Meghan. He likes scary movies, but they spook him. During one of the tense, quiet parts of the movie, a creak sounded from the back of the house. Christopher gripped my hand.

"What was that?"

"Probably a vampire coming in through the window," I told him. He gripped my hand tighter.

"Daaad!" Meghan scolded. "You're going to be sleeping with him tonight."

"It's just the furnace expanding. If you had let me order garlic on the pizza, you wouldn't have to worry about vampires."

Midnight was approaching, both kids sleepy. Maybe the old movies have plots, but without the special effects and gore, they *are* a bit boring. "Let's turn this off and crash," I told the kids. "You can watch the ending in the morning. You guys look sleepy."

"We're not sleepy."

"Come on. Cut it off, and let's get ready for bed. You can sleep late. I'll cook you a good breakfast. What about lablebbe?"

"Cereal, dad," Meghan said.

"No, I promise. I'll fix each of you a big, hot bowl of lablebbe." Lablebbe is a Tunisian breakfast gruel, made of bread, chick peas, olive oil, hot sauce, lemon juice, capers, cumin, and a slightly boiled egg. Looks like vomit.

"No dad. Cereal will do."

"I don't mind fixing it. Not for you guys."

"I'll eat some," Christopher said. He has inherited a few of my taste buds.

"I won't," Meghan said.

"What about pork brains and eggs?"

"Cereal!"

"What about green eggs and ham?"

Meghan considered that for a moment. "Cereal."

I punched the stop button on the remote. The VCR clicked and hummed before static filled the screen. "Up. Let's get to bed. Brush your teeth. Christopher. How about running out to the car and bringing in my keys?"

He smiled, then shook his head.

"You're going to be sleeping with him all night," Meghan warned.

Finally, both kids were under the cover in my big bed. They don't mind sleeping together still, so I don't mind. I opened the closet door, acted like something had grabbed my arm and was pulling me inside.

"Daaad!" Christopher said, "You're going to be sleeping with me tonight!"

I sat on the edge of the bed. "Let's say the blessing."

"Prayer!"

"Let's say the prayer. Same thing." Each of us said a few sentences. I tucked them in, kissed foreheads. "Sleep tight. Don't let the vampires bite."

"DAAAADDDD!"

"I love you two boogers. I'll be right in the next room."

I turned the light off, left the door cracked. Turned the television on and listened to the late news. Through the wall, I could hear the kids talk for a few minutes, but soon they were silent. After thirty minutes of watching the world's chaos, I turned off the tube and let Roy Lee in. He tried to hump Lilly. "You pervert," I said, scratching his ears for a minute. I locked the garage door, then checked the burners on the stove and the oven to make sure they were off. Checked the door again, then the stove once more. The coffee pot was unplugged. Petted the dogs again, then turned off the kitchen light and closed the dogs inside. Newspaper was spread on the floor, and I hoped Lilly's aim was true. Brushed my teeth.

The kids were sleeping. I listened to make sure each was breathing, then closed the door, turned the thermostat down. Stripped and crawled into Christopher's twin bed. I lay on my back and stared into the dark ceiling and let my mind wander. Wondered what Diane was thinking about.

It was going on two years now since I'd been with Merrie. I thought about the black-haired woman again. Ronnie. She had won second place in a fiction contest I judged, is about my age, grew up in DC. Raven hair nearly down to her waist. Slender. Looks younger than her age. We'd had lunch a couple of times; she seemed to like me. I debated whether I should ask her over to the house one night and cook her dinner. Two years is a long time sleeping alone. But there are benefits. I have the whole mattress to myself. If I need to fart, I fart. Christmas is cheaper. Still, two years is a long time. Finally, I rolled over to my side, farted, and within minutes was sleeping.

Weak daylight through the window. I heard a bird singing outside. The furnace fan was blowing warm air. I drifted in a gray layer for several more minutes, but the dogs were bumping in the kitchen. Getting up, I pulled a bath robe over my nakedness. Halfway down the hall, I turned up the thermostat, then quietly opened my bedroom door and looked upon the kids. Christopher was in a fetal position; Meghan had stolen most of the covers again. Both were breathing. I gently closed the door; they would sleep till noon if I let them.

The dogs romped when I entered the kitchen. Taking

two slices of bologna from the fridge, I led them to the pen. The ground was shiny with frost; I stepped quick. Back inside, I made strong coffee, poured a cup and added enough skim milk to cool it. Turned on the television and flipped to ESPN to a fishing show. For the next hour, I channel surfed while downing three cups of coffee.

No lablebbe this morning. I didn't have chick peas, anyway. Fried some mild pork sausage, then poured the grease from the pan. Mixed flour, an egg, teaspoon of salt and tablespoon of oil with enough milk to form batter. No Aunt Jemima here. Poured twin cakes into the pan and cooked until bubbles were breaking through the top. Flip and browned the other side. Placed the hot cakes on a plate beside the sausage in the oven, then poured another round.

Standing above the kids, I mimicked a rooster. Meghan groaned, then lifted her head, stared at me and smiled. I crowed again. She dropped her head back to the pillow. Christopher lifted on one elbow. "Rise and shine," I said. "I want to hear toenails tapping on the floor."

I remember my Dad's same words on Saturday mornings when he wanted us to do something like pile brush — or help castrate piglets. I wanted to choke him. "Rise and shine! I want to hear toenails a'tapping on the floor."

"What time is it?" Meghan asked.

"Ten o'clock. I've cooked you a good breakfast."

She arched one eyebrow.

"No, not lablebbe. Sausage and homemade pancakes." I crowed again. "Rise and shine and pay your fine."

Christopher went past me to the bathroom. His boxer shorts were sticking out. Meghan's hair was spread across the side of her face. I leaned and kissed her head. She was so warm and smelled like soap. "Did you sleep good?"

"Yeah."

I patted her hip. "Time to get up. We've got a good day planned. I'll fix you a plate."

I scrambled some eggs with bits of onion and green pepper. Filled up glasses with milk and loaded up two plates. By the time I brought the plates into the living room, both kids were on the couch watching Power Rangers. I wondered what happened to Bugs Bunny.

"I wanted cereal," Meghan said.

"You need a good breakfast. Breakfast fuels the whole day. Power Rangers eat big breakfasts."

"Thank you," she said.

"Where's your breakfast?" Christopher asked. "You need to eat, too."

"I'll get it soon as I finish this cup of coffee."

Christopher ate all of his food. Meghan ate half the sausage, one pancake, and about a spoonful of the eggs. She pushed the bits of onion and green pepper into a little pile.

"Meghan, you eat like a bird."

"A swan," she informed me.

"Swans eat worms and mud."

"No they don't."

"Yes they do. You'd learn that if you watched the Discovery Channel instead of cartoons."

I ate the rest of Meghan's food. Didn't even have to dirty another plate.

There was a new show at the planetarium at UNC, one about the exploration of Mars. I also had noticed in a sales paper from Sears, a Ping-Pong table on sale for just fifty-nine dollars. The Ping-Pong table would fit in the garage, and would be good kid-bait away from the television.

The planetarium matinee started at two. We arrived a few minutes early and got good seats on the back row where we could see the whole dome-shaped ceiling. The black, dumb-bell shaped projector in the middle of the planetarium looked like some robot from a science fiction movie. The lights went out, we settled back against the headrests, and suddenly the ceiling was a replica of a starry, night sky. Crickets chirped, and in my mind I was again ten years old and lying in the pasture behind the house I grew up in, gazing into the universe and wondering what it all means.

My Uncle Ken gave me a telescope he brought home from Air Force service in Germany. The scope was a nice

German glass, and could lower the moon and planets until they seemed to fit inside my palm. The pale quarter moon became a world of brilliant shadow and light, sharp mountain ranges and coin-shaped craters punched out by meteors. The dim, yellow shine of Saturn was transformed into a tiny, white orb split by razor-sharp rings. As I looked through the scope, into infinity and time, I grew larger as I realized I was part of a universe without boundaries. My world did not stop at the tree line of sweetgums and oaks, but swelled beyond the tobacco fields and across the river, and raced at the speed of light away from earth to where even my telescope could not probe. Maybe I lived in a four-room house minus plumbing, but I was linked through light years and millennia with an existence beyond miles and minutes.

In the gift shop after the program, I bought a thousand plastic luminous stars to stick to the walls of my bedroom ceiling and walls.

"We'll make our own planetarium," I told the kids. "You guys can lie in the bed at night and go to sleep looking into the Milky Way." As a teenager watching the moon landings by the Apollo crews, I sincerely thought that during my lifetime I would travel to the moon, that by my present age, Pan Am would have excursion flights to a lunar colony where I could gaze upon the blue and white marble of Earth. That trip will never happen for me, but for Meghan and Christopher, it can. I want them to want to go, to choose the Sea of Tranquility over the Aegean Sea.

The Ping-Pong table for fifty-nine dollars at Sears looked about as expensive as the price tag, made of chip board with flimsy aluminum legs. The kids seized upon a different table, sturdy and heavy, it folded at the middle and could be rolled on steel castors. It also cost $175.

I considered the tables. The first I wasn't sure would support Thanksgiving dinner. The second was sturdy enough to crawl under during a tornado. I fingered my wallet. I had paid off the Sears card when my land sold. Ping-Pong was a good draw away from the television. As Katie taught me to think — a good table will outlast three cheap ones, especially when I'm going to have Christopher leaning all over the playing surface trying vainly to reach those backspin shots I lob at him. I took out the plastic; this is America.

I needed a truck even more than I needed a heavy-duty Ping-Pong table. I strapped the cardboard carton on top of my car, and drove way below the speed limit. Within an hour, the nuts and bolts were tightened and the matches began. My backspin wasn't what it used to be, but neither was my jump shot or my hairline. But I did have a house and a garage with a heavyweight Ping-Pong table/tornado shelter, and two kids growing fast and strong enough to soon best me at the game.

I started to cook supper while the kids laughed and argued and played. Chicken fried in sunflower oil, mashed potatoes with the skins left on, a tossed salad dosed with fat-free Ranch dressing. The meal was similar to the ones my mother cooked, minus bacon grease and most of the salt — minus some of the flavor, too. I did make biscuits from scratch, self-rising flour, salt, buttermilk, ended up with about as much dough on me as on the baking pan. But with a slab of butter and strawberry jam, they would be quite edible for biscuits made in 1999.

We ate sitting in front of the tube watching the adventure movie. I'd seen the flick before, so when the action wasn't heavy, I went to my bedroom and pasted stars on the ceiling and walls. By bedtime, I had a pretty good-looking rendition of the Milky Way stretching across the beige paint.

"Let's say the blessing," I told the kids when they were beneath the covers.

"PRAYER!"

"Same thing." Each of us lifted a few sentences. I switched off the light, and suddenly a swatch of stars glowed where the room was dark before.

"That's coooolll!" Meghan exclaimed.

"Neat, Dad!" Christopher said.

Along with the stars, I had bought a Frisbee-sized replica of earth. It glowed blue and white amid the man-made galaxy. In a far decade, I imagined Meghan standing at a portal of the moon colony gazing toward Earth's glow. She is old, and I am already dust, and as she looks toward home she thinks, *This is what Dad wanted me to see when I was fifteen and he captured the heavens in his bedroom.*

"Go to sleep," I said.

"Thanks for the Ping-Pong table," Christopher said.

"Yeah, thanks," Meghan echoed. "I'm sorry you had to pay so much."

"Don't worry about it. It's already paid for itself."

"These stars look so real," Christopher said.

"Yeah. I like 'em. They sort of look like eyes staring at you."

"DAAAAD!" in unison.

I let the kids sleep even later than on Saturday. Just before noon, we went to eat brunch at a restaurant. Meghan ate a full plate of grits, scrambled eggs, bacon, and biscuits; somehow restaurant food always tastes better. At a popular black-owned restaurant in Chapel Hill, white people pay eight dollars for a bowl of chicken and dumplings with a side of turnip greens and cornbread, but many of those same patrons would likely turn up their noses at the same fare for three-fifty at a Fayetteville truck stop.

More Ping-Pong in the afternoon. I slacked off a little and let the kids beat me once in a while. Soon, I won't have to fake. Played with Lilly, tried to get her to learn to sit. Too soon, five o'clock was approaching, time for the kids to pack up so I could take them back to Katie. We dropped the movies off at the video store; Lilly was riding with Meghan in the back seat.

"Dad," Christopher said, "I want to start staying with you more."

"Well, I would like that a lot." I squeezed his knee; he rested his hand on top of mine. If I had no other reason not to drink in the world — and I had a hundred other reasons — his words alone would stay my thirst.

• • •

The river beside the campground flows swift and white over rocks, cold water that comes from the mountains, early in its long journey to the sea. I am once again reborn in the early morning, cast into consciousness and flesh. We are going today into the mountains, to the snow fields that still bury the high fields and flanks, but I am content for the moment to stand here by the current before diving into the hustle of the day.

Last night I finally drifted back into sleep, lulled by the memories of a former night beside a different river. And this morning, I stand beside a river that contains at least part of the flow of all waters I have touched in this life, merely channeled between different rocks. I look toward the mountains to where the river disappears around a bend, and then follow the course eastward to where the flow curves and disappears again. But I know beyond my sight in both directions, the current comes and she continues. Early this spring, in those suspended days between the twilight of winter and the dawn of the blooming season, on another water-road I gained insight into the knowledge that in this life and mortal form, I can never see beyond the curve of the river, but I can rest in the assurance that the flow will come to me, and will continue beyond me after I am gone.

Seven

All the world seemed cast in pewter, a thick gray sky that leaked cold rain, brown, naked trees that stretched against the clouds, soggy earth and a chill wind from out of the northwest. Cars crossing the bridge above the river were amplified by the twin concrete pillows that rose from the water to support the structure. The river flowed silent as time, coffee-colored, the current swift and rising.

My canoe was packed to the top of the gunwales, enough gear and food for a ninety-five mile run from here down to Wilmington. Tuesday at noon. If everything went as planned, I would paddle with the current through the turns and loops of the narrow upwaters for three nights until the river widened, and the fresh, rain runoff mixed with salt ions washed inland with the ocean tide to Wilmington where I would tie up to the wharf beneath the Hilton Hotel and a room waiting for me on the ninth floor.

The bow of my canoe was in the water, the stern grounded against the concrete boat ramp. I checked over my gear once again, making sure everything was lashed down in the event of a spill. Within reach of my hands were a jug of water and a dry-sack containing a couple tins of sardines, soda crackers, a six-pack of Snickers bars, and a topographical map of the river. I was dressed in long underwear topped with jeans, a flannel shirt, coat, and waterproof hat. I pulled on my brand-new life preserver and tugged up the zipper.

I pushed the canoe further into the water, then climbed into the seat, dug against the mud with my paddle, and suddenly I was afloat. For a couple of seconds, the boat tottered, until I planted my feet and centered myself. Already the current was pulling me downriver. As I passed under the bridge, the sound of tires crossing the concrete seams was loud, but within minutes, I rounded a bend, and the world was silent. That's the way it would be for ninety-five miles, a stretch of water at a time where I could scout any obstacles, with always a curve in sight before and one behind, balanced between what I have just passed through and what lies unseen ahead.

The rain picked up a little bit; the temperature was about thirty-eight. Sure, I was doing what any safety expert would advise against, canoeing solo through wilderness in inclement weather, but I know few people who would want to join me, and I did not want company. Maybe I was letting my testicles think for me, but I whispered the words of Henry V before he and his men went into battle with the French. "The fewer men, the greater share of honor."

The faintest touch of spring was in the trees, knobby buds that tipped the branches. The sap had begun to trickle upward, and Nature was waiting for this cold snap to pass before bursting into bloom. Wild crocus and daffodils had already flowered, the scattered spots of color stark against the drab day. Life grows from such small seeds.

I set myself into a paddling rhythm, one stroke after another, occasionally pulling harder to one side to correct my course. Let my arms act like a machine, and don't think about the motion, how many thousands of times I must flex my biceps before I arrive. Instead, I thought of Meghan and Christopher, how they hugged me especially hard the afternoon before when I was leaving. I told them I might not pass any place where I could call them during the trip, but that I would phone as soon as I arrived in Wilmington. My pulse was strong and steady.

Ten years ago, I was only a few months away from being diagnosed with myeloma. I already knew something was wrong with my body. When I jogged, I did not have the usual stamina. Occasionally, my heart would start beating irregularly for several minutes. A couple of EKGs showed no problems. As the weeks passed, I noticed my semen had lessened to a few drops, then totally disappeared. Then my urine turned dark, and a kidney biopsy diagnosed the problem.

The river was only about fifty feet wide this far inland. I worried about downed trees blocking the channel, left over from the hurricane that ripped through here two autumns ago. Within the first few miles, I did have to squeeze through tight places, but someone had already cut through the worst with a chainsaw. Beavers were evident, cone-shaped trunks plentiful along shore, the only wildlife active in this weather seemed to be a few songbirds flittering in the branches. But, at least I didn't have to worry about mosquitoes. In the mouth of a creek flowing into the river, I surprised a male wood duck. He burst from the water and flew low downriver to where I couldn't see him. The duck was so brightly plumed that he looked as though he had been drawn with crayons. I hadn't seen a wood duck in a long time and took the sighting as a good omen. He must have hidden, because I did not sight him again. Mating season, probably already had a frowsy, brown hen nesting eggs against this damp chill.

I thought about the current I was riding, and how right then I seemed to have my future planned like the dependable course of this river. Five more years and Christopher would be in college. I'd apply for a Fulbright Fellowship to India to teach for a school year in one of the universities. During break from college, Meghan and Christopher could come for a visit, and by train we'd tour the country. When the Fellowship was over, I'd sell my house for a handsome profit, and with the proceeds, buy a secluded piece of land on the Dan River near the Virginia line, and build me a funky, little post and beam structure with a wraparound porch. Continue teaching two days a week, write some more books, grow a large garden and can or dry most of my vegetables. Hell, maybe even be more radical and buy a little house down on Cat Island in the Bahamas, live there September through April, then go north and teach summer school at State. The kids would have a great place to come for spring break. I'll see the kids well into adulthood, then have the Big One and go out of this world before I was decrepit and broke. Couldn't be like that wood duck who can herd his flock around for about three months, then fly south for the winter, leaving his brood to fate.

The rain picked up, and I took a plastic tarp from behind my seat, spread it across my lap and legs and draped the edges over the gunwales. I was mostly dry and warm, except for my feet. Wiggling my toes, I tried to circulate the blood. Bend after bend, mile after mile I paddled, knowing I needed to reach a certain point on the map to stay on schedule. I was already a little behind from tarrying too long that morning. Six miles into the trip, I passed under another bridge, and knew I needed to paddle at least another ten miles to the next bridge and a ways beyond it before I started looking for a campsite. No sun in the sky, but by my watch, I should have enough time to get there if I speeded up a bit. I dug a little deeper into the water and cruised at about the pace of a fast walk. The current and wind were at my back.

Saw a lot of ducks. Mallards. All of them paired up. A heron watched me from his perch on a log, but didn't fly. Maybe he thought I was just another log washed downriver. I was. My ears were starting to tune-up to the silence; I heard a woodpecker hammering away on a dead limb. Once in a while, a songbird would burst into chorus, as if he knew as well as I did that eventually this rain would pass and the skies would clear and Spring soon would take off her overcoat and reveal her frock of pastel colors. Suddenly, against the vertical line of the forest, a shape formed, a buck deer standing with his head down, muzzle in the edge of the water as he drank. An eight-pointer, he had not seen me or scented me yet; his ears were pitched forward and tuned to the sounds of danger. I froze my paddle and drifted with the current. I thought of a story I wrote the spring before I was diagnosed with myeloma, the disease already spreading through the core of my bones. The journey I was about to embark upon where I was sucked down into a nether-world in question of fate and God, dependent upon faith and modern medicine and willpower to emerge. Of anything I have written, that story always seemed to come from a place within me I did not know. And it is finally now, in this year and on this water, that I am beginning to see the relevance to understanding my own life.

• • •

The river was not yet visible in the thick darkness prior to dawn, only the moon on the water, golden and full. For a quarter hour Mack Breece had been in the tree stand waiting. He watched the moon sail the water, saw Venus blink on and off as she moved through leafless branches in her climb up the eastern sky. The sun was rolling up, Mack could see his hands now, his .243 rifle cradled in his lap. As high clouds gleamed pink, Venus began to grow dimmer. The world was silent, he was far enough into the woods that the sparse Saturday traffic was muted. The first bird twittered, one single, pure warble, and that call was answered. Within minutes, the world was awake, doves began their sad cooing, a large fish broke the river surface. Mack could see into the limbs now, and a squirrel was climbing down a tree trunk to the ground to feed. The deer would be moving, and if that big buck was coming, he would arrive in the half light before the sun crested the horizon.

Mack had not moved a muscle in several minutes. The seat in his deer stand was padded, he had placed both feet on limbs wide apart, back erect. He always wore enough clothing that he stayed warm. Deer didn't live long enough to grow ten points by being stupid. Plenty of dumb hunters twisted and squirmed in their stands trying to get comfortable, blew breath into their cold hands, which to the ear of wildlife sounded like blowing trumpets.

A faint rustle of leaves, then silence, another few steps. Mack tensed his hands on his rifle and peered into the forest below him. More steps. Sounded like a deer, a large one. A man would make much more noise.

The buck stepped from a reed thicket into the open bank. He turned his head from side to side and searched, his nostrils flared. Mack judged the distance to be forty yards. A few saplings grew between them, but if the buck would move on down to the sandbar, nothing would stand between them but air.

Walking onto the sandbar, the buck searched both

ways on the river, then slowly lowered his head to drink. He was the one all right, that rack itself like a tree. Mack had spent hours scouting him during the off season, learning his trails, where he slept and where he came to drink. Only when he lowered his head to the water did Mack lift his rifle and peer into the sight. The buck was magnified four-fold. Mack pushed off the trigger safety, planted the cross hairs just back of the buck's shoulders, then squeezed off the round.

Thunder in the forest — the shot was true enough that the buck did not even wheel. His front legs buckled, he dropped flat to his belly and his muzzle and eyes sank into the water. In the great silence that followed the gun, Mack clicked on the safety before even taking his eyes from the scope.

Despite the massive blood loss, at the wildlife checkpoint, the buck still weighed in at eleven pounds above the county record. The rack was a perfect ten points. Noon had passed; Mack's belly gnawed with hunger. He studied his watch and decided to swing by Mary's Place for just one hour. She made the best cheeseburgers in town, and a cold beer would sure taste good. A lot of the fellows would be there by now, too, and Mack wasn't ashamed to admit to himself he wanted to show off. The guys sometimes kidded him about how well he prepared for and planned everything he did, but didn't it pay off? He'd started ten years ago as a bricklayer's helper, and now he employed a five man crew. At twenty-eight years of age, he owned his own house, loved his wife, had a three-year-old son, and hoped it was a daughter that was due to pop out in two weeks. Lying here in the bed of the truck was the carcass of the county record deer. Who would laugh last?

Mary's Place was a squat, frame building painted white and decorated with neon beer signs. The dirt parking lot was scattered with a dozen trucks and cars. A cluster of people stood at the tailgate of one of the trucks, mostly men, a few women in tight jeans and layers of makeup. Mack knew them all by name. He'd grown up in this community, had worked with, or now employed, nearly everyone who came to this bar. Mack parked and got out of his truck and walked over to the group. They were looking at a buck with a four point rack. The truck belonged to Claude Phillips, a loud-mouth guy about Mack's age. Mack had gone to school with him, had hired Claude twice and both times ended up letting him go. The deer hadn't been gutted yet. Mack saw where the bullet had struck the buck in the lower back. probably severing his spine. Another close range shot in the head had killed him.

"He made it about a hundred yards," Mack heard Claude say. "Strong sucker, pulling himself forward with just his front legs."

Mack figured Claude would haul the deer around for a couple of days, then throw it into a ditch.

"Bossman," Claude shouted. "You like my little trophy?"

"He's a pretty one, all right," Mack answered.

Mack saw that Claude was studying his hunting clothes, the skinning knife still strapped to Mack's belt.

"You look like you might have been doing a little hunting yourself," Claude said. "Have any luck?"

Everyone looked at Mack. He wished he hadn't stopped by now. Billy Peters, Mack's cousin on his mother's side, stared at Mack's truck and saw the canvas covering the deer.

"Looks like you got something back there, Mack," Billy said.

Mack shrugged one shoulder.

"Hey, Claude," Billy said, "bet ya a beer on the spot that what's under that canvas is bigger than that fawn you murdered."

Several people laughed. Billy worked for Mack, was dependable and loyal and hardworking.

Claude eyed Mack's truck, the ample sheet of canvas. He smiled, but his smile was fake. "What you got, Bossman?"

"'Bout the same as you."

"Two beers," Billy chimed in. "Two beers, shots of whiskey, your choice, that Mack's got a bigger deer under that canvas than you've got."

"You're on," Claude answered. "Show us your kill,

Bossman."

Mack led a parade of people to the rear of his truck. When he pulled back the canvas, a collective gasp, then a round of whistles erupted. Mack couldn't help but grin.

"County record by eleven pounds. Call Sam down at the station if you think I'm lying. I been scouting him since last summer."

Billy slapped Mack's back. "I wish I'd bet a case now. I know this man. He doesn't underbid a job or waste bricks. Come opening day, he goes out and takes the county deer record."

"Heart shot," someone said. "That buck didn't know what hit him."

"What did you shoot him with?" asked Jimmy, a teenager who had worked last summer for Mack.

"243 stainless steel."

"Can I look at it?" Jimmy asked.

"She's on the rack."

Mack grinned while listening to people praise him. He glanced at Claude who was still smiling, but his eyes were drawn narrow.

"Yeah, the Bossman's tough," Claude said. "But when you own the company, you can afford time off to stalk the woods. Me, I gotta work for a living and hunt when I got a few extra hours."

Mack recalled how Claude was bad for laying out on Mondays. He had often smelled whiskey on his breath following lunch. Behind Mack's back, Jimmy opened the truck door and took the rifle from the rack behind the seat. The boy admired the heft of the weapon. He shouldered the rifle and sighted on a cloud, then slid the bolt back and then forward, as if he was fixing to shoot his own prize deer. Smiling, he put the gun back on the rack.

"Shit," Billy said. "Yours was probably a road kill, Claude. Let's go in. I got some free beer to drink."

"I cover my bets," Claude snapped. He reached into his back pocket and pulled out a pint of Kessler's. He unscrewed the cap, then took a long draw. He held the bottle *out to Mack.*

"Have a drink, Daniel Boone."

Mack shook his head. "Naw. I stay away from the hard stuff."

"Hell, Bossman, my whiskey ain't good enough for you? I can't afford Jack Daniel's."

Claude shook the bottle. Mack exhaled and took it and turned the bottom up. The whiskey burned going down and felt like fire in his empty belly. He handed the bottle back and Claude sucked on it again. He left two fingers in the bottom.

"Finish it."

Mack recognized the duel, but he took the bottle and drained it.

While driving home, Mack concentrated on the center line. He was way over his usual limit of four beers. The whiskey had done it — two more shots inside the bar, then round after round of beer — never did eat a hamburger. The last hour had been sort of a blur. He remembered Claude finally bringing up the subject about him getting fired, but before the argument got bad, Billy cold-cocked the guy. They slugged it out for a minute before Billy dropped Claude. The two of them had been itching to fight all afternoon. Mack left then, weaving between tables and out the door to his truck.

He rolled down the window and hung his head out in the freezing air. Damn deer still had to be hung up. Madge would be mad. Though Mack was drunker than he had been in years, he still wanted another beer. He drove slowly the last mile, taking deep breaths and trying to clear his head.

Mack stepped inside the living room and studied Madge sitting in the Easy Boy. She wore the calico frock with the peasant neck that he liked, her thick brown hair rounding both sides of her neck. She was singing a song to Marty, the three-year-old straddling her knees. The large book was perched atop the fullness of her belly, round and taut as a melon after eight months of pregnancy. She was beautiful, her skin holding the luster of a pearl; the boy was handsome, carrying Mack's mouth and chin, Madge's blue eyes.

Madge looked up and smiled, but her face was tight. The boy squealed and grinned at his father, but clung to her.

"Hey," Mack said, glancing at the clock. He leaned his rifle against the door jamb, then slowly removed his coat and hung it on the rack.

"I was starting to worry," Madge said. "I called Ruth, but she didn't know where you were."

"I'm sorry, babe. I got a buck early, then decided to stop by Mary's for a beer. I ended up staying a lot longer than I wanted to."

"I saved your supper."

"I ain't too hungry." Mack tried to steer a straight path to the kitchen. He looked in the fridge, but there was no beer. "Damn!" he muttered. A good fight was on HBO later that night, and he would want some beer. The cat rubbed against his leg and yowled. In the cabinet was a single can of cat food. Mack slid it behind a box of saltines. Then he took another sobering breath.

"We're out of cat food, and the cat is hollering," Mack said, walking past his family. He began putting on his coat. "I'll run out and get some and be right back."

Madge looked at him with eyes that were clear and knowing. "You don't need any more beer, honey."

"Who said anything about beer? The damn cat is hungry." Mack opened the door, then turned back to her. "We need anything else?"

Madge stood slowly, cradling Marty in her arms. "Mack, please don't go out again," she said softly. "You shouldn't be on the road."

"And let the cat starve?"

"I'll fix the cat something. I'd rather you be with us." Mack stared at her, and for a moment hated lying. She was so damn pretty standing there hugging the boy, ready to burst with his second child. But as suddenly, he turned angry. Shit, all he wanted was a couple more beers. Sit down and watch a good fight. Any man that laid bricks fifty hours a week deserved a couple of beers.

Mack looked outside at the darkness, then back at Madge. He stepped inside. "Well, hell!" he said, grasping the knob and slamming the door violently.

The impact jolted the rifle, causing it to begin sliding down the wall. Mack stepped forward to grab it, but in his drunkenness he kicked the stock and the weapon fell toward the center of the room. Mack grabbed for the barrel but missed, the gun came down hard against the arm of an oak rocking chair.

The cartridge Jimmy had chambered earlier that day discharged with a roar. A bullet stinging as a wasp splatted into the center of the boy's chest and threw up fingers of blood that dotted the ceiling and wall. The lead punched through his shoulder, then buried deep to the right of Madge's heart. A huge, ringing silence followed the blast; the boy instantly sagged in her arms. Madge's eyes opened wide with astonishment. She took two steps toward Mack, one arm raised pitifully. He caught her as she fell, tucked the boy under his left arm, bent slightly to wrap his free arm around her buttocks and lifted. Somehow, he opened the door and began running for the light on the neighbor's porch. The boy felt loose like one of his teddy bears, his blood draining down Mack's trouser leg. Madge's arms were clasped around his neck, but her grip got weaker and weaker while he kicked at Sam's door and screamed.

Mack watched the ambulance man pump hard against Madge's still chest. At the hospital, he threw up on the floor. His mother held to his arm and sobbed into her scarf. The doctor walked slowly into the room, holding the tiny girl he had cut from Madge just before her heart quit. The child was blond and blue-eyed with her brother's pug nose. Mack turned in horror and rushed from the hospital. At the funeral, the preacher talked of God's will, of how we were not meant to understand the goodness in all of his plan. Mack walked away from his words and began a two-month drunk that ended when he was carted off to Butner to the mental hospital, twenty pounds thinner and vomiting blood.

• • •

The rains fell like a bitch for awhile. My gear would
stay dry, but water flowed backwards and puddled at my feet,
so I bailed it occasionally with an empty Spam can I brought
along for such purposes. But with the rain, the wind picked
up on my back and I tracked at a pretty good clip. A mouse
could probably ski behind me. My watch read five o'clock,
and I knew it was time to start thinking about a campsite.
With the clouds, it would be dark by six-thirty, and I had to set
up the tent. I ate a candy bar in three big bites, then dug deep
into the water. My pulse was fast and steady in my ears.

Katie did not like the story of Mack Breece that I have
begun to tell you. She said she thought I was subconsciously
killing off our relationship. I strongly disagreed at the time,
but I wonder now if the future was not speaking to me. The
neck of a whiskey bottle is similar in shape to the bore of a
hunting rifle.

Five-thirty, and the bridge appeared around a bend.
Just beyond it were several nice sandbars where I could camp,
but I didn't want to hear cars thumping over the bridge all
night. About a half-mile past the bridge, I spied a low bank
with an outcrop of sand, not as good as what I passed upriver,
but an early twilight was settling among the trees. I ran the
bow up into the sand, rose carefully and stepped out of the
canoe into ankle-deep water. My boots leaked, and I cussed.
At least the rain had stopped.

I selected a piece of land that was fairly level, kicked
sticks and rocks away. Unloaded what I needed from the canoe.
Tarp went down first, then I erected the tent, pushed the stakes
into the soggy ground. Unpacked my sleeping bag and air-
mattress and threw them in the tent. The rain was starting again.
My feet were numb, fingers cold and clumsy. Near the tent
door, I placed the lantern, my pack stove, and a large tin of
beef stew. The water jug went inside, a flashlight, my large
military K-bar. Beginning to shiver, I reminded myself of
hypothermia. Removing my boots, I burrowed into my bag
and zipped it up to my neck. I lay there, slowly beginning to

warm, as the twilight deepened into pitch-black night.

In a half slumber, I dreamed. I'm holding a tiny baby. The child has long hair, and resembles one of those troll dolls that used to be popular years ago. The child smiles at me, already possessing a full set of teeth. I want to drop the child, but understand it is my own, and would not do so. Finally, I awakened and struggled against the confines of my bag before realizing where I was. I pressed the light button on my watch and saw it was eight o'clock. Unzipping the door, I shined the flashlight upon the river. The water was black and flowing fast from all the runoff up river. I hated to get out of the bag, but knew I needed to eat and stockpile carbohydrates for the coming morning.

My boots were stiff and cold. Holding the flashlight under my armpit, I located matches in the drybag. I pumped up the gas lantern, then turned the throttle until I heard a hiss, struck a match and, *WROOF*, I had a bright, yellow light. I warmed my hands above the glow for several minutes. Perched on a folding camp stool, I pumped up the stove and lit it, then adjusted the carburetor until the flame was low and blue. I peeled the label on the can of stew, then opened it and set the can on the burner. Within minutes, the gravy started to bubble. The glow from the lantern formed a cocoon around me, the darkness beyond the light as solid as a wall. From the river, I heard a splash, but was not startled. Just a beaver smacking his tail against the water.

I ate the stew from the can, spooning the chunks of beef, potatoes, and carrots with crackers, washed the food down with Kool-Aid I mixed in a canteen. This was supposed to be fun? No. This is about being alive and strong and sober. The stew tasted especially good when a person was hungry and tired. The warmth from the lantern was magnified after sitting all afternoon in near freezing rain. If I looked toward where the sun had set, I could trace a path backwards in time and distance to that window I gazed out of in the detox ward when I would have gladly traded that place for here.

The rain picked up again. I stowed the gear and got back in the tent. Inflating the air mattress took about ten minutes and made me lightheaded, but the effort beat the alternative of sleeping on the hard ground. I stripped down to my long johns and burrowed into the bag. I brought along a little radio headset that I tuned to a country music station. The weather forecast called for the rain to end tomorrow. I lay there for a while and listened to songs about people who were doing without, but here on this river bank, my belly was full, and I was warm and dry, and I had no time clock to punch in the morning.

Dogs barking. Roy Lee and Lilly yapping at someone walking past the fence? Suddenly I realized I was not in my bed at home, and those couldn't be my dogs; I fought the zipper on my sleeping bag and looked out the back window of the tent. Two beagles stood in the woods looking back at me. I clucked my tongue and the dogs barked more and retreated a few yards. I didn't see any humans.

Laid back down and let my head collect for a moment. Unzipping the front flap, I saw that my canoe was still tied to the tree, my gear where I left it. Seven o'clock. Gray sky, the trees dripping. Dawn swelled late with the cloud cover I could see my breath, and I lay there in the warmth of the bag, dreading to get up. I knew I needed to make about thirty miles today to stay on my schedule, and should already be breaking camp.

I tuned the radio to a strong frequency and listened for a few minutes. Traffic reports I didn't need. News of Kosovo I'd rather not hear. The weather report came on, and the man said there should not be much rain today, that by tonight the clouds would clear. I thought of a Simon and Garfunkel song about getting all the necessary news from the weather report. Life was a bit simpler this morning. From deep in the woods, I heard a turkey gobble. After about a minute, he gobbled again. He was perched on a branch somewhere, his keen eyes scouting the undergrowth. The breeding season had begun. If I had a slate-call, I could mimic a female warbling seductively from the undergrowth. The Tom would fly down from his perch, gobble again; I'd answer on the slate-call with words of sweet love. Ole Tom would puff up his chest, his head would swell with blood and turn purple, and he would come strutting, scratching the ground, tail feathers erect, wearing his best courting suit. So much like a male; he probably already had a couple of females in his harem, but he just couldn't resist the temptation of one more sweet thang crying for attention. If I were good with the slate-call, were very still, he would come to me, jute-stepping and gobbling, "Hey mama. Big daddy coming to ya." And when he stepped between two trees, puffed-up and lusty, leaving what he already has for what he imagined, with a shotgun I would blow him away. Karma.

I took a deep breath and unzipped the bag. Pulled on my jeans and shirt, then slipped on my damp, stiff boots. Crawled out of the tent into the chill air. Must be a real shock to a baby when it slides out of a 98.6 degree environment naked and wet. I'd cry, too. I did.

Started the stove to heat water, then began breaking camp. Ate breakfast of instant bacon and cheese grits and lots of strong, instant coffee. An hour later, I was packed back up, and pushed off into the black current. Paddled hard for the first mile to jump start my circulation. My feet were still cold. I said my prayers, concentrated on Meghan and Christopher, asked that I make it safely back to them. I quit praying after I was diagnosed with myeloma, until I returned from Seattle. I wasn't mad at God, but I didn't think the disease was fair. I had always pretty much played by the rules, did more good in life than bad. What good could there be in a thirty-five-year-old man with two small kids having cancer? The die was cast; I would either live or not, and I wasn't going to beg.

But as I lifted my words, a certain joy filled my chest; these past few months — years — had certainly had their ups and downs, but here I am again, alone on a river, my heart pumping and blood hot, how many miles I travel that day determined by how many times I pull backwards on the paddle.

Every mile I traveled southward seemed to draw me deeper into the emergence of spring. The willows that hung over the water's edge seemed to be sprayed with the slightest green mist, tiny mint leaves barely beginning to unfurl. Redbud trees were blooming, crimson blossoms unusually bright against a mostly brown and gray world. In an eddy behind a downed log, I surprised a female mallard with four fuzzy brown and yellow ducklings. She squawked and circled her offspring, then flapped her wings and skimmed the water to land fifty feet downriver. The ducklings huddled close to the log. The current took me quickly past the log; the hen squawked again and flew further from me. She held one wing outward, as if she were wounded, trying to lure me from her brood.

"I'm not going to hurt your babies," I said to the hen. "You get on back to them before a snapping turtle pulls one down." After another short flight, she doubled back to her brood. In a tree top, about fifty yards past where the mallard turned around, I spotted a red-tailed hawk. I knew the predator's X-ray eyes had probably spotted the brood of ducklings; I hoped the mother kept one eye on the sky.

• • •

Mack stared through the curtainless window of his room into the gray courtyard. His room was bare except for a bed and dresser and the chair in which he sat. The first of the year had passed and snow had fallen last week, but most of it had melted now, or turned to slush. The sky was cold and blue. Mack waited to watch the black man bring out the kitchen garbage. Always the same time, give or take a few minutes, he carried out a large can full of breakfast scraps and dumped it into a dumpster. Afterwards, he always turned the can upside down and banged it against the ground. Left were chunks of grits and egg whites and scraps of toast.

The rats lived in burrows under the dumpster. In seconds their heads appeared, black eyes gleaming; their noses twitched at the smell of new food. They massed at the edge of the dumpster, about two dozen in a cluster, nervously turning in circles, snapping at one another, starting and stopping and acting as if in debate. Then, as if on one particular command squeal, they ran for the garbage, tails lifted off the ice, heads skimming the ground. They were upon the spilled food in seconds, grabbing and biting and swallowing.

Mack always saw the hawk's shadow first. He could not see the bird of prey's perch — probably a tree limb where he had a clear view of the courtyard — but the shadow was his calling card. The rats saw the shadow too, and froze, hunkered even lower and waited. The hawk swooped in, talons splayed, his wings shaped in a V and skewered one rat. He never missed.

The other rats scattered. Jaws packed with food, they raced for the shelter of the dumpster. Their unlucky brother squealed and struggled for a few seconds as the red-tailed hawk consolidated his grip. In a few moments, the rat went limp, the hawk flapped his wings and rose until only his shadow was visible again, winged to his perch where Mack saw in his mind the bird slowly ripping his prey.

Day in and day out, one rat died in sacrifice for the spoils, his brethren to digest their meal in the dark, warm earth tunnels. The hawk seemed to target one rodent from his perch; he might be on the edge of the group or tight within the middle, but he was the chosen one — he died.

Mack heard footsteps behind him, the soft patter of gum soles.

"Mr. Breece, it time for your 'pointment," the attendant said.

The psychiatrist's office was filled with a large, stacked bookcase, a desk and two stuffed chairs. Her Duke University diploma hung on the wall. Mack took his chair and stared at the floor. The psychiatrist looked to be only months out of school, wore glasses and loose sweaters, but probably looked good at home in tight jeans and a t-shirt with a beer in her hand. She opened Mack's chart and scribbled something.

"Mack, is there anything you'd like to talk about today in particular? Why don't you tell me what you've been thinking about since our last session."

Mack stretched out his legs. He thought about the rats he'd seen devoured each morning. He looked up sharply into the doctor's face.

"The rules don't matter."

The doctor startled, leaned forward on her desk. *"What do you mean, Mack?"*

"What I said. There ain't no rules. I understand that now."

"Well," the doctor answered, *"there are rules. People don't follow them all of the time, but plenty of rules exist."*

Mack combed his fingers through his hair. His scalp was oily. *"I used to believe in rules. Used to believe in them. If I knew the rule, I wouldn't break it."*

The doctor stared at Mack's chair, then back at him. She opened her mouth, paused, then spoke. *"Do you think you broke a rule, Mack? Are you talking about the accident?"*

Mack shut his eyes tight. *"One time. One Goddamn time, and my whole world explodes."*

Mack snorted in through his nose to stop his tears. *"I never drink whiskey. One damn time I drink too much. I always unchambered my rifle as soon as I came out of the woods. Why in the hell I sat it by the door loaded, I'll never understand."*

"Mack, that was an accident. A terrible accident. But you're not to blame." The doctor placed her hands palm down against the desk. *"Fate, God — I'm not a theologian, but events happen sometimes that seem senseless and tragic and without meaning."*

Violently, Mack shook his head. *"They* are *senseless and without meaning. Shouldn't be any rules because they don't hold up. All we can do is hunker down and hope the shit doesn't fall on us — that we ain't the one picked. He doesn't respect the rule followers. Fuck up one time and you're out."*

The doctor adjusted her glasses. *"Who is 'he,' Mack?"*

"You know who 'he' is. He's a son of a bitch."

The snow melted in early March. The first blush of spring began in the courtyard, green onions, then spears of daffodil leaves. Each morning Mack watched the drama of hawk and rat. Occasionally, Mack walked in the courtyard in *long circles. One afternoon following his walk, Mack used the pay phone for the first time.*

"I do believe you're crazy now," Billy said and grinned. He took a seat on Mack's bed, then reached into his coat and pulled out a small cardboard box. From another pocket, he pulled out a small steel-jawed muskrat trap.

"One Pet World pedigreed rat. One spring loaded varmint trap. Man speaks to me for the first time in two months and asks me to bring him a damn rat and a trap.

Mack took the box and lifted the lid. He stared at a medium-sized white rat with black markings. He closed the box and slid it under his bed. He took the trap and put it under his pillow, then looked at Billy and nodded.

"I owe you."

"You don't owe me nothing. A man in the crazy house says he wants a pet rat and a trap. I bring it." Billy leaned forward and slapped Mack's arm. "You 'bout ready to come home, ain't you?"

"I been thinking about it."

"You look good. Hell of a lot better than when I brought you here. You were on some kinda drunk."

"Wouldn't you have been?"

Billy's smile died. He exhaled slowly. "Yeah. Probably. I'm sorry, Mack."

"You ain' t got no reason to be sorry."

Billy slowly rolled up his shirtsleeves. He began talking while staring at his arm. "I saw your mama and the baby yesterday. That's a beautiful child, Mack. Marty seems to be doing real good."

"I don't want to hear about them, Billy."

Billy's eyes jerked to Mack. "Man, they're your children. You're all they got, Mack."

"They got Mama. Mama can raise them."

"Your mama is old. They need their daddy."

Mack stood from his chair and walked to the window. He gripped the sill and stared outside.

Next morning, Mack watched the rats again, saw the hawk swoop in and skewer the chosen one. The morning was bright, the daffodils in bloom, a dogwood tree glowed with blossoms. After lunch, he returned to the window until the sun was in the western sky. Mack took the pet shop rat from the box and studied it in his hand.

"Sorry, man. My time's coming. I'll get mine. You can bet."

Mack circled the rat's neck with his thumb and index finger and squeezed. The rat gaped his mouth open and struggled. Within a minute, he ceased to fight. His pink eyes glazed over and closed halfway. Mack held his grip another minute until he was sure the rat was dead. Then he slipped the rat and trap into his coat pocket and walked to the nurse's station to sign himself out into the courtyard.

Mack walked his usual circles for several minutes. He scanned the trees for the hawk, but saw only robins and other song birds. When he was sure no one was paying him any attention, he let his circle carry him behind the dumpster. Quickly, he kneeled and emptied his pocket. Using his heel, he pushed the trap stake into the ground, then set the jaws. With care not to touch the trigger plate, he laid the rat within the jaws. Mack scattered some twigs and grass over the steel. He turned and walked straight back inside.

Mack sat by the window the rest of the afternoon. He got drowsy and twice slapped his face to wake up. The sun was low when Mack was jerked bolt-up in his chair by a flash of wings.

The hawk hit the rat with both feet, springing the jaws. They snapped closed, meshing rat and hawk talons. The stunned hawk flapped his wings and tried to take flight, but the chain kept snatching him back down. The bird spread his wings and lashed at the trap with his beak. As dusk fell, the hawk's efforts grew weaker. He panted, occasionally emitting shrill cries. Finally, he was swallowed by the night.

Mack awoke with a start, a shaft of sunlight coming through his window. He bolted from bed and hurried to the window. Rats covered the hawk's carcass. Not much remained *but a mass of bones and feathers.*

• • •

Mack sat straight up in his chair in the psychiatrist's office, arms folded defiantly. The doctor stared at him while tapping a pencil eraser against the desktop.

"You got to be the one making the rules," Mack repeated. "I understand that now. If you're the one making the rules, you make rules you like."

"But you can't make all the rules, Mack. Other people make rules too, and some of them you have to follow."

Mack unfolded his arms and leaned forward. "Control. That's what you gotta have. I lost my control for a while, but I know how to get it back now. You got to make the rules before the other guy does. I'll be all right now. I'm ready to get out of here."

The doctor looked down at Mack's folder for several moments. "You know you've been free to leave any time. Mack, I'm glad you feel well now."

Mack stood from his chair. The doctor smiled at him, but her smile was not reflected in her eyes.

Eight

Less than four months had passed since that morning when I awoke at dawn to stare through the window of the detox ward. Staring at the red line of the horizon, I knew I was at an intersection where I had to make a decision in my life, the choice of whether I grasped a paddle in my hand and took control of the course of my remaining days, or let myself be sucked again into a whirlpool of alcohol. Right now I had a blister at the base of both palms, but the hurt I felt there was a good pain.

I thought about nature and the parenting instinct. I've known a few humans who flew from their flocks, but never doubled back. I could not walk from a child of mine, even if the mother was a street whore. I would know that child was half me, blood of my blood. But it sure would change my life right now. I could forget about a Fulbright to India or a little bungalow in the Bahamas for about twenty more years, and I'll probably be lucky if I get twenty more years out of this body, all I and God have put it through.

I hit a section of the river that must have been razed by a tornado during Hurricane Fran two years ago. A lot of trees were down in the forest, several blocking the river. The first two I managed to squeeze through branches where the water was still deep enough for the canoe to float. Then I came to one that was especially large; the trunk extended from shore to shore except for a point in the middle where the water was flowing over in a six-inch waterfall. The current was bunched together there, like last summer with Merrie when we shot the white funnels between large rocks. I backpaddled and scouted the chute. It looked passable, about a yard wide. A tangle of dead branches were above the opening, so I would need to lean backwards as I slid under. I made sure my life vest was zipped up, got straight with the chute, then paddled hard. The bow had already breasted the log when I saw that the water was shallower than I had thought; the canoe sat lowest under my seat and the boat grounded against the trunk.

The current piled against the stern, then pivoted the canoe sideways, causing it to act like a dam. Water rose against the gunwale and started to spill over; I grabbed a branch and tipped the canoe toward the leeward side to stop the overflow. The craft toddled on the fulcrum, completely out of balance and would have rolled if I hadn't had hold of the limb.

This is a fine mess, I thought. Can't back up. Can't go forward. The current was swift, and the water deep in the middle of the river. I sat for a long minute and thought. The bow was sandwiched between two limbs, and even if I were able to bump my weight over the log, the canoe would be sideways, and would swamp in the current. If I flipped, I could get tangled up in the limbs, or in the least, I and all my gear would be soaked, and the temperature was hovering around forty degrees. In the water beneath the log, I could see a thick limb. What if by holding to the branches overhead, I stepped out of the canoe onto the branch getting my weight off the boat? I could pull the bow straight with the current, inch my seat past the fulcrum, then reach forward to another branch overhead and maneuver myself back into the boat.

Ought to work. I just had to be very careful. I studied the branches above me and selected one that looked sturdy. Gripping it with both hands, I lifted my weight and swung my right leg over the gunwale. Cold water flooded my boot as I submerged my leg, my toe on the limb. Deeper than I had thought, water up to midway my thigh. Gripped the limb tighter and swung my weight out of the boat with my left leg inside to keep the craft from floating away. CRACK! The limb broke, and suddenly I was up to my hip in water and would have been completely under had not my boot jammed against the submerged limb. My other leg had the canoe tipped so far to the side that water was spilling over; I grabbed for another branch and lifted myself enough to take the weight off the gunwale. I hung there for several seconds, drawing long breaths.

My submerged boot was stuck, jammed between what seemed like a fork in the limb. Don't panic, I told myself. Take some deep breaths. I'm not drowning, not even close to drowning. I wiggled my caught foot, felt out the situation. By twisting my foot, I was able to slide my boot out of the fork. I felt the limb with my foot, then positioned my heel against what felt like solid wood. I put my hands on two separate branches and tugged on them to test my weight. Using my left leg, I drew the canoe backwards until the bow was free. Gripped a solid branch a foot further forward, let the canoe slide until my seat was beyond the log. Now all I had to do was select a branch another foot or so forward that would hold my weight and swing myself back into the canoe. I paused. Lifted a silent prayer. The current murmured as it slid over the log; birds were chirping in the trees above me. Fuck the Indian philosophy. This wasn't no good day to die. Not as long as I had Meghan and Christopher to raise, and I had a room waiting on the ninth floor of the Hilton at the end of this trip.

• • •

The canoe cut the smooth river water with hardly a sound, Mack handling his paddle with the experience of three days afloat. Mid-morning had passed, the April air heavy with vapor and pregnant with the fragrance of honeysuckle. The sun was yet upon the water, the shady depths reflected a bank lined with mixed stands of black oak and sweetgum.

The river had made things right. Here on the water, under the clouds of early spring, he had taken charge again. The water flowed east as steadily as time. He could ride that passage, leap ahead with several hard pulls on his paddle, or let the canoe drift broadside, moving slower than downed leaves that skittered across the surface. He felt he had become a man again, a man in control of his fate. A strange peace had taken over his mind.

Last night huddled near the fire, he had handled the pistol for the first time. A .38 long barrel, the chamber full of wad cutters; he liked the way the cylinder clicked each time a shell locked into place. The gun was heavily oiled and blued, the handle made from handcrafted walnut. A man's weapon. Here, swallowed by the song of crickets, he felt far separated from preachers speaking of the unblaming will of God. Tomorrow when the trip ended, when the tremor was out of his hands and he was docked in Wilmington, he planned to rent a room in the Hilton that overlooked the water. He would buy a fifth of Wild Turkey and drink it slowly while watching the twilight settle over the river. Then he would take out the big gun.

The day slipped by with the current. The trees gradually gave way to marshlands, hundreds of birds singing in the rushes. From his map, Mack knew he was on schedule, needed to make about five more miles before he camped for the night. Then in the morning, all that would separate him from Wilmington was about twenty miles of wide, brackish water, where that evening in the hotel the journey would end.

The sun was getting low when Mack realized that something was strange. The canoe wasn't tracking as it had upstream. Whenever he paused rowing, the canoe lost speed quickly as if she were dragging dead weight. He glanced at his watch and realized he should have already passed beneath the bridge where 117 crossed. He dug deeper with his paddle. After a half hour of hard work, Mack stopped rowing and scanned the bank. Immediately, the boat stopped tracking, skirted to one side, and began to drift backwards. What the hell? The current was flowing backwards. Why is the Goddamn river flowing backwards? Then the answer struck him.

This close to the ocean, the high tide swelled so much that it actually turned the current in reverse for a couple of hours. The April full moon was tonight, and Mack remembered how occasionally the spring tides drew unusually high. From exposed mud flats, Mack could see that the tide was still a couple of feet from cresting; the water might roll in reverse for several more hours.

Damn. Everything has gone so well and now this,
Mack thought. *I'm exhausting myself rowing against this*
fucking tide.

Setting his jaw, Mack stabbed the river with his paddle.
"I'll be damned if you'll whip me," he shouted. "Not now!"
The canoe inched forward.

Mack fought the current for another hour until his
neck and shoulder muscles were knotted. He had finally sighted
the bridge when a large sandbar appeared on the right side of
the river. He turned and drove the bow of the canoe high on
the white sand, his chest heaving down air.

Mack stood in the boat, his knees popping, then
stepped into the shallow water. He walked several yards, then
flopped against the ground. The sand was damp and moisture
slowly soaked through the seat of his trousers. The sandbar
was littered with trash that had been carried downriver. He
picked up a handful of sand and slung it toward the river. The
sun was barely above the horizon, and he could not camp
here. But he could make the bridge, could camp beneath the
concrete, and by morning the tide would be flowing out and
he could finish the run.

Mack stood knee deep in water after swinging the bow
of the canoe downriver. He placed both hands on the gunwales,
then began trotting as he pushed the boat toward deep water.
The toes of his boots dug into the soft sand.

Mack's first thought as he fell was that he had stepped
off a shoal into deep water. As he pitched forward, he almost
lost his grip on the canoe, but managed to hold on with one
hand. His upper torso pitched forward under water, his
headlong plunge stopped suddenly by a searing pain in his
lower back and right leg.

Mack pulled the canoe close to him, hung his arms
and head over the side, then passed out from the pain. When
he opened his eyes again, the sun had dipped below the
horizon, and the water was up to his neck. Doves had begun
to coo. He looked wildly about. Instinctively, he struggled
against his bond; a searing pain in his hip caused nausea and
dizziness to roll up from his gut into his head.

Mack steadied himself against the canoe, then reached into the murky water. His left leg pointed straight forward, the right one buried to the groin. He ducked his head under water, scraped at mud around his thigh, his fingers reached what felt like narrow slats of wood. Gently, he felt around his wounded leg, touched sharp splinters thrust into his flesh; a wide rusted iron band ran along the inside of his thigh. Whatever he had busted through rounded to both sides as if he straddled the back of a very wide horse.

Mack realized he had smashed through the hull of a wrecked skiff, years ago washed upside down upon the sandbar. His hip was broken, his leg held fast between the keel band and aged, treated wood. With no leverage, fighting intense pain, he saw little possibility of pulling free. The water lapped at his throat. He ducked under again and jerked at his leg, but the murkiness and daggers of pain made him lose all sense of direction. He surfaced, gasping for breath. Mack studied the sandbar. The tide would crest about a foot over his head.

Blind panic made him jerk upwards violently. He screamed as the pain made white sparks dance before his eyes. He shouted for help, but knew no one could see or hear him from the distant bridge. The cold water cleared Mack's mind quickly; his panic replaced by rage. He took several deep breaths. Soon, he was going to drown in a manner totally out of his control. Some fisherman would find his body, a preacher would stand over his casket and say it had been God's will, that now Mack Breece had found peace. Mack opened his mouth and cursed. The current had cleaned the murkiness from around his legs; Mack noticed something red beneath the surface. He ducked his head again and saw about a foot of garden hose sticking out of the sand. He reached for it and pulled two yards of rubber hose to him, the end fitted with a tarnished, brass coupling.

"I ain't whipped yet, damn it all," he mumbled.

Mack studied the hose. He swished it back and forth in the water to wash out the sand. After studying the sandbar again, he took his knife from his pocket and cut through the hose three feet above the coupling. Putting the coupling in his *mouth, he sucked in. He could breathe!*

The water was up to Mack's chin. He tipped the canoe toward him and reached into the boat and grabbed his canteen. He stripped off the canvas cover, then emptied the plastic canister. Screwing the cap back on, the hose slid tightly through the strap that held the cap to the canister. Mack pulled the canoe forward till he gripped the rope tied to the bow. He cut off a foot-long length of rope and held it in his teeth. He then looped the end of the bow rope around his waist and tied it. From his pack, he took out a small, waterproof flashlight and put it into his pocket.

Mack's mind was now as clear as ice water. He let go of the canoe and let it drift away from him several yards until the rope tightened. Sliding the hose through the loop about six inches, he lashed it tight with the piece of rope he had cut. Mack put the coupling into his mouth, then leaned backwards as far as he could until his face was submerged. He could breathe!

Mack tried to focus on the notes of a mourning dove as the water lapped over his mouth, then his nose. A golden moon was sitting above the eastern horizon when the water topped his ears and eyes.

• • •

I chose a limb that looked sturdy, took a deep breath, then swung myself up over the canoe and lowered myself into the seat. Let go of the limb, grabbed my paddle for balance, and within two seconds, the current had shot me through the opening out into clear water.

Whew! Lifted a prayer of thanks. My leg was wet and cold, but my hair under my hat was clammy with sweat. Bailed the canoe with my Spam can. I started paddling again, rounded the next curve and — lo and behold — another tree blocked the river, this one a more solid barrier than the one that had just tested me.

Lord. Is this necessary? I guessed it was, or the tree wouldn't be there. This time, I portaged. Pulled to the bank, unpacked my gear, toted it beyond the tree, drug the canoe through the woods, then repacked everything. The process took about an hour. I stuffed down some sardines and crackers before getting back on the water. But around the next bend, the river was clear; I stabbed the water and tried to make up some of my lost time.

Felt good to gulp air, my mouth and eyes open to the world above water. I thought about Meghan and Christopher that night when they came to me as I lay drunk on the couch, and Meghan said to me, "Let us be your addiction." Myself suffocating in liquor, and her voice passed down to me through the drowning tide to where I had snagged myself in a log jam in the river that I should have known for years I was approaching.

The hours slipped by and twilight was descending when I came upon a small sandbar in the mouth of a creek. I beached the canoe and erected the tent, then built a hot fire from an abundance of driftwood that had washed against the sand. Took off my boots, my socks steamed as I held them close to the heat. The sky began to clear just as the sun was setting; the last shreds of clouds were streaked with colors, and I was hungry and tired and very happy to be alive.

I dreamed a baby was crying. I was in my house, and the floor was stacked high with old newspapers. Against one wall was a pile of spent wine and liquor bottles that reached almost to the ceiling. A baby was crying, and I was searching through the trash trying to locate the child.

I awakened to the cackle of an owl from a branch near the tent. Not the lonely "who, who," more often heard, but the strangled, screeching cry of a night bird who has maybe sighted a stalking fox or bobcat. If I did not know the terrible cry, I could easily imagine it to be some fanged, demonic beast or tormented, wandering spirit. But I knew it instantly as only an owl; I am more at ease here in the deep forest than if I were sleeping near what is called civilization. The owl moved on; the forest was silent again. I thought of the dream, the baby crying in the same pitch as the owl, all those newspapers and liquor bottles piled nearly to the ceiling. Next thing I knew, I was aware of light through the tent walls. I unzipped the door and saw the river, blue sky and pink cirrus clouds reflected upon the water.

By the time I had the tent packed, water was boiling. Fixed coffee and grits, fried a potato I baked in the ashes last night with bits of onion. I needed a good breakfast. I was behind schedule, and needed to make more than thirty miles today, if I was going to arrive at the Hilton when I said. But the sun was still below the tree line; I slept well despite babies and owls crying, and all I had to do was pull backwards many thousands of times on my paddle and keep looking toward the next bend in the river.

I packed the dry-sack with the rest of the candy bars, a can of peaches, Vienna sausages and potted meat, and what was left of the onion I had cut earlier. Topped off my canteen from the big water jug. Picked up a few bits of trash from the sand, and all I was leaving here by the water were footprints and memories. Pushed off into the current with a good breeze to my back, as the sun was beginning to glint through the trees. Ran through my prayers, then tuned my radio to the *John-Boy and Billy Big Show*. Set into a rhythm of paddling and the miles slid by as I chuckled at the redneck antics of the two disc jockeys, their jokes and monologues interspersed with selections of classic rock.

I saw my first boat about noon, two men heading up river. Except for cars crossing bridges and the back porches of several lodges, the fishermen were my closest encounter with humans in two days. I stopped paddling, drifted and ate several crackers topped with Viennas and slices of onion. Gulped diluted Kool-Aid. I used a plastic jug as a urinal, so I didn't even have to beach when nature called. By landmarks on the map, I knew I was making good time, but where I needed to be by dusk was still a long way off. Kept paddling steadily, and by mid-afternoon, the river was pretty wide. I could quit worrying about downed trees, but a section on the map concerned me. For a few miles, the river divided into several channels that looped and curved around islands. Although I was still more than thirty miles from Wilmington, I could tell

I had already entered the tidal region. Tree trunks were black a couple of feet above the water, darkened by tides that raise and lower the depth. I knew that close to Wilmington, the current can actually reverse and flow inland.

Another mile, and the river divided at a point of land, both channels equally wide. I studied the banks and went with the channel that had the most trash and debris alongshore, knowing the current was stronger to that side. After a half mile, the other channel looped back in, and I knew I had chosen right. Then the channel divided into three channels. I picked one and paddled a quarter mile before realizing it was beginning to narrow, the water too slow. I cussed and fussed at myself and backtracked and took the right channel that remained fast and clear. For several miles I kept having to choose, but I knew none of the channels would be a disaster; all of the water eventually flows back into the main stream if you keep going. Finally, I was past the maze, and ahead was a bridge I had been waiting to see. Beneath the bridge was a wildlife ramp, a small country store beside the road. I ran the bow onto the concrete and maneuvered myself standing. My feet felt like wood, my legs stiff from so many hours of cramped sitting. But boy did it feel good to stand upright; I limped toward the store to a pay phone where I dialed the kids' number. Nearly five p.m., they would be home if I were lucky. Two rings and Christopher answered.

"Hey buddy, it's Pop!" My voice cracked from not using it for so long.

"Hey, Dad! Where are you? We were worried."

"I'm at a little store beside Highway 210."

We talked for a minute, then Meghan came on the other line, her musical voice like a jolt of sunshine. I told both of them not to worry, that I would be off the river this time tomorrow. In the store, I bought a couple of cold Cokes and a cigar, chatted with the woman behind the counter like any guy on his way home from work. I was back on the water by five-fifteen, drifting sideways while studying the map. Normally by now, I would be thinking of a place to camp, but the sun was still high and the break from paddling had brought rejuvenation. I was well into the tidal land now, the shore low and wet with marshland. I knew I needed to do another ten miles to make my planned campsite that night, but there was not enough daylight left for that. If I camped at the sandbars below the bridge, I'd have to listen to traffic all night and would have more than thirty miles to do tomorrow in water that might turn backwards. I thought about my schedule, of one person I had told where I planned to camp the third night. Fuck exhaustion. I dug into the water and sighted on the inside curve of the next bend.

No moon in the sky, stars studded bright against the black expanse; Saturn, Jupiter, and Mars were clustered in the western horizon. The tide was rising so I had no current to push me. I stayed to the middle of the river by centering on the black curtain of trees to each side. I wasn't tracking nearly as fast as when I had the current and wind behind; eight p.m., and I rowed like a machine, tired to the bone. Finally, rounding a bend, the lights of the bridge appeared a half mile downriver. I pulled closer to the left bank, took out my flashlight and clamped it between my knees so it punched a yellow beam ahead into the blackness. Didn't want to run into a snag. A wilderness landing was supposed to about 100 yards upstream from the bridge.

I spied the concrete boat ramp finally. No one seemed to be there. A tiny sandbar lay a few yards upcurrent from the landing, only about as long as my boat and twice as wide. Not enough room to erect the tent, but the sky was clear. The sand was dry and spotted with leaves and twigs, so I knew it didn't flood with the tide. The moat of water would separate me from any carloads of drunkards that might come in the night. I brought the canoe broadside to the sand and carefully stepped out.

In another hour, I'd eaten a bellyful of stew and stomped flat the apex of the sandbar where I would sleep. I was too tired to blow up the air mattress, so I just laid it down as a ground cloth. Leaving on all my clothes but my boots and coat, I snuggled into the bag. My feet were cold, my shoulders so tired and sore it hurt to lift them above my head.

But I began to quickly warm; my feet tingled. Orion was sliding toward the tree line. From the undergrowth onshore, I heard steps, probably a deer, but as I looked into the dark heavens, I fantasized....

...Poke Salad Annie stood on the shore, her bosom and face illuminated by the glow of a kerosene lantern.

"I saw you pass as I was checking my trot-line," she told me. "Are you lost?"

"No. I know where I'm going. It's just taking awhile to get there."

"Would you like to come home with me and rest?"

I left all my gear; she took my hand and led me along a path through the woods to a one-room cabin built from cypress logs. The cabin was warm and smelled of wood and smoke; Annie was willow-thin, her face and forearms spangled with freckles, her long hair braided down her back. She wore a long, green dress woven from mimosa leaves. She told me of her lonely life as she cooked a supper of fried catfish and cornbread.

"You can sleep with me if you like," she said. Her mattress was stuffed with down from migrating birds.

She unbuttoned my shirt and rubbed my shoulders with liniment. Turning the lantern down, she looked into my eyes as she unbuttoned her long dress and let it settle in a pile around her feet. The flame illuminates the sides of her breasts like half-moons; a curved scar marked her.

"You were hurt."

"That was years ago. I'm well now."

At dawn, she made strong coffee, hotcakes and sausage. My socks dried by the fire overnight. "I'll come back to see you," I told her.

Annie smiled sadly and shook her head. "No, you won't. No one ever travels back upriver...."

...Just a deer in the woods, but I am human with a mind that can take me briefly from this bed of sand. As I lay almost in the water, my eyes traveled among the stars, and I understood I was part of something so infinite and timeless that I can only accept and try to understand.

• • •

Breathe slowly. Innnn. Ouuuut. Innnn. Ouuuut. Don't panic. Just breathe slow and easy. Keep your mouth closed tight around the coupling.

The water seemed especially chill to Mack as it slowly topped his scalp. Twilight faded, and he was in a world of darkness, of muffled sounds, the river coursing around his body like a constant wind. He could hear his heart beating in his ears, rapid, but regular and strong. He breathed in long hisses, as he worked to pull and push air through the hose. To reduce his panic, he counted each breath, no longer aware of the pain in his leg.

Just breathe slowly. Don't think about it. A few hours and the tide will start down. Innnn. Ouuuuuut.

Something bumped into Mack's back. He jerked. Water leaked into his mouth, momentarily gagging him. He swallowed the water, but had missed a breath and now had to suck longer and harder on the pipe. Panic rose and for a moment he thought of trying to once more wrench his leg free and burst upwards to the moonlit surface. Mack raised one hand above his head until it surfaced into the cool night air.

And you'll drown trying, he told himself. Drown and he'll have taken everything from you. Even your choice of death. Mack saw lights dance before his eyes as the lack of oxygen lightened his brain. When he looked up, he could see the moon shimmer high above in the sky.

If I ain't careful, I'll pass out and still damn drown, he thought. Mack concentrated on several long breaths.

Innnn. Ouuuuut. Mack wept, his tears instantly swept away by the river. His sinuses ached, so he momentarily removed his fingers from his nose and blew out clear snot. He was one with darkness, only aware of his heartbeat, his long, tortured breaths. But he hated himself even more for again losing the upper hand, and hated God more, and hate would keep him breathing until he was able to finish his life his way.

The universe became softer, quieter, dimly lit by moon glow as if Mack floated in some diffused portion of space where existence was only the sound of a heartbeat and breathing. He became drowsy, so he concentrated on those sounds, rolled the taste of metal over his tongue, counted each breath. Again, he felt something bump his back. Seconds later, another object bumped him, then another. In the dim, washed light, he saw objects moving past, silvery shapes that undulated through the water. Mack wondered if he was hallucinating. He felt for his light and switched it on. The bright, round beam punched into the darkness.

Stripers. Dozens of them were swimming upriver. The fish migrated each spring into the rivers and creeks to lay their eggs and the first huge school was passing him, fat, pregnant females pushing against the current to that spot where they would spawn. Mack clicked off the light and thought of those good days when he had fished the river for stripers and shad, the schools so thick, he snagged some with a grapple hook. More and more fish bumped him. Their scales caught the moonlight, causing each fish to resemble a pale ghost.

Mack stared in amazement. Hundreds of fish moved by him now. He clicked on his light again and saw that many of the females were already spewing eggs. The eggs streamed behind them like strings of bubbles, catching and casting their own reflected light. He felt movement against his leg and turned the light there. The female was laying eggs, the mass sticking to him as it would to a submerged stump or log. The current flowing around Mack was thick with eggs. Some stuck to his shirt, to his arms, to the skin of his face. Fish passed him by the hundreds, the river shimmering with roe. In his light beam, Mack saw smaller, predatory fish sucking in eggs, but for each egg eaten, a thousand more were laid. Mack stared in wonder at the spawning of so much life.

The universe was now a world of reflected moonlight, the fish passing like comets, the eggs thousands of life-supporting planets. He felt as if he stared into the night sky at distant galaxies, nebulae, to the far boundaries of the cosmos. The eggs whirled in the current like a blizzard, millions of potential lives flushed from the womb into the currents of fate. The females swam against the current, released their eggs, many eaten within seconds, thousands more to float on the ebb and rise of tide and hatch. Some would grow into adult fish and go to sea, only to return to this same river and spill their own young. The cycle would go on and on. Mack shut his eyes hard. The fish bumped him, engulfed him and coated his body with clouds of roe. He concentrated on his breathing, in and out and in.

The wind on Mack's face brought him around slowly. Beyond his closed eyes he became aware of light, of bird songs; the breeze tickled the small hairs on the back of his neck. He wondered if he was hallucinating and hesitated opening his eyes. The light made him squint and blink before he saw water lapping around his legs. He sat hunched forward, the hose still clinched in his mouth. His skin and clothes were slick with fish eggs. The canoe trailed behind him, drawn seaward by the ebbing tide. He lifted his head; his neck muscles burned like fire. Another fire burned below the horizon. Mack took the hose from his mouth and breathed deeply of cool, morning air.

Now Mack could clearly see the boat hull. His leg throbbed with every heartbeat, but the pain only made him more alive. Mack studied the wood, the keel band. Pulling on the rope, he drew the canoe to him. From his pack, he took out the big gun.

Doves called from the brush; a woodpecker hammered a dead limb. The river surface was flat as glass and stilled by low tide. Mack listened for a moment to the grind of morning traffic crossing the bridge.

Mack rolled the cylinder several times, aimed carefully and squeezed the trigger. The first shot punched out a hole two inches in diameter in the hull, splintered the grain, rushed into flight the woodpecker, several doves, a pair of mallards hiding inside a reed thicket. Two more shots rent the keel band, curled downward the ragged edges. Another slug to the right of his leg splintered the hull inches behind his buttock. Mack felt the trap's jaws release; he slipped his leg upward several inches. Hot pain flooded his hip as the circulation flowed, but he smiled as he slid further back upon the hull, dragging his leg from the vise.

Mack lay on his back in the mud and straightened both legs. He felt splinters of bone grind in his hip, but was relieved that none had pierced his skin. He pushed himself sitting, fired the last shot above the water, then threw the pistol into the river. Downstream, he spied a small fishing boat coming his way.

Mack half dragged himself, half rolled until he lay on his back in the middle of his canoe, one leg over each side, his head resting against his pack. He shoved with his good leg until the canoe slid to deep water and began to drift. The wind swung the canoe in slow, wide circles; the sun in the branches warmed his face. The birds resumed singing, their tune oddly familiar like a lullaby. Mack cocked his head toward the song and began to mouth the words.

• • •

Dawn lifted blue and clear. The radio weatherman forecast temperatures in the mid-sixties. Hastily, I packed the canoe and left the tiny sandbar. A bubble of joy swelled in my chest. Despite what these next miles of water held for me, regardless of what years I have left in my life, on this morning I felt peace. I'd waded through some muck in the past months, but felt clean right then, despite sore muscles and soiled clothes. Whatever awaited me at the end of the river, I would accept it as part of the plan. I wished I could say to Katie how sorry I am that I allowed alcohol to push her away. I wished I knew all the secrets of fish that spawn, of why some eggs are eaten seconds into the current and why some grow into large stripers that return one night to this same river to spew their own clouds of milt and roe. But at least they do return, and I had returned, and I could settle for my nose above water and my eyes on my children and my love for them and my duty to raise them to keep me breathing.

The river widened, the banks were low and blended

into brackish salt marshes. Lots of birds; fish broke the water. At noon, the river took a big swing toward the south. Wilmington was a straight run with the wind to my back. I didn't need to hurry. I had made up the time I lost; occasionally, I didn't even paddle, just stayed straight with the wind and let it push me slowly downriver. A year ago, I would be thinking of whiskey, anticipating how when I checked into the Hilton, I would order a fifth of good bourbon and drink the whole bottle. I don't want that now. Boats with fishermen appeared, crab pot buoys; the skyline of Wilmington rose above the marsh grass.

Life flows like the water, turbulent and again placid, pulled between the sun and the moon, through light and darkness, but always into a new day.

Nine

The Going to the Sun Road through Glacier National Park was built early in this century by Swiss engineers and is still considered a feat. It's also a feat to pack six people into this compact car I rented so we can drive over the snow fields of Logan Pass, the grade too steep and winding for thirty-foot Winnebagos.

"You OK, Ma?" I say to her. She has one palm pressed against the dash.

"I'd be better if you would slow down a little bit."

"You keep collecting rocks, the brakes might fail from all of the weight."

We already have three rocks in the trunk, and we are only about halfway to the pass. We've stopped for two waterfalls and a mountain goat that begged for handouts. We found out from people at the campground that the pass was just opened the day we arrived, so I know that luck is riding with us. Christopher is snapping away with the new camera Katie and I bought for his birthday, which is coming up next week. I keep warning him about getting too close to cliffs. His voice is creaking and squeaking from the torrent of male hormones that is filling his blood, and in the past month he has exceeded Meghan in height. Christopher has a natural eye for the camera, knows when to frame the distant peak between tree limbs and fingers of rock and when to let his subject stand stark and alone.

Logan Pass is buried in snow, the road cut through vertical walls of ice twenty feet high. I think of when Katie and I hiked Red Gap Pass and the trail had disappeared months earlier with the first autumn storm. But we knew the saddle in the ridge above us was where we were to go over, so we trudged upwards, our boots breaking through the crust ankle deep into dry powder. And at the top, we knew there was no way to go but down, and that somewhere in the lower elevations, the snow would end and the trail would reappear for us to follow. We spoke to the guy sitting on a rock smoking a joint and looking toward the way we had come. He offered us a toke, but we declined and started the descent. When the snowfield ended and the ice only remained in scattered patches, we walked switchback as though following the spine of a serpent, searching for the trail we knew would reappear. Within a mile it did, washed clean by the runoff, new pebbles exposed to the sun, the path that would lead us back to cars and houses and the world we had walked away from three days earlier.

I think about how today I live the closest to the world I seemed always to be walking from. A small brick house in a quiet neighborhood. Two dogs and a new truck payment. The newspaper is delivered to my driveway each morning. But, I did not buy that small house because I was told that is what I should want from life. I came to that home knowing at age forty-five I could at last be content with that lifestyle, the mortgage, the raised-bed garden, the *News and Observer* sheathed in plastic. I could actually like it and be proud of that small place because I had lived the options, and not just for a two-week exotic vacation. And that mortgage I am not liable for the rest of my life. Home is internal and eternal, and where I am best happy with my heart and the people who love me is where I should rest. And if I am blessed, maybe by not settling for what is close and comfortable, but instead waiting for she who plucks my heart strings, I may be rewarded by spending the last of my life living music instead of listening. I gamble, but I have chosen to gamble.

West to the boundary of Glacier National Park where I turn the car around and begin the fifty-five mile passage in reverse. At a pull-off, Christopher scrambles to a rock ledge where he has a clear view of a deep valley and the peaks beyond, choosing to frame this picture with nothing but open air. I watch him and mute myself of my concern that he stands so close to the cliff. If he were to slip and fall to the rocks below, I would fall and die with him, but he will not see all of the valley if he stands always where he is safest.

I have a snapshot of Katie in the snow field high in Glacier. She is drinking from a canteen, her eyes trained beyond the canister toward the valley into which we were about to descend. She is framed by white ice, her blue eyes and the red bandana in her hair especially bright. We were just a week married then, and already seven days closer to our divorce that was still several deserts and peaks beyond our vision. As inevitable as the course water takes when it is warmed beyond the crystalline state to a temperature more akin to the blood of humans and their differing views of where the trail should end, we had already chosen separate paths.

• • •

Late April in the afternoon. I was with Meghan and Christopher and Katie had just gotten home from work. I hugged the kids and was just about to leave when Andy, Katie's boyfriend, drove up. He's in his early fifties, prematurely gray, a lawyer who attended Davidson College, the same school Katie graduated from. I shook his hand hard. I like Andy, but he's not the type I would pick to be on my team.

I was walking to my truck when Katie called my name. I stood by the truck and watched her come to me. She's still an attractive woman. I felt a couple of butterflies in my stomach. Usually when she follows me outside, she is pissed about something I have done or not done. Katie and I get along well, but there is always a flash point of anger between us barely beneath the surface that must be suppressed. She smiled at me.

"I wanted to tell you something before you heard it from the kids." She took a breath. "Andy and I are getting married. We haven't set a date yet, but we've made the decision."

I nodded. "Well, I'm not surprised. I've been expecting that for about a year."

"I just wanted you to hear it from me."

"Well, I'm happy for you. Andy is a good man."

"I hear you and Ronnie aren't together now."

"Yeah, but that's OK. My life is full enough already. I've had about enough female attention to last me the rest of my life."

"We'll see how long that lasts."

I laughed. "No, really, Katie. I'm happy for you. I hope you and Andy have a wonderful marriage. You deserve a good life."

Her blue eyes were shiny. I looked at her for a few moments and thought about how I once loved her and how today she seemed to be a complete stranger to me, someone I knew no better than if I passed her on the street.

Driving home, her words ran through my mind like a loop of cassette tape. I wasn't hurt. Not jealous. We're so totally different, and have always been so. Our relationship always seemed like two dissimilar atoms that when jammed together through fusion produced great heat, but within an instant were blown to smithereens.

At least she's marrying a man who fits the type I knew she always wanted. A lawyer, liberal in his political views, neat, thinking about tomorrow more than he does today. I always said that if I had been an accountant or an attorney, Katie and I would have had a wonderful marriage. It's not the profession, but the mind-set that she wanted.

Katie divorced me for the same reasons she wed me. She said I was different from other men when we first met. I had quit an established job to seek an education, talked of one day wanting to write books. I drank hard and played hard and spoke of wanting to see what was beyond the next tree line, never satisfied with what already lay within sight. I told her time after time that I was not going to change, that I had already lost one wife because I couldn't fit into the mold most people accepted. She'd get mad sometimes, say she didn't want to change me.

I believe it was when I talked her into joining the Peace Corps that she realized how crooked my path could be. At the time, I was one year away from graduating from UNC. And I eventually did graduate, but I quit a newspaper job to rise early in the morning and write fiction, then go and frame houses. And it wasn't long after that when I began to publish, though, the reality of my writing soon became apparent. Unless I changed what I wrote about, I was never going to make much money from my words. And I kept drinking, until alcohol became about as much a part of my life as breathing. And finally at age forty, she had a man who played hard and drank hard and wanted to write books, even though they didn't sell, and was still wanting to move to some place like Australia and homestead, when we already had two children and a pleasant home in a suburban neighborhood.

Marry Andy, Katie, and I sincerely hope the two of you live long and happily and have that retirement home on the Outer Banks with the sailboat, and when you vacation it is in Paris or Madrid, and what you find within reach is exactly what you always searched for.

It ain't me, babe; but I think in your heart you always knew that.

We roll southward after three days at Glacier, toward Utah and a different frame of raw beauty. It was fitting to come here to where Katie and I climbed the first mountain together, the beginning of a series of heights and depths that strengthened our muscles and wore at our bones and eventually broke only our hearts. It is said that opposites attract, the reckless and the regardful thrown into union so that one can scout the forward path while the other watches the rear for avalanches. And what results is an opposite vision, alter egos that must eventually slay the other in defense of the id.

Do you think you and Mom wouldn't have gotten divorced if you hadn't drunk so much?

I don't know for sure, Christopher. But I do believe if I hadn't drunk, we never would have gotten married at all.

A breakfast stop again; we left out too early for me to cook pancakes and scrambled eggs. Bruce and I hand the kids money to buy biscuits and hashbrowns.

"What you want, Donnie?" I say to him.

"I got my food."

I roll my eyes. The kids stare at me. "Go ahead," I tell them. "We have a lot of miles to do today." They leave and Bruce slowly gets to his feet and goes outside. I know what he's doing. Giving the kids some money to buy Donnie breakfast. This is the third time. Anger burns in me. I told Donnie before the trip that he couldn't expect to go on a two-week vacation for a hundred dollars.

For all the times I've been to foreign lands, the stints in the Marines and Peace Corps, appearances on television and radio, I am the least prepared for old age of any of the men in my immediate family. Donnie and my brothers have worked career jobs since the beginning of their early twenties. They work hard, but have labored their ways up to the higher pay scales of their professions with good retirement, health and vacation benefits. Only three years ago when I began full-time teaching at State did I start contributing to a retirement fund, and only then because it was mandatory, about two hundred dollars a month. I have a hundred dollars in a savings account that was necessary to get my house loan through the State Employees Credit Union. My yearly salary at State is no more than the blue collar wages my brothers earn. What I make off writing and speaking varies from year to year, but has never been enough to brag about. And here I am spending several thousand dollars to finance this trip. I better have the Big One at about age sixty-five, or else I'm in for the poor house. But as soon as Bruce walks from the Winnebago, I feel guilty. We're talking about food here, not a mink coat.

Donnie complains when Meghan hands him a biscuit and hash browns, but he eats them. We hit the road again, Bruce driving fast and aggressive the way he does at work in his semi. We travel a series of long valleys where we roll up and over passes where the motor strains to make it across the lip. Each time we pass another Authentic Plains Indian Crafts store, Ma reads the propaganda printed in large words and watches the roadside attraction fade. Finally Bruce wheels into one of the stores.

"Everyone back in fifteen minutes," I announce. "We have about three hundred miles still to Salt Lake City."

I'm back in about twelve minutes, Bruce a minute later, then the kids and Ma about on time, her lugging another paper sack.

"Ma, you don't have to bring all of Fayetteville something," I tell her.

"Well, I saw these beads and I thought about Kim's birthday coming up. The sign said they're made by real Indians."

I wonder if the beads were really strung by Native Americans, or by Native Taiwanese. I'm being cynical again. If Ma believes the beads were crafted by American Indians, they are. I look at my watch and feel the pressure gauge in my head tip the danger zone. Donnie has been gone twenty minutes, everyone sitting here waiting on him. I crank the generator so the air conditioner will work. Another five minutes passes before Donnie exits the store, clinching a couple of bags.

"That's just Donnie being Donnie," Ma says in his defense. "He does a lot of work for me around the house."

"Y'all waiting on me?" Donnie says, as if he is surprised.

He puts his purchases in a cabinet he has designated as his own.

We roll on down into Utah, toward the Great Salt Lake and the Mormon Tabernacle, the Mecca for a religious group that Donnie explains to us is bound for hell.

Morning again. I roll to my back and lie there watching limb shadows against the canvas. Something is especially good about this morning, but the good thing won't come to the surface of my brain. Like when you wake up and are going to the circus that night and know it deep inside your brain, but several seconds must pass before the realization bubbles up.

Lynn. Her image opens suddenly like a flower. I think of her for a couple of minutes. Lynn is like the circus, even though I don't know when I will see her again.

Sitting over cups of coffee at the picnic table, Bruce with his usual cigarette, me smoking a cigar. The campground is beginning to stir, people filing off to the restrooms. Our Winnebago is still quiet, although I know Ma is awake, lying in bed thinking about whatever she considers on this early morning so far from home.

"It sure feels good to sit here drinking this coffee, the day just starting and not hungover," I say to Bruce.

"I'm proud of you for stopping drinking," he answers. "I know that was mighty hard to do."

"You know, it wasn't. I just quit. Just like that. There hasn't been one time in the past six months that I've even considered drinking. Haven't had the slightest desire."

"I'm going to quit these cigarettes. If you can quit drinking, I can quit smoking."

I know he's tried to quit several times, goes a few days until his body hurts so bad and his mind is in such shambles he starts again. I wish he would quit. I know with our family history he is destined for lung cancer in his late fifties, will go hard like my Dad and two of my uncles, withered and hurting until he welcomes death as a blessing.

"Smoking is a lot harder to quit than drinking," I tell Bruce. "They say it's harder than heroin."

"Yeah, but that had to be hard what you did. Cold turkey, just like that."

And I think about his words, and I know there are people who would say I am fooling myself, that I am just the right bad moment from taking up a bottle again, that I should be attending AA for support, have a phone number in my pocket of someone to call and talk me out of drinking when the urge strikes. They are wrong. For me, they are wrong. I know there are folks for whom AA is a lifesaver. I know some personally. But the only twelve steps I need are the months of the year that I know will not come to me if I continue to drink, the book I must follow, the pages I have yet to write. Call on a higher power? The rising sun is a higher power, and it called on me this morning to share communion with my brother, clear headed and exuberant. For twenty years I drank simply because it felt good to drink, and I can offer no truer explanation. I expended that pleasure till it was as dry as powdered bones and in the dew of the first light I discovered the supple, pleasant waters of myself. That is the elixir I now choose to drink.

A beach on the Great Salt Lake. Meghan and Christopher and Bruce and I float upon the briny water. It's true. You can't sink. I can lie on my back and lift both feet and arms out of the water, and still I float like a cork. I'm careful not to get the water in my eyes.

"This is so cool, Dad," Christopher says. His voice has changed. The squeaking has suddenly vanished and overnight he speaks in the deeper tone of a young man. Like changing the frequency on a radio his voice has re-tuned, a sprinkle of gravel in that sweet child's lilt he spoke just yesterday. I am proud of him, and I am saddened. As with Meghan in New York, when I lost the little girl momentarily in the crowd and discovered a young woman standing right in front of me, my little boy is no longer. I want to take him in my lap and hold him like Mary held the body of Christ in Michelangelo's famous sculpture.

Ma and Donnie stand on shore, taking pictures of us. We float together in a little pod, a small flotilla of vessels, all containing similar blood, all of us with the same brown eyes, like the colors struck on ships of a shared mission. I think about the salt in the water and the salt in our blood, of the old phrase that blood is thicker than water, and that my family is like this ancient basin between these mountains, fused through time into one body that is buoyant in even the deepest sea.

At another souvenir shop this morning, Donnie was the last to get back to the Winnebago. I was pissed again.

"I was just about to leave your butt," I said to him.

"I'm sorry. I finally found what I was looking for."

Donnie laid a sack on the table. Then he went to his cabinet and took out all the bags he had stored there. The engine was running, but I hesitated at putting the transmission into drive. Donnie sat down in front of the bags and began taking things out. "I been searching for a jewelry box for Karen to put her stuff in. Finally found one I like."

A wooden, flip-top jewelry box painted with Indian symbols of turtles and horses and the sun. Probably didn't cost a lot, but it was pretty. Before him, he spread out an assortment of items — earrings, a matching necklace, a deerskin bag, colored rocks, a clay replica of Mt. Rushmore, bracelets, a ring. Most of the jewelry was made with beads and silver, probably in the twenty-dollar range. The skin bag had a buffalo painted on it. Ma picked up one of the bracelets.

"Karen is going to shoot you for spending all this money," Ma said.

"Some of it is for her birthday, and some of it I'll wait and give her at Christmas."

He stared at the gifts with a smile lighting his face, his eyes distant as if he were seeing my sister as he handed her the filled box. Donnie and Karen got married when Karen graduated from high school. Their honeymoon was two nights in a motel beside Interstate 95. Their marriage has been spent very close to home in the doublewide mobile home where they have raised three boys. Following the birth of her third child, Karen went through a couple of years of depression, mostly due to being overweight and stuck at home raising another baby boy when she had hoped so much for a daughter. But she buckled down and lost that weight and raised that child. She is not with us on this trip because she now works a full-time job that she likes. Mike, the oldest son, graduated from State, then Bible College. In August, he and his wife are due to leave for missionary work in Pakistan. As I watched Donnie admire the gifts he had bought, I grew ashamed of myself for getting angry when he took a few minutes longer than the rest of us to shop, even more bothered that I was irritated when Bruce bought him food. I realized now what fed my brother-in-law's hunger. Tomorrow morning, I will buy him two ham biscuits.

And I float here in a lake of water that will not let me sink, the same as I rest and breathe and toil always supported by a sea of blood that would never part and watch me starve or drown. Even my son's voice is now my own. And I know what I will cling to until my last breath, and I know there are good things and good people that are transient in my life, that I may enjoy and give to and take from, but in the balance of living, must be let go.

• • •

Early March. The morning light filtered through the shades. Ronnie was asleep with her head on my shoulder. Her long, black hair fanned across her face and onto my bare chest. I lay still and looked at the ceiling while listening to her slow breaths. She's a bed hog, slept glued to my side until I ended up on about a foot of the mattress. But she is warm and pretty, and there is much that I like about her. I knew I needed to get up. The clock read a bit past eight, and I needed to be packing for a speaking gig I was leaving for later that day. I also needed to pee.

I made the plunge about two months ago, called Ronnie and asked her to have lunch with me. After a couple of lunch dates, a weekend came up when I didn't have the kids; I invited her over for supper and the night, told her beforehand she could have my bedroom while I would sleep in one of the other rooms. In the morning, I brought coffee, sat on the edge of the mattress and asked how she had slept.

"I love the stars on your ceiling and walls. It's like camping out."

We met for lunch again midweek, the next weekend rolled around and Meghan and Christopher came to stay. I had already told them I was seeing Ronnie. When they were lying in bed Friday night, I talked to them about her coming over the next afternoon.

"Is she going to stay the night?" Meghan asked.

"No. Just for supper."

Meghan nodded, but stared beyond my face at the ceiling. Christopher seemed more accepting. "She's really got a tattoo?"

"Yep. On her upper arm."

I thought about when I moved into the house on Kilcullen with Merrie. The first night the kids stayed there, I tucked them into bed as I had done this night, but they were three years younger then.

"Why don't you sleep with us tonight?" Meghan asked.

"You guys will be asleep in no time," I assured them. "I'll be just down the hallway."

"What if I can't go to sleep?" Meghan asked.

"You'll go to sleep. I'll sit up awhile until you're asleep."

I knew what was in their minds. Their dad was going to go and get in a bed with a woman who was not their mother; any secret hopes that Katie and I would reconcile were being destroyed. I kissed their foreheads. "You know that you guys are the most important people in my life. Nobody, never, ever, will be more important to me."

"Then sleep with us," Meghan said.

"Baby. I'll be in the next room. All you have to do is call me, and I'll come."

They did call — about four times — each time I went before they finally were asleep. Merrie tried to understand, but she had never had children, was not so torn between her own needs and those of her offspring. Turning the light off did not turn off being a father, even if I knew the kids were trying to manipulate me.

Ronnie had never had children, either. When she came over the next afternoon, she was smiling and talkative with Meghan and Christopher. Meghan smiled at her, but only talked when spoken to. Christopher was more open to her. After dinner, Meghan settled into my lap with her arms around my neck.

Later, beside Ronnie's car, I hugged her and told her to be careful driving home. "The kids like you," I told her.

"Christopher seems to accept me," Ronnie answered. "Meghan was a bit distant."

"Oh, she doesn't mean anything. She's my little girl."

"She's also a young woman," Ronnie answered.

The next afternoon, Ronnie came over again. We played Ping-Pong. Meghan had gotten pretty good on the table; she didn't take any easy shots against Ronnie. At six, I took the kids back to their mother. I didn't ask Ronnie to ride with us.

"What do y'all think of Ronnie?" I asked.

"She's OK," Christopher said. "I like her tattoo."

"I don't think she is very pretty," Meghan said.

Later, I was sitting on the couch with Ronnie, making small talk, my belly full of butterflies. I've never been a Casanova, would not use up all my fingers counting the women I've been intimate with. I never gauged my masculinity by bed notches.

"You want to go look at the stars?" I finally said to Ronnie.

She smiled and nodded. Boy, that was a good line.

I exaggerated a yawn and wiggled my shoulder enough that Ronnie awakened. Time was ticking by, and I needed to pee pretty bad by then. Ronnie snuggled closer, and we talked a few minutes. I tarried in bed as long as possible, but the sun was inching higher. I needed to finish packing and get on the road. Finally, I got my arm loose and got out of bed with the promise of fresh, hot coffee.

"You said you would pay me lots of attention," Ronnie said, "and all you've done since last night is pack and buy things for your trip. You called your children twice."

"Yeah, but I was with you the whole time. I included you in everything I did."

"I was in the same room, but you were concentrating on other things."

"There's a lot to do to get ready for a four-day trip."

"You were with the kids all weekend and didn't want me to come over, and now you're getting ready to leave for four days, and I'm still second."

"Baby, I'm trying best as I can. I have a busy life, and I'm always trying to juggle things."

"I know. I see that more and more!"

I felt that I was trying to juggle four balls; Meghan and Christopher, my day-to-day life — and Ronnie. The kids would always come first. I had to meet the demands and obligations of the life I had chosen — teaching, writing, my two dogs, paying the bills a week after they were due. But, my love life was a luxury, female companionship something I enjoy and appreciate, but not essential to my existence.

Ronnie is a good woman. She's very intelligent, a talented writer and pretty. I enjoy being with her. Like me, she is a Sagittarius, likes the outdoors, similar music; we share the same middle name. She is very understanding about my commitment to the kids and my work. But she wants her share of my time if we are to be involved, and I cannot blame her for that.

"You spread yourself too thin," Ronnie said. "You need to cut back on doing so many little things, and concentrate on what is important. We've been together three months now. We should be spending more time together."

What are the little things? Coaching aspiring writers beyond my office hours. Speaking to groups of high school students about writing — but more importantly about living. Occasionally having lunch with a friend; she cannot understand why I still want to be friends with Merrie.

"It's unnatural. It's weird!" Ronnie said. "Why do you still want to be friends with her. It's like there is still something unfinished between you two."

I'll never understand that attitude. First you are friends, attracted to each other for positive reasons, then you become lovers, and when that doesn't work out, should you erase the good you saw in that person and act as if she never existed? Seems a lot more sensible to continue being friends, particularly if the physical relationship did not end because of betrayal or abuse.

I also need to fish. I need to sit sometimes and blank out my mind by watching something senseless on television. Once in a long while, I need to go on a four-day canoe trip right by my lonesome. I can't be on duty all the time, a puppet jerked by different strings so that I am dancing around the clock.

"I'm getting very tired of feeling like I am last on your list," Ronnie said. "You have to realize that I have needs and a life of my own."

"You're not last, Ronnie. You're in a special layer all your own that is unique. I want to be with you all I can, but if that is only once a week — or less — that time is special, and I look forward to it."

Easter weekend. Katie had taken the kids to visit her family in Memphis. Ronnie and I were at Raven Rock State Park, getting ready to backpack three miles to a campground by the river. My pack must have weighed close to sixty pounds, a big jug of water stuffed in the bottom compartment, carrying canned goods instead of the more costly freeze-dried stuff, but three miles is not so far. On many pack trips in the past, I was humping ten pounds of beer.

Ronnie was carrying Christopher's pack. Her load probably more than thirty pounds; she's in good shape, works out at a gym several days a week. A good way to get to really know a woman is to see her carrying a load, whether it is physical or mental.

"You ready?" I said to Ronnie, cinching some of the straps tighter.

"I'll race you."

She was in a good mood. I was in a good mood. The weather was warm and the forecast was for clear skies. The kids were safe with their mother, the dogs secure in their pen, teaching and writing suspended for the weekend. I could finally concentrate on just the two of us. And, the next day was Easter, the religious holiday I find most symbolic and healing. I hoisted my pack and tightened the belly strap, then helped Ronnie get hers on. Ronnie smiled as she stuffed a water bottle under the top flap on my pack where she could easily reach it. Another couple of pounds, but that was OK. I enjoy testing myself.

The first half mile *was* a test! I hadn't carried that much weight in ten years. Humped the pack higher, tightened the hip and shoulder straps. Got used to my balance being top-heavy. Wished I had a walking staff to use like a third leg. Sweat stung as it popped out where the pack was rubbing against my back. Just needed to get in a rhythm, like when I'm rowing a canoe, one step, then another, don't think about the weight, but enjoy spring in full dress now. The dogwoods were at peak, white cross-shaped flowers centered with a crown of thorns. Purple crocus bloomed low to the ground. Easter lilies in patches where the soil was shaded and moist. All the trees had blossomed, leaves that delicate mint green, still tender from the bud. The resurrection of life from the ice. Whoever picked the season for Easter could not have chosen a more symbolic time. I felt like the Phoenix, rejuvenated from the ashes, my body scarred, but rewarded with eyes that gleam with clear vision. Maybe my back and shoulders burned, but my hip sockets were fluid, fire drenched with water. Better to hurt and walk than float numb in a vacuum.

"Bluets," Ronnie said, pointing at a small patch of delicate blue flowers.

"What are they?"

"Bluets."

"Bluets." I liked how the name popped off my tongue. Ronnie knew a lot about plants. She used to own a plant store in DC. She specialized in exotic varieties like Venus flytraps and pitcher plants. "Bluets."

The trail snaked down a long ridge and dropped to a creek that flowed into the river. Across the bridge, the trail divided, the left one a shorter route to the campground, but crossing several ridges, the right one followed the creek in a longer, flat loop. We took the shorter path, more strenuous, but we would arrive quicker, could set camp and settle in.

Halfway to the campground, we dropped our packs beside a stream flowing between two of the ridges. The sudden change in weight made me feel like I was on a rapidly descending elevator. Hair soaked under my cap. Ronnie chugged from the water bottle. I realized again why I prefer canoe camping.

"Look, a trout lily," Ronnie said, pointing at a delicate

white flower. She pointed at another of the blue flowers. "What's this?"

I'd forgotten already. My forehead wrinkled. "It's not a crocus."

"No, it's not."

"My short-term memory isn't so great."

"How much *did* you used to drink?"

"Enough."

"Bluet. Bluet, bluet, bluet."

"Bluet!" I repeated.

"What's this?" she said, pointing back at the white flower.

I squinted one eye. It's not the booze. I can remember details from my childhood, but someone can tell me his or her name, and the word instantly slips through my ears.

"This should be easy for you. You like to fish. Trout. What's your dog's name?"

"Roy Lee."

Ronnie narrowed her eyes. "Your other dog!" She's pretty when she's agitated, which means she was often pretty around me.

"Lilly. Trout lily. Yeah, I can remember that."

It felt good to sit down. The stream fell over a rock and babbled. Frogs were singing. The trail climbed a steep ridge to high ground where a breeze trembled the leaves.

"That's a fern," I said, pointing at a curled plant at the edge of the water.

"A fiddlehead fern."

"Yeah, fiddlehead. And that is a bluet, and that is a trout lily."

Ronnie smiled as though I were one of her students. "See, you're trainable."

We hoisted the packs and strapped in again and began climbing the ridge. An hour later, we arrived at the campground. My shoulders were tired and my shirt was damp, but I knew more about wildflowers.

• • •

The moon was full, luminous and golden and swollen as it rose through the tree branches. I'd built a big fire, tons of dry wood downed by Hurricane Fran. There were a couple of other parties camping, but the sites were well-spaced; the only signs of other human beings were an occasional flashlight as someone walked the loop to the toilet, a dog that barked sometimes. Part of the load I toted was a twin air mattress. It probably weighed ten pounds, but when inflated was large enough for Ronnie and me to lie on together, suspended on air above the rocks and hard-packed ground. You make choices about what you are willing to carry on the trail. Took about fifteen minutes to blow it up, drew on my lung capacity bettered by humping hills. Finally, the fabric was drawn taunt and I capped the mouthpiece. Ronnie and I settled down on it, close to the heat of the fire, the moon burning higher and higher. She had her head against my shoulder, and I felt my pulse where she pressed against me. I heard the buzz of a mosquito scouting my face.

"Do you think plants and bugs have souls like humans?"

She was quiet for a moment. "I don't think anyone has the answer to that."

"I think we're all part of the same life force," I said. "Bluets, that mosquito buzzing around — the same solar wind blows through us all."

"That's not what your mother would say. Mine either. I think more like you, though. I think religion has to be personal to every individual."

It was only a few hours until midnight, the beginning of Easter. Seems like the whole journey of religion is bent on escaping death, the resurrection, rolling back the stone and stepping into eternal life in the same form you were born in. The concept of infinity, of eternal life has always been mind-boggling to me, and a bit terrifying. To forever exist, in the same mind I possess today; that concept is not comforting somehow. Better it seems to spend time as a bluet occasionally, a duckling hatched into spring on the banks of the Cape Fear, possibly a speck of matter in some blue-shining star sighted upon by a mariner navigating difficult waters on a far-flung planet.

"My mother would think it's a sin for me to lie here with you like this. We're not married."

"Do you think it's a sin?" Ronnie asked.

"No. It would be a sin if we were intentionally hurting or betraying someone else, but we're not."

"How could there be a sin in loving someone? You can't live by someone else's definition of sin. You have to listen to your conscience."

I thought about that as I watched the moon through the branches. I think the Ten Commandments would eventually be carved out by any civilization that evolved on any planet in the universe. The rules are simply basic laws of goodness that help society work. Don't kill other people or steal from them. Tell the truth and don't break families apart. Whether the words came from God on a mountaintop or from the creases in someone's brain, the difference between good and bad seems universal. And if I am to sin in this life, I would rather be judged for faults of commission than omission. If I encountered a woman on the street who asked me for money for food, and I invited her home and fed her and bathed her and gave her refuge with me in my bed, there are those who would say I sinned. But is it not worse to turn from the woman and give her neither money nor refuge?

"This fire is pretty hot," I said to Ronnie. "I think I'll take my shirt off." She chuckled. The heat felt good on my bare skin. I watched a light bob as someone walked by.

Ronnie sat up and unbuttoned her shirt all the way down. "I'm hot too." She looked over her shoulder. "Do you think people can see us?"

"Probably. If they stood and stared. Do you really care?" She shook her head and smiled. In the flickering light, her skin resembled copper. When she lay back against me, I suddenly tasted salt in my throat.

"I feel so alive out here," Ronnie said.

"That's because you feel your senses. We're not surrounded by clothes and walls." I placed her hand against my heart and put mine between her breasts. "Right now, the whole world is right here. I can feel your skin and your heart beating. It's so quiet, I hear your breath. Your face is part shadow and part light." I pressed my nose and lips against her neck. "I can smell you, and you smell like hickory smoke, and your skin tastes like earth and water. Nothing exists right now but what we can see and feel and taste and smell and touch."

Ronnie laughed. "Are you trying to seduce me?"

I arched one eyebrow.

"You're getting there."

The glow from my watch read three a.m. Lying on my back, I had awakened to the chant of a whippoorwill. Some of the air had leaked from the mattress, and I could feel the firm earth against my hip; Ronnie was asleep, her breath coming in long, slow whispers. Moonlight filtered through the net window. From the innermost cell of my brain, invisible lines streaked outward at every degree of a circle, beyond this tent, through the earth and heavenward, stretching into infinity. Am I not then the epicenter of the universe? If those lines reached out without an end, how could I not be the axis around which all matter revolved? And if infinity is impossible, if the lines eventually curve and come back to me, I am not still the hub, smack-dab at the center of all that exists? Reality is only what I am able to comprehend.

But from the vantage of her brain, is not Ronnie the center of the universe, myself lying two feet from the nuclear axis? Christopher, in the bed at his grandmother's house, the center of existence, Meghan, ten feet away in her own bed, just steps away from the convergence of the axis. But from her perspective the centered one, her brother slightly off the bead.

That is how I felt, there in the early hours before sunrise, a web of silk extending from my consciousness to include everything in creation. And whatever I do in this life, whatever action I take or do not take, a reverberation rolls outward from me upon the fingers of the net, a tremor that is felt, if ever so slightly, within the atoms of the furthermost star imaginable. And if reality is only what I comprehend it to be, do I not create the heavens and earth each time I awake from sleep; would not my death and the cessation of my consciousness destroy the universe as it is? And in the same sense, I am only a figment of the whippoorwills universe, a man one hundred yards away from the center of being, pulled into existence and reborn by the tremor of the birdmaster's song. Each creature that shares the living spirit one and the same as God.

I drifted in and out of sleep, awakening each time as the creator, until the hour arrived that I knew it was time once again to make the sun, and it slowly rose casting light upon the darkness. And when I emerged from the tent, naked and chilled in the weak light, I better understood Easter. Myself, Ronnie, my son and daughter, and the night bird, each equally possessing the fate of all mankind.

A fault line cut the river below the campground, black rocks and boulders that channeled the water through in silver plumes. Ronnie and I perched upon a rock shelf several feet above the water. A house-sized boulder in front of us split the river. A chute flowed between the boulder and the shore, smooth as a sliding board where it glided beneath us, then dropped about a yard into a deep pool where the current boiled up as if it sat above a fire. A cool mist lifted from the turbulent water; moss grew thick on the rocks where we sat. The camera in my head started, and I recalled scenes of Mike Hogg the day he rode an air mattress down this same chute.

Katie met Mike and Pat Hogg one New Year's Eve at a hotel on the Outer Banks. She had gone there with a girlfriend; I was backpacking solo in Big Bend National Park on the Rio Grande. A couple of weeks later we were invited by the Hoggs for dinner. They lived in a development in north Raleigh; Mike was a sales manager for Burroughs Wellcome, Pat, a realtor, very upscale in their lifestyle. They owned a large sailboat they kept in a marina at Minnesott Beach. Mike was brash almost to the point of being obnoxious, strongly resembled Billy Joel, spoke with the accent he had carried to America from his upbringing in South Africa. I could tell Katie was attracted to him, but it was the good type of competition that made me aware I was not the only man in the world. We grew to be friends.

The four of us were camping at Raven Rock when Mike got his air mattress, and without hesitation, rode it down the chute. I *had* to go next, and when I hit that boiling pool, I was not sucked down into a whirlpool or tangled amid the branches of a sunken log as I had feared.

On an earlier Easter, I remember being anchored with the Hoggs in their boat off Cape Lookout at sunrise, drinking beer for breakfast and listening to Jimmy Buffet. Mike dove off the boat and swam so far out into the sea I could no longer see him against the waves. Afterwards, he sat in his captain's chair, the sun glistening on beads of water in his hair.

"Hell of a sunrise service isn't it!" Mike said.

"I think so. The Baptist State Convention might not agree."

He cracked another beer. "The key to heaven is not penitence. It's participation."

I recalled a springtime three years ago, a week after Easter. Mike and Pat had divorced by then; he was living in England with another woman he had been with for several years, traveling much of Europe and Asia with his job. Katie called me one morning and told me Mike was dead. He was on a fox hunt when he suddenly reined his horse, coughed once, then fell from his mount. An air-evac team tried to start his heart, but he was pronounced dead at age fifty-one.

But sitting there with Ronnie, I could see him that second, coming down that chute on the air mattress, eyes wide open as he smashed into the wave, then surfaced shouting, one fist thrust toward the sky. And I followed him minutes later, through the door he had punched in a thing of beauty I had been afraid of.

Ronnie and I packed up, and we took the long trail

out that followed the creek. She pointed.

"Bluets," I answer.

Pointed again later.

"Trout lilies."

"Very good."

At a place where the trail was almost level with the creek, the soil moist, Ronnie suddenly kneeled. "Ohhh, look at this!" Tenderly, she touched the foliage of another plant I was not familiar with. "This is called jack-in-the-pulpit." Her voice bore a quality of reverence. "I didn't know they were found here."

I bent over and studied the plant. The flowers were shaped like two palms cupped with fingertips toward the sky. A yellow stamen stood erect in the center like a figure preaching the word. And the sermon at this moment on Easter came from the throat of Nature, not from a man or woman standing within the confines of a church, and I, resurrected and sinless, lamented only what I had not done yet in my years on Earth in homage to my gift of breath.

A couple of weeks following the camping trip. Talking late at night with Ronnie on the phone. She was angry, her voice carried that particular nasal Yankee accent I hate.

"You ignored me the whole weekend," she said.

"I didn't ignore you. I had the kids with us. I couldn't concentrate on just you."

"I was at the bottom of your list. Just like always. I asked you to put your arm around me at the bonfire when we were lying on the blanket, and you said you couldn't."

"I was propping on my elbows! I can't lean on one elbow and be comfortable."

"I was cold, and you put your arm around me for maybe one minute, then Meghan walked over and you said, 'Hoooney, are you cold?' and hugged her. How am I supposed to feel about that!"

Long moments of silence. What I wanted to say was, "Well, feel about it this way, if both of you fell in a freezing lake, I wouldn't even have to debate about pulling Meghan out first, even if she was further away." But, I didn't say that.

"Ronnie, I sleep with you. I don't do that with anyone else. Doesn't that mean something?"

"Yeah, you sleep with me when you want sex. I want a relationship. I need companionship. You want to see me on your terms, when you have time and don't have anything else on your agenda. I can't continue like this."

Several more minutes of argument followed. The same accusations repeated again and again. More support of my theory that all of existence is one big circle, because the same tired, exhausted arguments that have been discussed a dozen times come up again and again.

"Your relationship with Meghan is weird. She's fifteen. You don't hug and kiss a fifteen-year-old. You'll confuse her sexually."

That is the accusation that bugs me worst. I'm very demonstrative with Meghan and Christopher. I hug and kiss both of them, tell them I love them. They are just as affectionate. We'll be watching a sad movie and Christopher will say, "I love you, Dad." Meghan may come and sit in my lap for a few minutes and hug up to me like she has done all her life. We'll be walking down the street, and Christopher will reach and take my hand. That is bad, or confusing? My own dad was on his deathbed before we ever touched or really talked.

"Ronnie, you can rest assured that when Meghan sits in my lap and nuzzles my neck, she is *not* thinking of sex. The last thing in the *world* I am thinking about is sex. You don't understand. You've never had kids."

"I've been around plenty of kids. I've had relationships with men who had kids, and none of them centered their whole life around their children. It's unnatural. They're controlling you. You're never going to have a healthy relationship with a woman. No woman will put up with it."

A tired, drawn-thin sadness filtered through my bones. "Look, Ronnie. Five years from now, Christopher will be in college. They'll be grown. But right now, they need me. I just don't have enough in me to be a good father, write and teach, and be a full-time boyfriend at the same time. I *can't* be what you need right now in my life." Long pause. "Go out with other guys if you need companionship. I can handle that. I'll be with you when I can concentrate on us."

"You want me to go out with other men!" Her nasal accent went up another octave. "I can't believe you're saying that. You're willing to throw all we have together away?"

All we have together? I'd known her for four months. Katie and I went through the Peace Corps together, had two babies, and went through a bone-marrow transplant, and we threw it all away. I hardly knew Ronnie.

"I'm not saying sleep with other men. If you want to go dancing, go dance. I'll take my chances. I just can't be a full-time boyfriend to you right now."

"And I can't be a part-time girlfriend. And I'll not be your friend. You want me to be like Merrie. Some other man takes care of her, and you see her whenever you get the whim. I can't go backwards in this relationship. I'm tired of you turning on and off your feelings whenever you want to."

"I'm doing the best I can."

"That's not enough."

"Then I guess there's nothing more to say?"

"I guess not."

Long silence. "Then good-bye."

"Good-bye."

Another longer silence. I hung the phone up, and sat there feeling all hollow. The irony of relationships. You can't be together as much as you'd like, so you choose to never be together. That makes a hell of a lot of sense.

• • •

I seem to grow vegetables better than I cultivate relationships with women. Back in early March, I built two raised garden beds in my backyard and filled the rectangles with a rich mixture of topsoil, compost and rabbit manure. By the time I left on the trip, I was harvesting spring onions, spinach, mustard greens, turnips and romaine lettuce. My broccoli and brussels sprout plants were knee-high. My potato plants and squash were starting to bloom.

While thinning the turnip plants, I thought about some of the things Ronnie said. Am I destined to spend the rest of my life alone, unable to give to a relationship with a woman the attention it needs to work? Am I hurting Meghan and Christopher in the long run by not blending my time with them and Ronnie, allowing them a distorted view of the world where they will think their needs always come first? Possibly. But I don't really think so.

Yes, I think I've grown to be a bit selfish. After trying to make two marriages work, plus a couple of other serious relationships, I'm tired of compromise, wearied of trying to make myself into someone I'm not. With all my warts, I like myself. The best parts of me are strongest when not diluted. I'm not lonely. I get to sleep on the whole mattress instead of about a foot. I certainly still enjoy sex, but I've had my share, and will admit I am drawn these days more strongly toward getting up at sunrise and going fishing than snuggling in bed. And, I am tempered by the fact that statistically, I should be dead today from myeloma, that the bone marrow transplant gave me renewed life, but has probably taken from the total of my years; am I selfish to address first in my remaining years what I truly love best?

These turnips have to be thinned to about three inches in-between. Turnip seeds are tiny, so you sow them thick, and as they grow, thin them so they're not crowded. Too many in the bed, and all the plants will stay small, the roots too packed together to get the food they need from the soil. But thin them out, sacrifice some and the ones left will develop into healthy plants. The same with the spinach. Too many seeds for the soil, and they all grow malnourished.

Spoiling Meghan and Christopher? I'd rather them be spoiled by too much attention and love than deprived by too little. I have a couple of male friends who were divorced when they had young children, and who quickly submerged themselves into life with other women. I'm friends with the son of one of the men; he's told me how he was always playing second fiddle behind his dad's girlfriends, how he wished just he and his dad could go fishing or have a conversation between the two of them. When I am gone, I want my son to remember what I gave to him, rather than lament what I did not. May his arms ache from embracing rather than from holding them outstretched.

My tomato bushes were beginning to bloom. I love tomato sandwiches. White bread slathered with mayonnaise, slices of firm, red fruit, sprinkled with salt and pepper. Just like I ate as a kid, except now I like them with a little fresh basil. I didn't know what basil was as a kid.

I miss Ronnie. There's much I liked about her. I can't blame her for wanting what any other woman wants. But I am not willing to listen to my loins above my heart; if I end up alone, I will not have done so by valuing what I can hold in my hands above what already dwells in my heart.

She's still out there, anyway. That woman I have been walking toward since my birth, that perfectly matched soulmate who has been with me throughout eternity, only, so far, standing at arm's length in this lifetime. Maybe in some lifespans she only appears as the greeter at the Gate. Isn't that nice to think?

• • •

Back when May had settled across Dixie, pregnant with leaf and bloom, the days were warm and often spangled with rain. Nights were still cool; I often opened the windows of my bedroom and slept with a breeze filtering across me that smelled of damp earth and new foliage.

Another school year ended for me. This had been the most satisfying semester of my ten years at the university. Not once did I walk into a class hungover from a night of heavy drinking; not once did I call in with the flu when in reality I had "took drunk." And with a sharp mind, I was on top of my students' stories and pushed the young writers with more real commitment and interest than in previous bleary-eyed semesters.

On the last day of class, I tried to sum up this writing deal, to emphasize that they will learn to write more from involvement in the world than from sitting behind a desk.

"I consider each of you to be a friend of mine," I told them. "If you ever need a buddy, I'll be there. You ever get down and out and need a place to stay a few days, I'm in the book. Call me. Don't go and jump off the fifth floor of the dorm because your girlfriend dumped you, or because you're flunking a few classes. When life gets low, you just have to start climbing up. Believe me, because I've been there."

During the exam period, the usual parade of students dropped by my office with the familiar sob stories.

"I need an A so bad, Mr. McLaurin," Vicky told me. "I was on academic probation last semester and need to get my GPA up so I can reapply for financial aid."

She had green eyes and was buxom, wore a tight, blue-jean skirt. "I know I've missed some classes, but isn't there *anything* I can do to get an A?"

I talk very frankly with my students and often kid with them, and my first impulse upon hearing her words was to rub my chin and look into her eyes and say "Anything? Welll, there might be *something* you could do to get that A...."

But immediately, alarms went off in my brain. I wanted to fling open my office door and say loud enough that any nearby teacher or student might hear my words, "I can let you do an extra story. You can sharpen my pencils or mop the floor, but you cannot take off your clothes!"

Actually, I didn't think Vicky's "anything" meant "ANYTHING," but in this age of sexual harassment real and imagined, I don't take chances. She might have had a tape recorder hidden in her bra, and a joke could get me fired.

I took out the roster for her class and found her name. Five X's, two more absences than I allowed without penalty. I recalled that her stories were usually late, but she participated well in class. A grade of B would be generous. I told her again how this class was hard to judge, not like a math class where there is only one right answer to a problem. A story can be interpreted many ways. I might like it while half the class didn't, or vice-versa. I sighed, sat back in my chair. I recalled the story she wrote about a young woman getting an abortion, how student stories are usually based close to the reality of their lives. How that story took some guts.

"I'll tell you what. I'll give you a B+. Over this summer you do something you've never done before — it has to be legal and moral — something you were afraid to do previously, and I'll raise your grade to an A at the beginning of the Fall semester. How's that?"

Vicky smiled and nodded. As she walked out the door, I couldn't help but wonder if I were the type of man, what she might have consented to for that A.

I opened a letter from the chair of the English department. I was getting promoted to assistant professor after ten years of teaching as a lowly lecturer. I had never really pushed the matter. I'm from a caste that expects to be meritoriously promoted upon performance, and despite my drinking days, my student and professional evaluations have been nearly sterling. But that is not always the way of the academic world — especially if you are a white, heterosexual male.

An irony of my life is that if I had stayed with the roots of my blue-collar heritage, being a white man who prefers women would be the least of my problems. But by educating myself and entering a field of work that is dependent upon thought more than sinew, I had encountered a competition and prejudice alien to the first half of my life.

But, I would not reverse my path and go down again into that delta. I do not want once more to hump crates of CocaCola or pound nails into framing lumber. My brother, Bruce, drives a truck ten hours a day, pulls gears, his knuckles white upon the wheel that steers 100,000 rolling pounds. His salary is higher than mine from teaching, but he would be the first to tell you he does his labor only for the money. His dream is to one day win the lottery and buy a sailboat and let the wind push him far away from any rivers of asphalt.

And though I admire and love Bruce, I do not want to be him, and though I have let my denial of my roots spill gallons of liquor down my throat, the path I walk is the one I chose.

Why did I choose that route, when my home-boys would sneer that now I am in league with women and queers? Maybe I feared my back wasn't strong enough, my hands steady enough to drive sixteen-penny nails all day. Maybe my fear of mortality is too strong. Not content to leave my name only on a headstone, I must leave books stored for the ages in libraries. I don't know. Count all of the above. But maybe, just maybe — and this is what I think — if I wander far enough, the curvature of time and the land will bring me back home, full circle, to the man I walked from, and then he will know not only memories, but also before his next step, where he wants to go.

Ten

Meghan has an eye for this lanky cow-teen, Bo, and I'm also keeping an eye on him. He's a few years older than she, lean and rangy-looking in his tight jeans, cowboy boots and Stetson. He guides the trail rides at the KOA in southern Utah close to Bryce Canyon where we've camped for two nights. Bruce, Meghan, and Christopher have mounted up on bored, automated mares, Bo on his paint gelding that prances sideways. They're about to do an hour's ride through a red canyon that is flaming with the late sun. Ma watches them ride up the trail into the high canyon, her tired, aging eyes suddenly harkening back to another time and gait.

"He'd sit on his horse in the woods beside the road and wait for my school bus to come by," she says recalling her courting days with my father. "Through the trees, I could see him racing the bus on that bay gelding he rode. I'd hurry and put up my books and saddle up my pinto, then meet him down the road at a clearing in the trees. Daddy would have had a fit if he'd known where I was going."

Ma was sixteen at the time, lean with large, brown eyes and a full mane of dark hair. My father was twenty, fresh out of the Navy where he had served out the end of World War II on a destroyer in the South Pacific. I like to imagine them racing together on horseback across the green fields, the wind streaking my mother's face with tears, to a shaded creek bank where they lay on moss beside the water and held each other and talked of the life they would build together. They married a year later on Valentine's Day, my mother with her senior year to finish, my father employed by a local dairy.

Ma was pregnant with her first child when her pinto

waded into the same creek where a few years earlier she and my father had dreamed of the future. The horse got mired up to her belly in silt and tangled in the web of a wild grape vine where she drowned after becoming exhausted from her struggles. Over the next eight years, my mother gave birth to five children. My father went to work in the Merita Bakery as a machine operator and farmed on the side. Although we always had a horse or two on the farm when I was growing up I have no memory of my mother ever riding. She was too busy always carrying a baby on her hip. The only memory I have of my father riding a horse was the night when he came home drunk and decided to ride the young Appaloosa stallion he had bought. I heard the rapid hooves from my bed, then the silence that followed after he fell. He was seeing double when he came into the house and had to spend two weeks in the hospital. I remember the box of canned goods the woman delivered from the church.

Ma watches Meghan ride across the ridge following that young cowboy. The ghost of her youth rides with my daughter, the spirit of having the whole world in front of her on the trail, all the can-be not yet drowned by the will-be. Today my mother rides a wheel chair instead of the blood-hot back of a galloping mare. She is probably eighty pounds heavier than when she used to hurry to saddle her mare, her long hair now cropped short and gray as a tombstone. I hope that when Ma dreams, sometimes she is that girl again, the ache in her legs the desire to clasp them against warm flesh. I hope I live to see my grandchild, a boy with my eyes who stoops to pick up a green snake knowing full well he has been warned not to. I hope I am like my mother. She does not shout at Meghan to rein in her mount and turn around. Maybe this time the mare will not drown, the serpent will not bite. But if history is like a carousel that goes round and round, I believe Ma would still say to Meghan and Meghan's child, "Jump on and ride. Even the fall is better than to have stood limp-armed while watching the horses gallop by." I think of Lynn again, and of a morning only a few weeks earlier, but now only memories. All of history is but memories — mere dreams —

and if I am the architect of my future, should not my recall contain not only the lessons of loss, but also of what I hope to gain?

• • •

Mid-morning and the phone rang, and when I lifted the receiver, at first I heard only static, then Lynn's voice delivered long on the wire. After we chatted for a few moments, she paused, then said, "I don't know if you can do this or want to, but I am going to be in LA in early June, and wonder if you would like to meet me?"

I asked her the dates and told her I would think hard on the opportunity, and we said good-bye, and I clicked off the phone, but the line between us remained open and humming, unaffected by many miles and a different hour on the clock. That line has remained live for five years now.

I first met Lynn the summer after Katie and I had parted, and I was living in the cabin. She called one afternoon and introduced herself, told me she was a fan, was in North Carolina visiting relatives, and hoped to meet me. Noon at Breadman's restaurant in Chapel Hill, she had told me I would recognize her from her description of herself and I did among a hundred hungry strangers. Slender and pretty with large brown eyes so similar to my own, we could have been mixed from the same pool. I saw her singular against the crowd, as if her form had been cut from a different portrait and pasted upon the picture before me. And when I spoke to her, she extended her hand and told me I looked exactly as she knew I would. And that strange sensation washed over me that I had stood here before with my hand clasped around this woman's fingers, staring into eyes that could have been my own.

I figured she would decline my offer to stay at the cabin with a hotel room already paid for, luxury exchanged for a night in a structure with no air conditioning, no toilet and an assortment of summer bugs. Nevertheless, I offered her my bed, saying I would sleep on an air mattress on the floor. She said the offer suited her.

—207—

That night we talked until past midnight, sticky with bug repellent and the sweat from a long walk we had taken. I told her about how I took a bucket bath each morning before driving to teach summer school, and how cold the well water felt. I had recently built the porch we sat on; above us were the bare rafters where I intended to nail sheets of tin, the stars and an oval waning moon shining white and framed through the ribs. She debated whether I should ever actually apply the sheets of tin, the shelter in exchange for the sky?

That night I listened to her sleep upon my narrow bed a few feet from where I lay, and that tired ol' male voice whispered to me, "Why you sleeping alone on the floor with this good-looking woman within reach. You ought to at least try, you wimp. What are you, a homo?" But that voice has never had much control over me, and the next morning when she was leaving I told her to take it only as a compliment, but I had wanted to touch her during the night, and Lynn smiled and said she had thought of the same thing. Those simple, sincere words were better than the memory of an act performed through insecurity with a woman I did not know, but suspected already I had always known.

After hanging up the phone, I sat and stared into the room with Lynn's invitation still in my ear, and my Baptist upbringing was there in balance, like Jesus listening to the Devil's offer of the Kingdom. This was too strange. I had recently been invited to Los Angeles to speak to a book club. One of the dates they suggested included the weekend Lynn would be there. A paid fare to the city of angels where it just so happens that a woman would be in town whom I consider divine. Nearly even odds I have venom in my blood again. Lynn has been married now for many years.

I thought of every reason I should go to L.A. while Lynn was there, and every reason I should not. I have never met a woman I enjoy being with so much. Lynn is married. Her intellect intrigues me. She is married. Lynn lives life artless in her application. She is married. Each time I am with her I see beyond another layer of mortality and closer to two souls that seem simple and guiltless. She is married. My mind seems to fit into the folds of her own in ways I have never experienced. Lynn is married. My body fits her in ways I have never experienced. She is married — I want to be with her, and maybe, the time I have left to do this in this life is trickling out.

Does it work that way? Is God really the type who would dangle a man above fire and forbid him to drink water. Would He say, "I have placed this burden upon you and before you I place this temptation, and if you resist the fruit, I may choose to remove the weight from your shoulders. Or, I may not remove the weight, and you may not carry a weight in the first place. I am the God of Abraham, and look what I did to him, at long last a son, then asked him to slit the boy's throat. Let's play games."

I don't think so. I believe the scenario is more like this. God places a weight upon one's shoulders and sometimes tries to counterbalance by allowing a ray of light to crack the shell of blackness, and that person can either choose to look into the light or turn and stare into shadows. Or probably even more likely is that God doesn't place the weight there at all, or lift it, but leaves these acts to nature and fate and sometimes the celestial cards fall in one's favor, and sometimes they don't.

Picking up the phone, I called United Airlines and booked a three-day turnaround. If I was to sin — and in my heart I could not believe going to be with Lynn was a sin — then I would rather the offense be committed in the flesh rather than just in thought. Does not the Southern Baptist God say each is equal? Let me be judged by acts of commission instead of omission. If I was thirsty and placed two cups upon the earth, one upright with its mouth toward heaven, and the other down with its mouth sealed against the earth, I would drink first from the cup that complies with the laws of nature and physics and is poised to be filled.

I was not listening first to my loins. My heart has always held power over the rest of my body. I have turned away more times than I have turned toward the women who beckoned me. And Lynn has turned; she is moral if the rain is moral. For three years she turned, and I turned, and then this past spring when she was home to Carolina, we chose to face each other, the embrace saved for that moment when what was right eclipsed what might be wrong. Rain fills the upright cup, and we may nourish our thirst or drown, depending upon how we choose to drink.

Friday afternoon, I hugged Meghan and Christopher especially hard before leaving. "Next week this time," I said, "we'll have the Winnebago and be getting ready to leave."

"It's going to be great, Dad."

I tousled Christopher's hair. His voice cracked about every third sentence. Hugged each of them again.

"Will you call us from L.A.?" Meghan asked.

"Of course."

For all my rationalization, I still couldn't shake a certain guilt that spoke to me. "Here, you're a week from taking a wonderful trip with your kids and mother, and you're risking flying all the way across the country to see a married woman. Karma. Would serve you right if the plane crashed."

That night I went to bed early, but knew I wouldn't sleep very well. I needed to be up at four to catch my flight at six-thirty. I lay in bed and stared into the darkness studded with man-made stars.

Lynn and I are standing waist deep in an ocean surf and the waves roll in huge swells that lift our feet from the sand and lap water over our chins. We barely make it over the crest of each wave, then are lowered into the trough to touch our feet to the sand briefly before the next swell threatens to engulf us. But when we join hands, we rise together out of the sea into high, rare air, miles above what threatened to choke us. But the oxygen is thin, and though we both feel weightless and immortal, we are in danger of falling. But by barely touching fingertips, we are able to float suspended between the rough sea and the heights; an energy crackles between our fingers, and in that layer of air between water and thin vapor, the air is cool and fragrant and flows in a breeze upon our faces.

I woke up to the stars and remembered fragments of the dream and wondered of the strangeness of it. I had never been swimming with Lynn, but then dreams are often based upon the never. I thought of my river trip last March, and of that third night following fourteen hours of rowing when the bow finally scraped concrete at the landing above the bridge....

...And Poke Salad Annie stood on shore, her face and bosom illuminated by a light she held. "I thought maybe you were lost, or that I had missed you," she said.

"No. It just took me longer to get here than I would have thought. I'm glad you waited...."

And I looked at Lynn and she into my eyes, and we threw that canoe onto the back of her truck and went to a motel down the road. Her bare breast against mine, her mouth against mine, her hair hanging damp upon my face, and the breath I drew was the drought she had expended, my wind given in return to her. I felt giddy, euphoric; we circulated one breath until we drew inward the same air as plants and were transformed into a life-form primal and simple.

In the morning, we ate breakfast and lingered over coffee, and then she drove me further downriver so that I could ride the tide and the clock on time to a friend waiting for me at the end of the river. As I slipped away, again carried by the current that had pulled me now for four days and for all of my life, I lifted my hand to her and smiled. No, we cannot go back upriver, so the stops we make in route should be significant.

Most of the world is made of water. We are born from water and when we die, most of our body eventually turns to vapor, so I guess to dream of the ocean and high clouds has something to do with the journey between the womb and the wake. I slept again, and this time did not awaken until my eyes opened with a start and the clock's face reads two minutes till the buzzer. I guess when my eyes are closed, my ears fine tune themselves to the pitch of the strained spring that is about to erupt and proclaim, "Go and live."

• • •

Another dawn with soft morning light through the window curtains. I lay in bed and looked into the light and thought of omission and commission, of choices made and chances passed. I knew what my mother would tell me to do. I knew what I wanted to do. I thought of dreams and wondered if all of existence is merely different layers of sleep.

I was especially glad to hear the yelp of the tires when the plane touched down in L.A. The flight had been long, but on schedule. The clock had been turned back three hours so that the time was only mid-afternoon. Safely on the ground. Didn't crash and burn in the Grand Canyon. The thoughts of sin aren't as bad as actually doing the sin, my guilt voice whispered to me. Turn your back to temptation, and you shall be delivered safely back home. Partake of the flesh, and there exists a strong possibility that on the return flight a bomb will explode in the cargo hold and you will fall for three miles screaming toward death.

As I was waiting to debark from the plane, I wondered if Lynn would be waiting for me. Our communication had been limited. She should have arrived yesterday, but who knows? She could have decided not to come at the last minute; possibly our union last March opened her eyes to a realization that I was not worth the trouble?

But Lynn stood waiting against a wall toward the back of the crowd, and her image leapt out to me the way it did that first time I met her. It's as though I'm looking at a photo of a group of people, black and white and flat and two dimensional, but her figure has been painted upon the glossy in thick paint of color. And I walked straight to her and hugged her and felt like someone had jabbed me in the stomach.

"I was afraid you might not be here," I said to Lynn.

"Well, I wondered a bit if you would be on that plane," she answered. "You have been known to show up late."

I smiled. "Ain't no river wide enough."

• • •

Late in the afternoon, and I had already checked us into a hotel at a beach outside of Malibu, and we were sitting on the sand watching the sun hang above the horizon in the western sky.

"Every time I see the sun set in the ocean, it's unsettling to me," I said to Lynn. "It's like I'm watching the world turn with my blind side to life as it unfolds. Usually when I see the sun above the ocean, the day is just beginning and is nothing more than speculation and hope. Here, it seems to be only memories."

Lynn nodded. My calf pressed against hers, but except for hugging at the airport, we hadn't touched. I felt shy around her. When getting the hotel room, I asked for a room with double beds, instead of a king. I didn't know what had gone on in her head in the two months since the river. Maybe she had asked me here to tell me she has decided there could be no physical relationship between us, that we must go back to the occasional phone call or letter. But I was glad we did not fall into the sack and rut moments after walking into the room; that is the television, carnal version of a relationship, and Lynn does not watch television.

"Maybe that's the difference between Southerners and West Coast people," Lynn said. "We live by the rising sun, think first of what we have to do and overcome, and people out here live more by what they've accomplished."

Lynn has fair skin; the low sun was red on her shoulders, and I squeezed some sunscreen on my palm and rubbed it on her shoulders. She lowered her head and I kneaded the liquid into her shoulders and up her neck.

"I wouldn't want you to burn," I told her, though I knew the weak sun wouldn't burn her. "I also want to touch you," I confessed.

Lynn laughed and pressed her leg against mine. "That's what beaches are made for. And I would prefer that the sun rise out of the water. I'd rather have the day, and all the potential, than only the memories."

• • •

Later that night at a Mexican restaurant, Lynn took a

pair of chopsticks from a napkin in her purse. Japanese chopsticks, short with finely tapered ends.

"I've never known anyone who carried around a pair of chopsticks."

She shrugged. "I like to feel my food. If it weren't for etiquette, I'd eat with only my fingers."

And I observed her hands, the part of her body that I find most sensuous. Lynn is almost my age, a very attractive woman who could easily pass for someone ten years younger. But her hands are timeless and ancient and ageless, and with one turn are those of a child and then an old, old woman, fingers that can deftly thread a needle and guide a welding rod. Those hands create art that begins with the concept of living and is framed a few breaths short of the final draw of the lungs. Sculpture that speaks of who I am, instead of who I was.

"I wish I had chopsticks. I've never seen anyone eat Mexican food with chopsticks. But I like it."

"I eat everything with chopsticks. Except maybe soup."

And she reached again into her purse and took out another pair, and for the first time I ate taco salad piece by piece instead of shoveling all the mixed portions together into my mouth. I thought of Tunisia when I would sop olive oil with pieces of bread and of Meghan so small then and how she would nurse the end of my finger when her mother was not there with her breast. I remembered my grandmother telling me of how at noon in the shade of an oak beside the field she would chew her food and in her fingers take a portion from her mouth and feed my infant father. And in that moment, what I wanted most to do to Lynn was feed her. Not strip her bare or be with her, but bring to her lips food that was satisfying and healing.

Later that night in bed, the hour was late, and I was tired, and I knew she must be. She was so warm beside me. I said, "I know you have to be exhausted from jet lag. We'll just go to sleep. There is time for the other things."

Lynn didn't speak. Her head was against my shoulder and our fingers of one hand were locked together and then it began. I circled one of her knuckles with my fingertip and she pressed her knee against my thigh and touched her fingertips against my lips, I tasted one with my tongue, then took her fingertip into my mouth. And she put her lips against my neck just a brush at first — then another that rested longer, and I took all of her finger into my mouth and that pulse began between us that is the same insistent meter as heartbeats and tides, and everything that follows between us was as natural and necessary as feeding.

Morning in bed; I had made coffee and brought two cups to the nightstand. The sun was up, but had not been there long. Light was thick and yellow through the curtain. Small talk about what the day would bring, the work she had to do, the time and place I had to stand up and preach the word.

"What's our relationship?" I asked Lynn.

She was silent for several moments "We don't have one, and that is the beauty of it."

I thought on that, then chuckled. "Well, it seems to me that something is going on between us."

"But, it doesn't have to have a name. We just are."

Eastern philosophy, to name anything is the first act towards killing it. "OK," I said. "We just are."

She sipped from her cup. "In words, I can't offer you any kind of commitment."

"I understand that. I don't need that, either."

"But, I'll tell you this. For three years now, your name has been my mantra. I don't have to think of you. You're there within me before my thoughts can occur."

I told her about the loop inside my head that had been going around in a circle constantly since March, her name over and over without cessation.

"That's the same voice I hear. We just are, and that existed before people invented time and clocks and rings."

• • •

I had to enter again the world of clocks. The house

where I was to speak of words and books sat on a hillside with a view of the ocean and Catalina Island on the horizon. I was parked in front of the house with five minutes to spare, the first sparkles of the two Valium tablets I ingested were beginning to circulate; I was about to transform into the man I am most not — the one who has the answers.

I don't really need the Valium anymore. In the old days, I would begin to suffocate when I spoke in front of people, would exhale more than I inhaled, unless I was stoked and calmed with a couple of pills and about a half pint of vodka. The vodka is history now, but I usually still take the sedative.

Several cars were parked along the street. Nice cars, a Cad, Lexus, vehicles that would cost about the same as a doublewide a whole family would live in back in Fayetteville. The house I was certain cost somewhere in the range of a million dollars. I'd gotten pretty used to the type of people who would be inside — mostly white, upper-middle-class women who were educated. Those are the sorts who buy books. Few of them will know anything about the people I write about, but I have to give the women credit for buying the books. Folks want to read fiction about people who either live worse or better than themselves. Where they have climbed up from, where they hope to go. Few want to read about lives that are close to their own. That would be too frightening. I looked at my watch and saw that I had five minutes till I was supposed to begin my act. I knew that inside the woman who invited me was watching her own clock, afraid that I would not show and that she would be embarrassed in front of her friends with all that fancy finger food and bottles of good wine. I grabbed my book and stepped from the car.

Knocked on the door, and it opened almost immediately. The woman standing there fit the bill — about fifty and well-preserved, on her wedding finger a diamond I could retire on.

"You must be Tim McLaurin?" she said and smiled and extended her hand, and I said yes and shook her hand.

"How was your flight out?"

"Oh, it was real nice. We flew over the Grand Canyon."

I was escorted to the den where about a dozen similar women were standing and sitting. Two men were there. I was introduced to the women first. All of them were handsome and tailored and polished; they observed me with keen eyes, then the men. They looked like the women dressed in drag. Both gripped my hand, and I felt a certain tension between us like two male dogs who run up on each other in neutral territory, each waiting for the other to jump.

"North Carolina," one man said. "I lived there for two years. Got my MBA at Duke."

"Yeah. Duke. That's a good school." I thought — well, if you went to Duke, you didn't live in North Carolina. Not the real North Carolina.

"You're a younger man than I thought you'd be," he said.

He was probably referring to my book jacket picture. "Yeah. I'm forty-five. But, I look about fifty-five. I've got a lot of miles on me."

"Would you like a drink?" the host asked. She waved her hand at a well-stocked bar. All the black label stuff was there.

"I'm giving my liver a rest," I said. "I wouldn't mind some coffee." In the past, I would have poured myself about a double shot of bourbon to upgrade the high I wore in. I told her I would like the coffee black with an ice cube to cool it. And then we exchanged about ten minutes of small talk, and when a lull in the conversation occurred, I knew the time had arrived for me to click on and become the knowledgeable one with X-ray eyes who knows the answers. But, in reality, I am the opposite, the man with all the questions. And I started talking, trying to explain why a working-class Southern man would stoop to writing books.

I told them about growing up, and how the stars and snakes whetted my appetite for learning, one eye on the ground and the other staring into the heavens. I told them about the time when I was twelve and my father asked me to thrust my arm to the shoulder up the birth canal of a sow and hook a breached piglet with a piece of wire and pull the baby from being stuck between the mother's pelvic bones and into the world. A loop of guts protruded from the piglet's belly where I had hooked the wire, and I followed my father to the house where upon the kitchen table in the hour following midnight he sewed the wound closed with sewing thread. And when we returned to the barn, we found that the sow had continued giving birth, but in our absence, a boar hog had stood there eating the newborn. And what had I learned from that experience? That birth and death seem intertwined, that we are all spit out into the world where luck seems more important than destiny. I told them that I write to understand my own existence, rather than to help others understand. That by writing a book, I confront a subject I feel strongly about, but am not sure why I feel that way, and by creating a cast of characters, a plot, and bringing that conflict to a resolution, possibly in the end I have found the words that define my gut feelings.

I read some. Then I fielded questions, and the questions I had heard each a hundred times, the inquisitions only recast and enunciated over a different person's tongue.

"What do the people you write about think of your books?" one woman asked.

"Well, the irony is that the people I tend to write about don't read my books. They normally don't read books, period. I remember one time a guy who could have been a character right out of my first book — he had a large scar on his stomach where a guy had cut him — he said to me, 'My wife read some of your book to me, and I think you need to start paying me royalties.' But he was smiling. He realized I thought he, and other people in east Fayetteville, were important enough to write about. But later, the mayor of Fayetteville, a woman who lived in Haymont, the rich section of town, said she thought the book cast a bad light on Fayetteville. That's usually the way it works. The people who didn't live the book are most critical of the story."

"How do you write?"

When I told her I use a word processor instead of a

pencil, she seemed disappointed, as though a real writer should hover and labor over each word, needs to feel the lead scratch out the syllables. But, does a rock climber use a hemp rope and an ice pick to climb Everest? No. She uses the best equipment that will get her to the summit. And I told them that I work best when surrounded by the chaos of daily life, which is the focus of what I write about. Meghan in the next room and the drone of television through the wall. I actually welcome a phone call in the midst of when the words are flowing, like *coitus interruptus*, a chance to stay the letdown after the dam bursts. That I have actually turned down the chance to seclude myself in a room with a view in Vermont or southern France, where the writers I know who went there admitted that they mostly stayed half-drunk and chased tail and talked about writing. That writing is low-paying, lonely work that usually ends up taking a toll on relationships.

"You said you are now writing a book about this year in your life," one of the men asked. "You seem to have lived an interesting life, but one year? You're not exactly Ernest Hemingway."

He smiled, and that is the kind of question only a man would ask. Well, what if I dragged you outside and rolled your ass down the street for about a block? Is that what you think it takes to write about one year in your life? I recalled the man at a party once who did not know my work and seemed insulted when I told him I had just written an autobiography. "How thick is that book?" he asked, and rephrased the question several times. "How many pages is in that book?" He seemed pissed off that any man could even consider writing about his life if he had lived short of sixty years and had not been at least a governor. I found out later there was a reason behind the man's reaction. He was losing a battle with cancer, his own life pages close to the end. Today, I describe my nonfiction as a memoir, not autobiography, and that is a truer definition, not so much the story of my life as it is the story of those people who affected my life. Not the general, only the messenger.

"No," I say to the man who reminded me of a woman,

"I'm not Ernest Hemingway, but I'm not trying to write about WWI or bull fighting, either. I'm writing about a forty-five-year-old man who is divorced, been through some trials, is trying to raise his kids and pay his bills and make it through life and retain his integrity. Does that sound like anyone you know?"

"Sounds like about half of America."

I smiled. "It ought to be a bestseller, then."

I told them it's not bloodshed and famine that most American readers can link to, but it is the stories that they too have experienced, the same fears and triumphs they have felt that bridge the gaps between all races and genders. And if for whatever reason, I can find the words to describe these experiences when they are unable, these readers can still say, "This is *my* story as much as it is your own, for memories and images are constructed only of words already used by a zillion tongues; you only recount tales spoken by my mother and father and my ancestors before. Therefore, these too are my words." I agree.

"You're not at all the way I imagined you'd be," the woman who was my host said.

"Who did you think I would be?"

She laughed, seemed a bit embarrassed. "I don't know. You have a strong accent — a pretty accent. You dress differently than I would have thought. You seem so down-to-earth. I'm not sure who I was expecting."

I hunched one shoulder. "I don't know. I'm just me." I was wearing a pair of worn jeans and a polo shirt and sandals with no socks. I wondered if she expected me to arrive wearing a smoking jacket and a turtleneck. I told them about the time I came to L.A. after my first book was published to talk with some people who had purchased the film option. Over cocktails, a young woman mocked my manner of speaking, repeating words and sometimes whole sentences in a Hollywood Southern accent that became increasingly unkind until she realized I was the man they were courting. Immediately, she stopped the harassment. Maybe at first she thought I was Tim McLaurin's chauffeur. I recalled another

time waiting to speak at a small college, and the president of
the school was seated nearby and I heard him whisper to a
colleague, "I wonder where Mr. McLaurin is. I hope he isn't
going to be late."

I don't own a smoking jacket. I speak the same
language as the people I write about. I've thrown away the
suit I had begun to wear too often when speaking in public —
and drunk. A couple of years ago at Middle Tennessee State
University, I was so intoxicated when I got up to talk that I
don't remember what I said.

"What advice do you give aspiring writers?" another
woman asked.

"Write what you know about. I would never write a
book about a Jewish man living in Manhattan, because that is
an alien world to me. And write in the voice you are born
with, but use the right words." I told them about one of the
first short stories I ever wrote when I was in school and
studying under a man who had published lots of stories in *The
New Yorker* and *The Saturday Evening Post.* In the story, a
young man had returned to a river where he had spent many
happy hours as a kid. But this time he sat with a young woman
he had played with as a child, upon rocks at the edge of the
current, his hair still short following his discharge from the
Marines. The river looked the same and sounded the same,
but during a romantic interlude between the couple, a large
turd floated by upon the current. My teacher hated that turd
and the image it presented, told me I needed to get the turd
out of the story. His advice bothered me considerably.
Symbolically, the turd was the heart of the story. But in a later
class under the writer Doris Betts, she told me to keep the
turd, but to craft my words so that the ugly image did not
dominate the landscape, the river would still be coffee-brown
and the doves would still sing, the turd no more intrusive than
the fact that the man now shaved and wanted to kiss the girl
he had once ridiculed, his innocence tainted, but his memories
intact.

And it occurred to me then that writing is more about
the individual words and syllables than the sentence. That a

turd can become a ship swept upon the currents of fate, if worded the right way. I thought of Lynn and her chopsticks and how eating is a metaphor for her life, the importance of dwelling upon the individual grains of rice instead of shoveling in and trying to digest the whole mass. And when I thought of Lynn, I wanted to be with her on the beach and not there with people I didn't know or particularly like, and I released the neck of the balloon I had inflated and let the air out.

I don't have answers any more than the people listening to me. If I am different, it is in that I am willing to ask the questions. And that inquest carries a price. My youngest brother, Danny, climbs power poles for a living, and when he looks into the night sky, he sees the night sky. I see beyond the velvet dome into quasars and through light years in question of why I exist. Maybe Danny doesn't need to know or already is secure in the fact of his being, and I pose the questions from an unhealthy dose of ignorance and fear. If I am honest, my need to craft words comes from insecurity more than confidence.

And then I was out of there after shaking another round of hands. The guy who questioned my authority to write about one year told me he had a book he wanted to write if he ever found the time. I hear that line all the time. If he truly needs to write that book, he will find the time, even if it means going without sleep or food. I hope for his sanity, his need to write never gets that great.

Mid-evening after I finished my speaking engagement, I found Lynn on the beach where she said she would be. An ocean liner was passing upon the dark sea, her many lights like some star cluster that had slipped down.

"So did you dazzle them?" Lynn asked. She intertwined her fingers into mine.

"I suspect I disappointed them more than dazzled them."

"I doubt that."

"Sometimes, I wish I climbed power poles for a living, or maybe was a steward on that ship out there. I think living would be much simpler."

"You really don't have license to say that. You and I both don't know what is in the steward's head."

"Yeah, and I don't really want to climb power poles. I'm scared of electricity."

"And I probably wouldn't know you if you climbed power poles."

"Do you like me because I write books?"

"I like you because you want to write books. I'm attracted to the man who sits down in front of that blank page much more than the man who signs his name to the title page."

"You think so?"

"I know so."

And too soon, Monday afternoon had arrived, and my plane was due to fly me back east and forward in time. At the gate, I hugged Lynn. She slipped a piece of paper into my shirt pocket.

"This is my itinerary for the next few weeks. I hope the trip out west goes well."

"It'll be great. When will I see you again?"

"I don't know. There is a lot happening in my life in the next few months."

"I wish you didn't live so far away."

She didn't answer, and I knew not to say any more. I took one final breath from her and walked to the door and turned and waved, and she was there, stamped out in bold relief against the mosaic of my life.

As the jet lifted off above L.A., dusk was over the earth, lights beginning to come on in the city. I already missed Lynn; I took the folded paper from my pocket. The loops of her handwriting mirror herself, straight up without leaning. At the bottom of her itinerary, she had glued the ticket stub from a movie we saw the previous night about a man who lived with gorillas in Africa so long he became accepted into the tribe.

McLaurin

Instinct
Eve. Adult

Straight words — the name of the movie, an evening performance, adult price. But she had circled "Instinct," and with the stroke of a pen transformed a memento into a slightly erotic statement of our time together. The trio of words can be weighty. Eve is always blamed above Adam for destroying Eden. If blame was directed toward my relationship with Lynn, she would probably receive the most heat because she is female. Adult. Lynn and I are both adults. We have no excuses.

"Instinct" was circled. Eve and Adult were not circled. Instinct dwells inside of me. Instinct causes me to touch my fingertips to the words Lynn had written, seeking heat left from the blood in her hands. And I touch my fingers to my nose and close my eyes and breath, trying to scent the direction of her trail.

The plane lifted and circled long toward home, suspended between ocean and clouds. And my window faced west, where the sun was yet visible from that high vista. And there painted was a sunset like no other I had witnessed in my life, the heavens and sea ablaze from a dying light bounced between and splintered by molecules of water both liquid and vapor. A glorious sunset that I suspect no one else in that aircraft saw but me, etched in black and crimson and shades of blue, violent and utterly peaceful.

A man and a woman in a dream were drowning in a sea drawn by tides, waiting for the surge to ebb. To tread water was to perish. But by locking hands, they grew wings and were able to fly, but the danger was equal in rising too high where the air was rare but thin, the vision muddled by lifting too far above the roots that pipe nourishment to all land creatures. But by touching fingertips and not clinging, by not holding to each other with a grasp that choked and fended, the man and woman found they could float in a strata reserved and private, suspended through delicate intercourse between drowning and falling.

—224—

I flew east toward home, thinking of omission and commission, of choices made and chances passed. I knew what my mother would have told me to do. I knew what I had done. For the rest of the flight, I did not fear the plane crashing. If I fell, my death would come from a faulty engine and not from a wrathful God punishing me for feeding a hunger he gave me.

Eleven

Even though I am viewing the Grand Canyon for the fifth time, still I am momentarily struck speechless. No other place on earth I have seen possesses such timelessness. The canyon drops away from the rim in a series of purple and vermilion cliffs, buttes and plains to a loop of the Colorado River glinting silver. Eons ago, where I stand, my toes would be in the water, and today the river flows miles beneath me. The air seems to resound with a continuous note of "ohhmmmm," like the earth exhaling in one eternal breath. Didn't I wade across this river in another youth when the banks were no steeper than those of the Cape Fear River I frequented just thirty years ago?

Our first sight of the Canyon is disappointing. Desert View, first tourist stop inside the east entrance to the park. The parking spaces are filled with tour buses and cars, seemingly as many people standing against the guard railing as the years time took to carve out this place. Exhaust fumes and voices, people elbow to elbow, snapping away with cameras. I drive us a mile farther along the rim and park on the shoulder of the road. Only a few yards through scrub piñon trees I find a rock shelf where we all stand, removed from the crowd and the whirring of shutters. Reminds me of New York when Meghan, Tema, and I walked from St. Patrick's Cathedral and I heard a dove coo right in midtown Manhattan.

Far below, a wiggly line snakes across one of the plains. "That's Kaibab Trail," I say to Christopher. "I hiked it once all the way to the river."

"Can we hike it?"

"Maybe for a little ways," I tell him. "It's miles to the

bottom. Then you have to come back up."

I tell Meghan and Christopher about the first time I came to the Canyon, and how I hiked all the way to the bottom and back up again all in one day. Down Kaibab at sunrise, carrying a day pack with a liter of water and a couple of candy bars and a sandwich. How I passed a sign warning me to turn back if I was not equipped to spend the night below the rim, trotting most of the seven miles downhill. Then along the river trail where I soaked my feet in the cold water, passing Phantom Ranch where people with enough money could come in by helicopter. I ate my meager lunch at Indian Gardens and refilled my water jug, then at noon began another seven miles of uphill switchbacks on Bright Angel Trail back to the rim. A year out of the Marines, Jenell waiting for me at the campground in our umbrella tent, I would not and could not quit walking, although my thighs were chafed and my calves were laced with fire. Back on top, my watch read four p.m.; I had mocked the warning signs. I had to will myself to walk the final mile back to the campground.

I don't tell the kids of how that night with Jenell, upon the air mattress, we made love with an intensity that has stood out in my memory through all these years. I cannot explain my lust for her that night, except that I had worked mightily to return to her, hiked for miles beyond what the signs told me was possible. I think of last March on the river when I paddled for fourteen hours because I hoped Lynn would be waiting for me at the landing, and how her standing there with a lantern justified my faith and exertion. At the motel the last thing I felt was weariness.

As I stand and gaze upon such beauty created by water rubbing against rock through the long grind of time, I fantasize about Lynn coming home, and of the house we would live in.

The kitchen will have a well fifty feet deep down to limestone where the water is cold and sweet. To draw the water, I lower a bucket on a knotted rope, that when the bucket is full, I lift hand over hand, the effort so that my biceps knot under my sleeves. For breakfast, I cook for Lynn and myself buckwheat pancakes, the flour milled from grain I harvested from our farm, sliced fresh peaches plucked this morning and hot black coffee. The toast is from bread I baked last night. I carry the feast upon a tray up a winding stairway with 365 steps to the tip of a tall oak, the bedroom roofed with glass, where I wake Lynn and feed her with my fingers while she in turn feeds me. At the end of the meal, I throw the plate and cup through a window to a pit in the earth below, where later in the afternoon I retrieve the shards of clay and pulverize them with my fists and shape the dust with water and fire the vessels again in an urn, so that we never eat upon the same plate. And every morning, the ritual will be the same; to feed her takes commitment and effort. And when we want to make love, we both climb a ladder one hundred feet higher to a platform built way above the tree, a single plank without sides where we have to lie very close and pay attention to what we do; if we were not attentive, we would fall a long ways, and we will fall together.

The second week on the road slips by. We tour northern Arizona, Ma collecting another rock just about each time we stop. I bet there are five hundred pounds of rock in this vehicle, but I don't complain, just as I have ceased to grumble when Donnie is the last person back on board. I have certainly tested many times their patience with me.

Then finally, three days remain until I am supposed to have the Winnebago back to the dealer and we join the tires to Interstate 40, nearly a straight shot across the heartland back to Dixie. We have one more important stop before home. Christopher's birthday is on Thursday, and the miles and time coincide with a stopover in Memphis to share a cake and candles with Katie's family. Last year on his birthday, he was so many miles and hours from me.

• • •

Mid-June had arrived, and frogs sang, audible between the roar of jet engines as they thrust passenger planes into the sky above the airport. My bad right hip burned, and I was eager for the second session of summer school to come and go so I could have a second operation to install another synthetic hip. Katie and the kids were leaving for two weeks of sailing in the Greek Islands on a chartered boat with her sister and brother-in-law. Almost sixteen years to the day had passed since Katie and I had boarded a plane in Fayetteville to leave for Peace Corps training. How different we had been — Katie rail-thin with long hair, me flawless in body, not one stitch ever put in my flesh, no broken bones or nights spent in the hospital. No thoughts yet of children. We loved each other.

Katie and Meghan and Christopher were already checking in at the airport, passports and tickets in hand, shuffling their bags forward as the line moved. At the security check, I worried that the steel in my hip would set off the metal detector, but it didn't. The monitor said the plane was on time; we took seats where we could see the runway. I kept hugging the kids, reminding them to wear life preservers when the sailboat was underway, already feeling a deep loneliness in anticipation of their two weeks away from me. Too fresh was my recall of the previous summer when they had gone to Scotland and of the vodka I had drunk in their absence, how I had rolled my truck, and my resolve not to do so this time. Father's Day and Christopher's birthday would pass while they were in the Islands. I sent a prayer aloft as I watched their jet disappear into the clouds.

On Father's Day, the kids called me from Eos. The weather was dry, the sky clear, but the sea was often rough and sometimes they hooked into harnesses while sailing. On the twenty-fourth of June they called again, Christopher's birthday, but I was in the mountains speaking at a library. But all day my thoughts were on him, my mind reliving the events of his birth twelve years earlier.

The apartment we moved into after Katie and I returned from Peace Corps seemed like a palace compared to the houses we had lived in during our two years in Tunisia. Three bedrooms, full appliances, hot water and a television

— back in Chapel Hill square on top of the American dream. Our readjustment to America had been hastened by the fact that Katie and I had returned as parents with a commitment and obligation to Meghan. Immediately I took a part-time job and returned to school; after Meghan had adjusted to the move, Katie went back to the job she had left, working with population control in the Third World. By the time that Christopher was a speck of life within Katie's womb, I had finished my degree, worked briefly as a newspaper reporter, and left that to frame houses after rising to write fiction in the hours before dawn. Meghan was walking and beginning to talk; her mother had moved swiftly through the ranks at her job and was now a boss with international travel as part of her work. Not long after conceiving Christopher, she left on a two-week trip to a conference in Turkey.

With my father little more than a year in the earth, I was even more aware of the value of time spent between me and my daughter. As a child, I have no memory of ever having a conversation with my father, or going some place as just the two of us. I wanted my child to grow up with concrete memories of her dad, of words exchanged and places visited. I did not want her to have to come to my deathbed to meet her father.

I did not have Katie's breast to comfort my daughter when her mother traveled, or the voice that Meghan had heard while yet inside the womb. But I tried mightily within the vessel of my body, sang to her and fed her, changed diapers and washed her bottom and listened for her breath in the still hours after midnight.

One night I stood with Meghan and watched the hunter's moon rise full and golden, and told of her mother and the budding child inside her waters.

"See mama in the moon?" I pointed to the shadows upon the large yellow face. "Mama and the little one are waving to us."

"Mama," Meghan chortled at the word. She squirmed in my arms.

I imagined Katie sitting by the hotel window in

Istanbul, in the predawn, that same moon settling in the sky to her west. She placed her hand upon her round warm belly and whispered, "Little one. See your father and sister in the moon. They are not so far away. See them reflected in the moon. They are waving to you."

Katie was an ideal mother-to-be while carrying both Meghan and Christopher. A lover of coffee in the morning, a couple or three beers in the evening, she gave it all up upon learning she was pregnant. I watched her stomach grow round, her breasts fill, her hair grew lustrous from the hormones that nurtured life. The months passed, and the baby began to kick and move and turn inside the womb. I would lay my palm upon Katie's belly and feel the wave. We talked to Meghan and tried to explain to her that she had either a brother or sister on the way, that soon there would be even more family to love. Of course, she did not understand — life to a two-year-old is what can be seen and touched.

As spring blossomed and the due date of early June grew closer, Katie and I began to look for a house to buy. The apartment was plush compared to the block and concrete house we had in Tunisia, but as we readjusted to life in America, we wanted more of what America offered. A yard, more room, air-conditioning, furniture that was more than collected odds and ends. Already I felt growing paternal instincts — to provide for my children a better way of life than what I had grown up in, the same as my parents had hoped for me. The house on Windsor Circle came available suddenly.

We had already looked at a few places outside of Chapel Hill. Rapid growth was turning woodland and fields into subdivisions. When Katie saw the ad in the newspaper, we decided to take a look. A brick ranch-style in an older, established neighborhood, the house had been built in the late fifties. The one-acre lot was filled with hardwoods, a deck adorned the back of the house. The price was right, and we closed on the deal almost immediately.

In my heart, I knew the neat little house in the orderly small neighborhood on Windsor Circle was not my ideal picture. I had always sworn I would never end up in a house on the corner of a block smack-dab in the middle of civilization. But my second child was on the way and we needed room, and the house would only be a stepping stone on the way to that farm in the country with a pond and a place for a garden and room to raise children as well as maybe a few goats and a horse and some laying hens. Katie and I would end up living on Windsor Circle all of our marriage, and in the living room where we signed the purchase agreement, we also signed the documents of our legal separation.

As with Meghan, Christopher had to be coaxed into the world. When Katie was ten days past the due date, labor was induced. And as she was with Meghan, Katie was again slow to dilate. We walked the halls of the hospital for hours trying to speed the process. After nearly twelve hours of light labor, the doctor ordered a sonar to make sure of the baby's weight. Katie and I watched the monitor as a nurse rubbed an electronic eye across Katie's belly.

"Do you know the sex of your baby?" the nurse asked.

"No."

"Do you want to know?"

Katie and I held eyes for a moment then nodded.

"See right here," the nurse said, pointing at the monitor. That is a penis."

Outwardly, we had both said the sex of the child did not matter. All we wanted was a healthy baby. Meghan was such a delight, how could we not want another daughter? But, inside I had been hoping very much for a male child; was it sexist for a man to want a son? I did not think so. Katie also wished for a boy, one of each, a road into two very different worlds of parenting. He was there, although still reluctant to enter the world.

Finally, in the early morning hours toward dawn, Katie went into hard labor. We had begun to worry that she might have to have another cesarean. But Katie was always a person who took her time making up her mind about a situation, then acted swiftly and surely. When she finally started dilating, she nearly gave birth without the doctor being present.

Katie's contractions began to get hard around three

a.m. Together we had taken a class in natural childbirth, studied breathing techniques and relaxation and words I was to use in coaching. But in the realities of giving birth, Katie seemed to draw within herself, and I was left only to watch and hold her hand as deep creases marked her forehead and she arched her back in pain. I studied the fetal monitor through wave after wave of contractions and listened to the beep, beep of our child's heart on a microphone.

Fathers who witness the birth of their children get shortchanged in the sympathy department. In no way will I try to compare my stress to what Katie went through, but as her contractions and pain mounted, my whole body seemed twisted in a knot. I had no way to release the tension. At least Katie had something to focus her adrenaline and pain upon. She had an object the size of a loaf of bread to push through an opening that was much, much smaller. Teeth gritted, face shiny with sweat, her eyes took on a glazed stare that seemed to link with her foresisters to primeval times. I had never before seen such focus and intensity in a face.

But I could only sit there with my accelerator mashed to the floor, my heart pounding; I wanted to put my fist through the wall. To complicate my anxiety, during contractions the baby's heartbeat would become erratic — for long seconds there would be no beep — and my own pulse would seem to freeze. The doctor had not been around for more than an hour.

"We better get the doctor in here," one nurse said to another. "This baby is coming."

I wanted to shout, "Hell, yes! Get the god-damn, son-of-a-bitching, cock-sucking doctor in here!"

Yeah, the baby was coming! Either a baby or a Mack diesel was fixing to roll out of my wife from the sounds she was making and the look on her face. And the doctor was said to be sleeping, certain the birth was still hours away, with my wife and son in a sprint at the end of a marathon. I wanted to choke him when finally he arrived, took one look and said, "You're right. We almost have a baby."

Watching Christopher being born ripped the veils of civilization from my eyes and reconnected me to the fact that mankind is still part of the animal kingdom. While growing up I had seen lots of animals born — calves, kid goats, piglets, foals — a human baby is born not so differently. Katie sucked in air and held her breath and bore down, his head crowned. "Push, Katie, push," the doctor urged.

My arm was around her shoulders, my head close to hers. "Push, honey. Push hard."

Another strong contraction. "OK, Katie," said the doctor. "Push real hard this time. Let's get your baby into the world."

I lifted Katie's shoulders higher and wished I could do this for her. "Push, honey. It's almost over."

Katie shrieked and the baby came out in a rush; sterile waters spilled and mixed with blood; an odor suddenly filled the room that reminded me of freshly mown hay. Christopher began crying immediately, and in his first voice — for one fleeting, split second — I understood all the secrets.

A few minutes later, I sat holding Christopher. The room seemed to ring with silence following all the action that had just occurred. The thud of my heartbeat slowed, but was still evident, like a clock in my ears. Once again, as when I first saw Meghan, I knew time had begun again, fresh and invigorated, that I was reborn along with my son, the images I would carry to my deathbed forever altered with his first cry. But with the curse of Eve, Katie had still to suffer. After debating his entry for hours, Christopher had bolted into the world, and in his haste, Katie had torn. And as I held my boy, the doctor sutured her flesh, and in my thoughts I gave thanks to the god that gives breath to piglets and firstborn sons.

And so you are far from me in miles, Christopher, on this day of your birth, but miles are only the count of steps that I would take to reach you if you called. Twelve years old, and in this age between boy and man, peach fuzz on your face and a voice that will soon chirp like young birds, the days are not so many before you lift the razor. I welcome it and yet I protest; my baby boy is soon to look me in the eye.

I see you in my mind, standing on the shores of

Santorini, as I saw you still inside your mother's womb under the moon's glow in Istanbul, again hours around the earth if I consider the clock, but only a millisecond in mental recall. A gift for you — I can hand you no warm puppy or balsa airplane this morning, and such might pale against the roll of dry mountains that poets say is where gods played. But this, I give to you, a present returned from that morning of your birth.

Fill your palm with black volcanic sand, as I fill mine with red Carolina clay. Sprinkle that soil and what remains are hands the same in flesh and molecules. Scoop the salty water of the ancient Aegean, as I take sweet rainwater from a puddle that fell yesterday, and in that mirror is not my face your own? You grasp a pomegranate and I palm a green persimmon and sling them against the sky, and the eyes that follow that flight are a similar chestnut brown and opened wide with wonder. You may be miles from me and the vision within your reach may differ from mine as bone from china, but you and I are of the same breath and blood.

Search the far horizons, son, and step toward them, but know I am always with you, as I am always there beyond the lip of earth waiting for your return. Bring me supper of figs and dates, and I will feed you in return from peaches that have ripened under this Southern sun. Tell me your memory of the volcano's throat and I will speak of the dust devil that rolled across the plowed field. Remember the old man who played wind music and danced by the sea, and I will recall the whippoorwill I listened to in the quiet hours after midnight. And my prayer for you is that one day hence you hold your own child on his first day, and with his small hand in yours, you then understand my words.

Two long weeks had ended, midnight had passed, and I waited at the airport for Katie and the kids to arrive home from their long flight from Greece. They had missed their connection in New York, and now they had been enroute for more than twenty hours. In a seat across from me sat a man with a large, purple birthmark that covered half of his face.

He looked up from the paper he was reading and caught my eye for a moment. I nodded at him.

Eight years had passed since the last time I was in this airport so late. Katie and I and the kids arrived once again after midnight on a flight from Seattle. I wore a baseball cap to cover my hairless scalp. My nose and mouth were covered by a hospital mask. My skin was pale from a summer devoid of sun, and my dark eyes looked intense with no brows above to soften them. A good friend of mine and his wife were there to greet us and drive us home to Chapel Hill. Gary kept his eyes fastened on mine as I approached him. I didn't like wearing the mask, but I had learned to hide behind it.

I left Seattle on day 100 following my bone marrow transplant — the first day I was eligible to leave. I felt that I had been sucked into a black hole and spat out the other side, the atoms of my body rearranged into the face of another man. But I left the VA hospital walking and disease free, a feat many men who entered the unit could not boast of.

In this world, the value of life is often determined by how pleasing to the eye the vessel is to another viewer. In doing snake shows through the years, I have been asked many times, "What does the snake eat?" I may be holding a corn snake or a boa constrictor or even a copperhead.

"Oh, I usually feed it mice."

The question asker nods her head.

"But when the season is right and I can find them, I feed the snake baby chicks. They're cheaper."

The reaction is almost always the same. Eyes widen, a shadow of horror covers her face. "Baby chicks! You mean you feed baby chicks to the snake?"

Mice are fine to feed to snakes. Rats are fine. People don't usually like mice or rats. Rats are not very attractive. But, baby chicks! Baby chicks are cute little yellow furry creatures that peep and will sit in your hand. Therefore, a chick's life is more valuable than a rat's. The eater of the mice or chicks is a snake, and to most people, snakes are ugly. Snakes are chopped into small pieces, run over with the car, then the tires squealed upon the carcass. But deer are pretty. They remind us of Bambi. Deer should not be killed, but hogs are fine to slaughter. Hogs lie in the mud and smell bad.

Humans tend to view other races and nationalities in the same way. If a person's color, religion, or politics don't appeal to our sense of beauty, he is less in our eyes. The perception of beauty can vary from country to country. A young woman in our Peace Corps group was a wallflower by American standards — overweight, shy, she didn't call attention with a comb and makeup to her pretty red hair and freckles. But in Tunisia she was a rose, a voluptuous armful of woman-flesh, and was besieged by Arab suitors. And when I came off that plane after four months of treatment in Seattle, I was ugly to the bone, by my standards and in the eyes of most others. I looked like Uncle Fester from the *Addam's Family*, a reverse metamorphosis, like going from the butterfly to the worm.

I'm not saying I was devastatingly handsome before the transplant, but my physical appearance caused me little concern. I had my share of girlfriends in junior high. I played sports in high school and dated almost every weekend. Hell, I found two women willing to marry me. My children are pretty. Katie is pretty. Life in general was pretty.

I remember standing once in line behind a man at a teller machine. He wore a suit with a hat atop his head. The man took his money, then turned around to leave. I was looking full into his face. I averted my eyes for a second, then stared back at the man. His eyes were on me; he nodded hello. I nodded back and tried not to show my horror.

He had been burned horribly, his face like melted wax. His ears were nubs, nose and lips shriveled lumps of flesh. But his eyes were blue and clear and intense, as if he still looked upon life with a mind unaltered by flames. I wondered what it must be like to go through such an ordeal and survive and still walk in the world surrounded by people unmaimed. I remembered kids from school who had been overweight or slow to learn or for other reasons stood out from the rest of the class and were subjected to ridicule for simply being different.

Maybe my reflection I had come to take for granted had changed, but the South had not. My senses were flooded when we walked from the sterile atmosphere of the airport. The air was wet and smelled of rain and laden with the odors of damp vegetation. Frogs sang in the road ditches. On the horizon I saw the flash of lightning from some storm too distant to be heard. I looked older, and I looked weary, but like the man at the money machine, I too had gone into flames and now stood again, scarred, in a world that did not value one maimed or dying or in retreat. But my eyes were still a rich brown, and the old woman at Heaven's gate could not snatch them for what I had witnessed and could better now envision.

I had been home only a couple of days when George came to see me. Several neighbors and friends had already stopped by. They hugged me or shook my hand gently as if I might be fragile and smiled all the time while saying how glad they were I was home. I felt like they were talking through me and beyond to another man who had stood in the house four months earlier. But George gave it to me straight. He is a former Marine, avid hunter and fisherman, shoes horses for a living. He has a tongue so honest it sometimes gets him in trouble.

George stood in the doorway staring me up and down for several moments. He shook his head slowly. "God Almighty, Tim. You look like you been through hell." He walked to me and pulled me hard against his chest for several seconds, then released me and stepped back. "Hey, you wanna beer?"

I had to decline the beer, but I was glad he offered. I also appreciated his honesty. I knew I looked like hell, and I felt like I had been through hell and acknowledgment was more healing than coddling.

I recall a time not so many years ago when I sought attention, a mask hiding my face the last thing I would have wanted. My senior year in high school, I was co-captain of the basketball team. A fraction over six feet tall, lean with muscular legs, I wore my hair down to the bottom of my neck

1

and sported mutton-chop sideburns. My chest was hairy.

I had established a ritual for entering the gymnasium for home games. First, I took my girlfriend, Jenell, parking behind the football bleachers. Mostly heavy kissing, I was lucky if I got a finger below her bra-line. She would leave her signature on my neck, a visible, but tasteful hickey. When we parked outside the gymnasium, my hormones would be fully revved with energy inside me for a double header. Timing my entry was important. I'd wait until the buzzer sounded signaling halftime in the girls' game. Jenell on one arm, my satchel in the other hand, my hair mussed just enough and the hickey showing above my collar, I'd lope down the sidelines in front of the home section, putting what soul I possessed into every step. All eyes were upon me — or so I imagined — the envy of every guy who couldn't can a twenty-foot jump shot — a source of lust for every female under thirty. Here I am! I am alive and looking good, and if you miss me now, check out my picture in the paper tomorrow.

One girl who did not lust for me was Sandy Phillips. She was too busy being the focus of many of the guy's nighttime fantasies. Sandy was pretty, and from a well-to-do family. She had been chosen Miss Cape Fear High, was in the Beta Club and a class officer. She dated college boys and ignored me and anyone else who ever sweated — one prim, stuck-up bitch.

More than a decade later, Sandy finally spoke to me. I was visiting my mother and was shopping in the community grocery store. I recognized Sandy as she pushed a food cart. She was still pretty, but lines at the corners of her eyes reflected some tough years.

"I'm sorry about your father," I told her. He had recently died after a long bout with cancer.

Following graduation, Sandy had seemed destined for more of the fairy tale life. She graduated from college, then married the son of a prominent family in Fayetteville. Her husband was driving them home from a late airplane flight when he apparently dozed off and hit a tree. Sandy had nearly died in the wreckage. Her marriage ended in divorce. Now, after years of operations, she still walked with a limp. A large moon-shaped scar crossed her cheek.

"I enjoyed reading about you in the paper," Sandy said. "I never thought anyone from our class would write a book. Especially you."

She smiled, and I knew she wasn't being malicious. "I was as surprised as everyone else," I answered. I shrugged one shoulder. "So, how is life with you?"

She brushed her cheek with one finger as if she wished to hide the scar, but at the same time point to it like a map of the road she had traveled. "Life is good. I'm teaching school." She pointed at a large bag of puppy chow in her cart. "I have seven baby labs at home."

We chatted for several minutes, asked about classmates we hadn't seen in years and laughed about events that I wouldn't have thought she was aware of. I said I hoped to see her sooner next time and turned to leave.

"Do you still play basketball?" Sandy asked.

"Some. I watch more on TV than I play."

"You had the most beautiful jump shot of anyone."

"You should have told me."

Sandy smiled again, a sad, long-reaching gaze in her eyes. "There is a lot I didn't say back then. I never looked ahead, only saw what was behind me in the mirror."

I quickly grew into my ugliness. Maybe strangers would give me a second look, some children might stare, hell, dogs barked at me. But my kids still sat on my lap; Katie still let me in bed with her. People who were real friends stopped noticing my swollen face and bald head; people who weren't real friends stopped visiting. Our basset hound still licked my hand. Behind my mask, my personality had survived despite the deluge of drugs pumped through me in the past year. And I knew my face would eventually heal — maybe my hair would never be as thick, but I would have sideburns again. My jump shot might not be so pretty, but I would still play. As Sandy had rejected mirrors, I had no desire to dwell on what lay behind me. When I was leaving the VA in Seattle, the doctor said statistically I had a higher chance of the cancer returning. But even a slim door was better than the closed door I had seen slammed in other patient's faces. Besides, a lot of the air had been taken from my ego, and with luck and grace and determination I figured to slide through the narrow portal.

The lights on the jet were like a summer Christmas tree to me as the big plane finally taxied to the gate at a quarter to one in the morning. People began to exit, faces drawn and pale in the sterile bright light of the lobby. A few of the passengers were greeted by family members, friends, or lovers, but most hurried past to their parked cars or into cabs. I waited, leaning against a wall and watching the weary people pass, usually gathered in clumps slowed by an elderly man or a woman herding small children. I began to worry — had they missed another flight, stuck in New York for the night? Was I wrong about their arrival, maybe in my eagerness to see the kids, I was a day ahead of their schedule.

Christopher was first through the doorway, his face turning as he scanned the room, Meghan at his shoulder. They were both dark, so very brown, the color of wheat bread. Their hair showed streaks of sun. I lifted my arm and Meghan saw me, and the three of us met in a circle of hugs and kisses.

"You guys are so tan! I can't believe how tan you are."

"It didn't rain a single day," Christopher told me.

Katie stood to the side and I smiled at her and she smiled. She was even darker than the kids, her blue eyes the shade of calm sea water. For a moment I wished to hug her too, but instead I held the children tighter.

"I bet you guys are exhausted!"

Christopher pointed at his watch. "We've been up for more than twenty-four hours. I didn't think you'd be here, Dad."

"Wouldn't be here? No way. I've been missing you guys for two weeks."

"We brought you some stuff," Meghan said, "but we'll probably wait and give it to you tomorrow."

"You two are the only thing I want."

I looked at Katie again. Her nose was red and had peeled. For the first time I noticed how her hair was gray above her temples. She stared beyond me and the kids, and I imagined she wished her boyfriend was here to hug her as I held the kids. I wished that for her, and thought less of him that he was not there.

"Thanks for bringing them back safe, Katie," I said . She nodded once, but knew there was no need for words.

Twelve

We drive long the first day and camp near Oklahoma City, get back on the road soon after sunup, and arrive at four p.m. at a KOA on the home side of the city Elvis died in, and where Katie and I married seventeen years ago.

I often dream of an empty house. Rooms dusty and bare of furniture, linoleum curled at the edges and cracked, the air chilled and musty and dim with only the light that leaks through a drawn shade. I am always alone in that house, and the doorway to the next room is even darker. But, I know I need to go into that room, because inside it is something I forgot to take with me, and I don't even know if it is even still there. The dream is always of a place I have left, and it is stale and barren and ghostly, and what I have come to retrieve is not in the room where I stand, but in a deeper chamber I wish not to enter.

I realize I'm standing at that door right now, waiting for it to open. Shreds of that dream whirl through my head; I've just knocked on the door of Katie's parents' house, and I hear Ladye Margaret's footsteps, then the bolt sliding as she unlocks it. I need to go into that room, because I left something there I need to retrieve, and I still don't know what it is. I step back and let the kids front me, Ma and Bruce and Donnie standing behind us.

"Hello, hello, hello!" Ladye Margaret hugs Meghan and Christopher. I see Van, Katie's stepfather, standing behind her, Peggy and Jim beyond him in the room. Ladye Margaret hugs me next, and her embrace is genuine. I shake Van's hand,

—243—

and his grip is firm. Peggy hugs me, then clamps my shoulders and pulls back.

"You're so brown, Tim," she says.

Jim shakes my hand and looks into my eyes and welcomes me. Both parties exchange greetings and we linger in the foyer, then move into the living room where I last stood six years ago. Katie's family looks the same, except that Van's shoulders are a bit more slumped with age. Jim's hair is mostly gray. Ladye Margaret and Peggy are ageless; they will always be ageless. The living room looks identical to the last time I was seated on this couch, the same furniture, television, and lamps. The only difference I see is the missing framed picture of Katie and me that used to sit among other pictures atop a desk against the wall.

"Well, tell me about your trip!" Ladye Margaret gushes. I begin a spiel about the distance we have traveled, the miles and the stops, the plains and the mountains and the rocks we have gathered. The air smells of fried chicken, and through a doorway I can see into the dining room to that same table I sat down to a hundred times laid out with plates and silver and glasses.

The conversation breaks into pieces between different people; I talk to Jim about how his work is going, what new buildings he is designing these days. I notice he is not drinking wine as he usually did on evenings before a meal, and I doubt he has stopped drinking, but feels he cannot do so in my presence. Bruce jokes about Ma's rocks with Ladye Margaret and of how he is going to need a back brace when he gets home. Peggy comments on how deep Christopher's voice is, and how timely the change seems right at his thirteenth birthday.

At the table, we clasp hands for the blessing in the tradition of Katie's family, then pass the platter of chicken, potato salad, asparagus casserole, green beans, and yeast rolls. How many times have I enjoyed this same meal at this same table? I've lost the count. Peggy brings the cake out with candles flaming, and Christopher blows the fire out and we sing him Happy Birthday, and he gets the first piece along with a bowl of ice cream. And then we give him his gifts, from myself, a rock of all things, but a small one, a nice opal I bought from a dealer in Sedona, Arizona; a quality jewel I tell him I will have mounted for him in a ring or a necklace when we get back home. Christopher turns the stone over and over in his hand, watching the deep colors flash. I am so glad he is here within arm's reach of me on this day, and not on the other side of the globe like last year. So very much has happened in this past year, so very much in these forty-five years of my life.

And then I see my shadow on the floor in front of the window to the garden where I stood that first morning so many years ago. My image laid upon the floor eighteen years reversed as I looked into the back yard brightened by the early sun. That shadow still there as if it is scorched into the hardwood, and I realize this is what I left in the inner room, that object I came to retrieve, not knowing for sure if it was really there or only imagined.

And I know now I cannot take that shadow; the stain cannot be simply lifted and retrieved or removed with Ajax and a scouring pad. I do not know how Ladye Margaret and Van and Peggy and Jim view the shadow, how Katie interprets it on her visits home. The last time Katie was here, she brought Andy. I wonder if he stood against that same window and left his image on top of mine, like a male dog marking his scent on top of one who arrived before him. I know this. Meghan and Christopher do not cast shadows, but throw the sun and the moon into eclipse, and for what darkness I may have brought to this family, I left to them two who are undeniably half me and fully radiant.

Last sunrise on this odyssey into my past and toward the future. I have saved a Cuban cigar from Lynn, and I smoke it with my coffee as Bruce and I talk in the quiet before one final 800-mile dash to home. I have gained much from this journey, but I have also lost some weight I did not need to be carrying.

"Been a heck of a trip, hasn't it?" I say to Bruce.

"There's a lot I've seen in this life that I wouldn't have without you," Bruce says. "That trip to Eleuthera with you and Merrie. This trip. The times you rented a beach cottage and invited everyone down. One day I'm going to take you somewhere."

"Shoot. We couldn't have made this trip without you, Bruce." I don't elaborate, but he probably recognizes the catch in my voice. It's not the trip he took me on, but the one he brought me home from that is why I sit here this morning. Home from Seattle where his bone marrow and almost daily platelet transfusions cured the fire in my bones. I have elected not to tell him there is a chance I may have another spark kindling inside, that I might have to call on him again. But if I have asked much of my brother, my consolation is my gratitude that I have been the one diseased and not he.

"I'm going to miss us sitting here in the mornings talking," Bruce says.

"Me too. You know, it's funny, but my best memory of this whole trip will not be of the mountains and the snow, but of me and you sitting here drinking coffee when it's quiet and cool and just talking about whatever comes to mind."

The door to the Winnebago opens, and Meghan comes out. I am surprised to see her up so early. I stand and walk to her.

"You're up early, punkin-girl."

"I want to take a shower before we leave."

"You excited about getting home?"

"I want to see Mom and my friends. But, I'm going to miss being with you and Granny and everyone. This trip was been sooo great, Dad."

Meghan hugs me, then pulls back and smiles while looking into my eyes. Her eyes are moist, and the light of the morning is soft, and in her dark irises I can see my reflection as if looking into a mirror. "I love you, Dad."

"I love you too, baby."

I watch her walk away from me, and I know that for all I have faulted at in life and come up short, if I were judged primarily by the merits of my two children, any benevolent

God would grant me grace.

We seem pulled by home as if in free fall, crossing the heart of Tennessee to the Blue Ridge where Bruce drives us across the mountains. Traffic is thick, and I play cards with the kids and don't look as we barrel around curves, through tunnels and down grades. At last, the earth goes flat again, and we are in the home stretch. About 150 miles out, I take over the wheel again. Darkness is falling, and soon the night is black except the twin holes punched out by the headlights. In the windshield, I can see my reflection and the image of my family behind me. I think again of Meghan early this morning when I saw myself in her eyes, of how effortless it was for me to say to her, "I love you." And to mean it.

Alone with my thoughts, my vision both in front of me and behind, my mind opens deep and blazing like the throat of a morning glory. This is the universe. This is the universe for me. All existence is contained within a many faceted jewel, each plane the eyes of someone I love, where my image is reflected back to me. I and all creation exist inside the jewel, and the surfaces of each plane are of the purest, whitest energy that allows no light, no thought to escape the mirror. Nothing exists outside the jewel, no infinite vacuum or endless lead wall, because reality does not exist beyond intellect to conceive it.

The Wizard of Oz told the Tin Man that a heart is judged not by how much it loves others, but by how much it is loved in return. I don't believe he was right, for even Hitler's mother loved him, as did Eva, who chose to die at his side. To be loved is inherent, but to love in return is to risk all that comes from opening one's life to another.

Suddenly, I realize how wrong I was last Easter morning in the darkness before dawn, when I imagined myself as the center of the universe. I think now that concept is a glimpse of hell, to be so totally, absolutely, utterly solitary without a loved one's eyes to fracture and bend and reflect back the image and memory of my life.

I think again about the old lady at the gates of heaven

who eats the eyes of those pilgrims without scars. They who must then live for eternity without the vision of seeing one's self returned, heaven and hell on the same plane, coexisting.

And suddenly I am wheeling the bus into the driveway at the home place. The door to the house opens and Karen walks outside to greet us, my nephew Matthew, Ma's dog, Fancy, who leaps and turns circles in her frenzy. I cut the engine and a deep silence envelops the inside of the bus for several moments, everyone aboard temporarily struck mute and immobile, caught between the gears of the road and home.

Within fifteen minutes, probably twenty family members have gathered inside the home place. Conversations roll and revolve around where we have been and what we have seen. Every traveler has a joke about Ma's rocks.

I feel strangely disquieted. I grew up on this land and in this house, but I am the only sibling to have moved outside a rifle shot from the crib where I was raised. And once again I stand here in this house that I have left so many times, and each time returned to.

I find a chair in a quieter corner of the room, away from the cluster of family gathered around my mother. Above me on the wall hangs a picture of the family when I was about sixteen. I stare into this young man's frozen eyes, and I recognize him and remember him and know he still sleeps in the first bedroom down the hall where his world revolves around Jenell and basketball and that red '69 Ford Fairlane he drives. I wonder if he knows I am here again — drawn back like the tide that keeps pushing and pulling between the tug of the moon and sun — that part of him that envisions the future and remembers the past and is forever suspended upon that exact heartbeat between the ebb and surge.

Katie saw my father standing in his bedroom looking out the window on the morning after he was buried. She said she backed up after passing the doorway and looked again, and he was gone. His shadow — what I left below the window in Memphis. We are all ghosts of who we were, the unborn fetus of who we will become. On the floor to the outside are footprints left in dust, some leaving, others returning. I've done it — walked full circle through the curvature of time and distance back to this chair. Do I know yet where my next step will lead me?

I think again of the story I wrote, of Mack Breece trapped under water and breathing through a pipe, of fish spawning and fish feeding, and his realization that he can never truly understand, but only accept and voice his existence in words he understands. I choose the jewel, myself one particle of a light reflected and refracted between the shining facets so many times that speed and time no longer exist.

Karen separates herself from the crowd and walks over to where I sit. She kneels and puts her hand on my leg. "I'm glad you got everybody back safely."

"Shoot, it wasn't just me. Everyone pulled their load."

"Some woman called tonight and asked if you were back yet."

"Who was it?"

Karen pauses and cocks her head. "You know, it's strange, but she didn't give her name. She just asked me to tell you she is home."

I nod and smile. Karen walks back to her spot beside Donnie. Where is home? I recall what Lynn told me that morning in L.A.

"But, it doesn't have to have a name. We just are."

Epilogue

Nearly a year has passed, and with my cup of hot coffee I watch the dawn rise red and silver through the treeline to the east. The front door is open, and the sounds and smells of early June spill inside. The air is still cool but humid, and thunderstorms may rear black and thunderous in the late afternoon. Birds are in chorus, their songs mixed with the grind of traffic from the nearby road. My nose scents the fragrance of damp soil and my roses, which are blooming. Roy Lee is outside, marking trees. I found Lilly a new home in the early weeks of last January before I got real sick. The five-milligram Dilaudid tablet I took is starting to kick in, and with the caffeine, swells within my brain a feeling of euphoria. I'm weaning myself from the drug, but five months of taking narcotics should not be stopped cold turkey.

I have much to be happy about. Despite being twenty-five pounds lighter than I was last year, I can eat now. For about two weeks, I could hardly swallow more than water. I have my voice. For a while, there was a chance that my larynx would have to be removed. Meghan is driving now, and Christopher is so tall that he stares me straight in my eyes. My lady is still sleeping, curled naked under a sheet, her wheat-colored hair spread like a fan across the pillow. She will not sleep much longer; a woman so full of life will not tarry in the dream world. But I am happy in these quiet moments, like the lull between heartbeats, content to sit and listen and feel the tide of life as it rolls up strong with the sun.

I had not planned to write these pages. I thought the story ended there in Ma's living room, where my mind still reeled from that last day on the road, my thoughts stretched between the high, snow-covered flanks of the Rockies and the flat, coastal plain of my heritage. But a number of people who had read the manuscript said to me, "Aren't you going to add one final chapter, seeing that so much has gone on since you shut down the motor on that Winnebago?" And I already anticipated the two questions that so many women probably would ask when I went out to sign books this fall: "How is your health?" And, "What happened between you and Lynn?"

A bluebird sits on a limb of the small cherry tree the kids gave me on Valentine's Day a year ago. Small fruits are beginning to ripen, and I hope the birds will leave me a few. An unusual number of birds seem to be living around my house this spring, as if the energy is strong and balanced now following the hectic and turbulent months of winter. How do I speak of the past twelve months, of what is important and what is simply another curve, hillclimb or descent through this crazy ride of life? I do not feel that my life is unique. I believe that if you are honest and open, your own life, whether you chronicle one year or the sum of all your breath, is as interesting and worthy of a book as mine. You just have to be able to string together the words. But most importantly, you must be willing to share your life, the flaws and virtues, knowing that people will admire you for the effort, will identify with your fears and hopes, will see their own lives reflected therein, regardless of whether they are of the same gender, race, religion, or whether they hail from the same neck of the woods.

I am willing to speak of my life, to tell where I tried to go, and show where I have gone, to be honest, and if the story at times seems unreal, then tell me what *is* real? I will tell you what has happened since the tires cooled on the Winnebago. I will tell you as honestly and openly as my judgement will allow. The words will be from my heart, and they will be true. Know, however, that "true" is a subjective word, channeled through my mind and wind.

• • •

I returned the Winnebago to the dealer the day after the trip ended. The man grumbled about the two weeks of bugs crusted against the headlights and grill, a couple of scratches on the floor where Bruce had rolled large rocks under the seats, a hole burned in the shotgun seat from a cigarette or cigar during one of the long hauls. I paid dearly for the abuse to the vehicle, but the dollars were worth the memories. Donnie and Bruce chipped in their share; Donnie even paid me and Bruce for the biscuits we bought him, although we told him it wasn't necessary.

Lynn was home for the summer on a trial separation from her husband, and what I can say of those couple of months is that they were magical. I can best sum up the time with this memory:

Sunday night at five minutes before midnight. She and I had spent the weekend together, and now I was alone in my bed, the sheets cool, the air conditioner whispering. Summer school had started, and I had to be in class at nine-twenty. Bone-tired, but happy, suspended in that luxurious layer of reality that comes before deep sleep, I was jerked back into the world by the phone ringing. I picked up the receiver to find Lynn on the other end.

"I'm sitting here on the porch and the full moon is in the sky and the frogs are singing and I was thinking of you," she told me.

"I wish I was there," I told her.

"I wish you were too," she answered. "God, I wish so badly you were here."

Then it hit me—she was asking, but not asking, for me to come. After a pause, I said, "I could drive down."

"No, you can't do that. It's too late. I love you too much for you to be on the road this late."

"It's only a couple of hours."

"I know, but it's late, and I know how tired you must be."

The hour was late, and I was tired, and the bed felt so very good, and at the same time I knew that Lynn was talking in female double-speak, which translated: "All this is true, but if you really love me, you'll get your dead ass out of bed and drive down here and be with me."

I also knew that life is fleeting and that one day—maybe not so long in the future—I might be lying on my death bed and would lament the night a good-looking woman beckoned me to come into her warm arms and I chose to sleep.

"I'll be there in about two hours," I told her, and hung up.

I stopped at a convenience store, bought a Coke, a couple of cigars and one of those roses wrapped in plastic, the stem in a water reservoir. I hit the interstate, tuned the radio to an oldies station, held the speedometer at seventy-five, and one hour and forty-five minutes later I was wheeling into the driveway of the cottage where she was staying.

We stayed up all night. At dawn, Lynn cooked breakfast. I got back on the interstate, and with five minutes to spare, was standing in front of my students as they slowly filed in. Although a bit tired, I felt totally alive. That night I turned the ringer off the phone.

Fittingly, the last place I saw Lynn was beside the ocean at the same beach where as a child I had stared across the wide waters knowing that if I ever started walking toward the horizon I might never turn around.

"You know, I may never see you again," she said, those brown eyes as liquid and flashing as the water by which she stood.

That probably will prove true. By then we had decided without so much as a single argument or unkind word that our relationship would exact too high a price from innocent people. Her life was tied to the exotic, the foreign and mysterious. My own was rooted in my heritage. I had already walked that full circle and knew that my destiny lay in Southern soil. Also, I am not the sort of man to be a once-a-year lover.

"Everything that happened this summer was meant to happen," Lynn told me. "And it was good, but not meant to be forever. Still out there is a woman who is walking toward you, and she is bigger than me and stronger, and she's not carrying the weights I have."

I think of Lynn now like John the Baptist, the for-bearer of another to come who would be greater. Lynn and I made the right decision. It was not an easy one, but the right one. And what we do right in life begets right.

Ironically, the protein that had showed up in my blood was back to normal in August when the retest was drawn. The fall semester started, and autumn rolled quickly into the chill of early winter. I found my life to be in a bit of a rut following such a passionate and adventuresome spring and summer. Teach, write, pay bills, spend time with the kids. I felt no draw toward booze, but I did find myself many nights at eight sitting in front of the TV, bored, nothing to look forward to but going to bed, sober and alone. But something did scratch at the back of my mind. When I swallowed, occasionally I felt a stinging pain in my left shoulder blade. When I gulped large mouthfuls of food, sometimes the mass seemed to stick in my throat. By late November, the pain in my throat and difficulty in swallowing had become hard to ignore. I finally made an appointment with the doctor. First an x-ray that showed nothing, then a barium swallow that revealed a definite obstruction in my esophagus. I endured with little sedation a flexible camera shoved down my throat to view the obstruction and take a snippet for biopsy. Another appointment was scheduled for a week later. I remember sitting in the examination room waiting for the doctor. I had grown optimistic. Several friends had told me that when biopsies were malignant, the patient was always called in early. I had already waited two hours beyond my appointment and still no doctor. Suddenly the door opened; he walked in and I inhaled long and slow.

"The biopsy showed cancerous cells," he said without much hesitation. As he explained that I had esophageal cancer, what the treatment would be and what my chances for cure were, I watched through the window as a robin hopped through the branches of a bush. Two rounds of chemotherapy spread out during six weeks of radiation. If the chemo and rads didn't work, the scalpel would be used next and the cutting would be extensive. My entire esophagus would be removed along with part of my upper stomach, and the two ends stitched together. My eating habits would change forever— no more big, fried catfish dinners. Instead, I would get by on a series of smaller meals spaced through the day. Depending upon how close the tumor was, my voice box might have to be removed. Through the thick pane of glass, I could see that the robin was singing, but I couldn't hear the notes. I wondered how it might be to open my mouth and have no words.

I hear notes from the bluebird, sweet with the exuberance of spring. A friend who is a massage therapist told me that diseases of the throat are suggested to be linked to the reluctance or inability to speak. And here I am a journalism major who has written seven books. Have I not spoken? Have I held my tongue? What should I have written? What story did I not tell? What truth did I keep buried until if festered and soured?

I do know there are stories I did not tell, truths not written because the telling would have been too deep an intrusion into the lives of people I loved. But cannot my voice in the future speak in actions instead of pages scribed, my hands actually reaching out to the lives and life I care about? I will strive to undo what is wrong and instill in place what is right. That which I can conceive, I am capable of doing, or at least attempting. Might such actions stave off the renegade cell that turned on me when I chose to sit and make up a world that could be instead of making that world so. Instead of seer, I will now be doer, my palms calloused as well as my fingertips.

A blush is visible on the cherries. If the bluebird and robin don't get too greedy, I plan to bake a pie with my first harvest. I may have to settle for a turnover. I recall last January when snow had buried the bottom half of the tree. Twenty inches fell, the deepest snow of my lifetime. I was well into treatment then, all of my hair shed, even my eyebrows. Weight was falling from me faster than the cherry tree shed its leaves in October. I had never seen such a snow and wondered if it were a sign. I didn't have the fight in me then that I had carried to Seattle in my first bout with cancer a decade earlier. I was weary and in pain and despite so many friends and family, I felt basically alone. Meghan and Christopher knew me as their father, had stories and memories they could tell their own children of me; seven books in libraries would whisper my name long after my bones were dust. Was this snow a gift from God, a sign that maybe the time had come for this life to end, my final mission to chronicle my demise with dignity and fearlessness, that others might make the transition more easily?

What goodness might I find in a second cancer at age forty-six? In the karmic return of one's actions, was the disease payback for transgressions, or was it simply another portal through which to view life as the wonderful gift it is?

Consider this. What if I were the only mortal, and every other person who had entered my life had been an angel sent to cause me to make the right choices before I draw my final breath. What if all the stars in the heavens were individual stages for solitary souls, each journeying toward enlightenment aided and challenged by personal spiritual guides who appear in the form of parents, spouses, children, neighbors, enemies and lovers. Maybe even pets. Does Roy Lee not challenge me to act in the right way, to feed him and scratch his belly and refrain from kicking him when he occasionally pees on the rug? The man who slaps me and calls me a son-of-a-bitch, or the woman who beckons me smiling to her bed, each on separate missions to cause me to think and decide what is good and what is not good, when to restrain myself and when to do just battle, when to blend myself into another's arms. In that framework, isn't a cancer in my esophagus simply another motivation in my life, one more test of choices and realizations, hopefully drawing me closer to the light and further from the shadows of ignorance?

Of all the treatments I received, I recall most vividly the minutes spent alone in the radiation room, lead walls separating me from other beings. The center of my chest right above my heart was marked with a spot of blue ink. A square of light illuminated the area to be nuked. I would hear the heavy doors close, then a few seconds would pass before the machine clicked, then began to hum as a ray of energy both hideous and healing passed through and out my body.

The first couple of weeks, as the rays passed through me, with eyes closed, I would view the cancer as a giant, ugly monster. I would be battling it with a machete, and when the machine ceased to hum, the beast lay chopped to bloody bits. But as time passed and I chose to see the ordeal as something positive, I changed tactics. I imagined holding hands with Meghan and Christopher, the three of us looking at the tumor as an agent of change. We would tighten our grasp as I thanked the cancer for the knowledge, awareness and commitment it had brought to my life. Then I would firmly inform it that it had served its purpose, that its influence was no longer needed. The tumor would begin to steam and shrink until it disappeared. Where it had been, I could see shoots pushing up, turning into vines that blossomed fragrant, colorful flowers. Love is the strongest healer.

Through the wall, from the bedroom, I hear Carol stir, lifting herself from sleep. I know within a few more minutes she will come to me, wrapped in her white bathrobe, her broad smile as warm and inviting as this dawn. In her pale blue eyes I will see reflected the song birds, this cool mist of morning, myself on the edge of a new day with all its fresh potential, virgin and sinless, yet to be sculpted by my mind and hands.

By mid-February, most of my treatment had ended, but recovery from the drugs and radiation was just beginning. I was hairless and skinny, my hands with a slight tremor. Carol did not know me, had never heard of me, was not someone who thought she knew me through my books. She had heard of my plight through a mutual friend and said she felt called.

I will never forget that day she first walked through my door. Thirty-six years old, born and raised in Michigan, she looked as if she had just stepped from the pages of a back-packing magazine. She is close to finishing a Ph.D. in business, but her art and passion lie in placing her hands on ailing people and drawing the poisons from their bodies.

I knew her already, although as she stood in the closed, stagnant air of my living room, this was the first time our paths had crossed. I knew her like an old friend, as if she had always been part of my life.

I know what some, no doubt, are thinking. This guy never stops. What is this, the sixth woman of which he has written? He'll be singing the virtues of another female a year from now. But I have asked that if I am willing to speak, you will hear me out. Honor this. Carol is as different from the other women who have entered my life as twilight is from morning. Dawn and dusk look similar, but each is different and special. She is both the sunrise and the sunset, one who comes singing a new song while speaking the words I have known throughout my life. She tells me that when she first saw my face, she knew that she was home.

Is she the reward for a life fully lived, if at times foolishly and negligently? Is she one more angel who stands before me now? Though weakened temporarily, I am in the best form of my life, weaned of alcohol, wiser, tempered, ready to mesh my life fully with another.

I believe I still have time left on Earth. I have children yet to raise, books to write, a voice I am now willing to use with action. I am with a woman who is my equal at a point in my life when I am both ready to give and receive. I am not willing yet to make that transition from life.

One day for certain I will die. My heart's thump will shudder and stop, my lungs will cease to rise. And the great mystery will finally be known, all the secrets opened. I believe the answer to all of creation will flower in an instant, the riddle so complex, yet so incredibly simple that I will open my ghost mouth into an oval and say, "Ohhh, so that was it!"

I like to imagine walking up to the gates of heaven. The old woman wiggles her gnarled finger and all my clothes are stripped away. In my nakedness, I stand before her, scarred and humble and proud.

"You have a lot of scars, son," she says, her bright, ancient eyes scanning my flesh. "How did you get so many?"

"Ma'am," I tell her, "I rode a frisky horse through life, and I rode hard. Sometimes I didn't hold on to the saddle horn, and my feet weren't even in the stirrups. Sometimes I fell off, but each time I pulled myself up, climbed back on and rode again. The scars are my memories."

The old lady nods.

"Son, you go on through the gate. You earned it. But you won't find rest there. It's just the beginning of another ride, and that's the glory of it."

She smiles, then leans and kisses me, her lips leaving a third eye in the middle of my forehead. The gates of heaven part, and through the lifting veil, I see not streets of gold, but green mountains and valleys, and dark blue rivers that roll on forever.